MONDO ELVIS

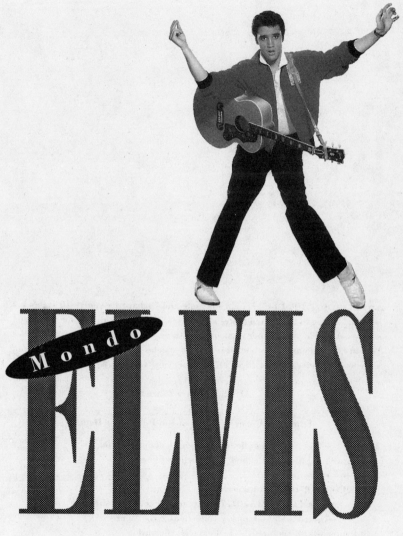

Mondo ELVIS

Edited by

Lucinda Ebersole

&

Richard Peabody

St. Martin's Press | New York

Design by Jaye Zimet

Library of Congress Cataloging-in-Publication Data

Mondo Elvis : a collection of fiction and poetry about the King /
   [compiled by] Richard Peabody and Lucinda Ebersole.
      p.   cm.
   ISBN 0-312-10505-3 (paperback)
   1. Presley, Elvis, 1935–1977—Literary collections.   2. Rock
singers—United States—Literary collections.   3. American
literature—20th century.   I. Peabody, Richard
II. Ebersole, Lucinda.
PS509.P675M66   1994
820'.8'0351—dc20   93-37887
                                                         CIP

First edition: January 1994

10   9   8   7   6   5   4   3   2   1

for Patricia and Allen Ahearn
—R.P.

for Cathy Byrd McCaleb
—L.E.

Kudos to our agent extraordinaire, Anne Edelstein, and our editor Michael Denneny, for believing. Plus special thanks to: Diane Apostolos-Cappadona, Jim Barnes, Lynne Barrett, Kevin Bezner, Lawrence Block, Joanne Brasil, Rebecca Brown, Stephen P. Brown, Mark Burgess, Ann Burrola, Janice Eidus, Joann Everly, Susan Hankla, Kathy Landwehr, Michael Martone, Oliver Morton, Robert Peters, M. Maja Prausnitz, Joyce Renwick, Lewis Shiner, Alan Spears, Dorothy Sucher, Phyllis Tickle, Robert J. Turney, and Phyllis and Michael Ward.

CONTENTS

*There's a guy works down at the chip shop swears he's
Elvis. . . .*

—Kirsty MacColl

INTRODUCTION

Elvis is everywhere, Elvis is everybody,
Elvis is everything.
—*Seattle Times*, May 1992

Love him or hate him, Elvis Presley will not go away. He's more pervasive dead than he ever was alive. Elvis has come to embody the American myth of success. He is the American Dream come true—where else could a boy, a lone surviving twin born in abject poverty, grow up to be King? He is also the comeback kid, the tortured sacrament for our modern sins. Destroyed by our attention only to be resurrected by the media—he drifts through the television wasteland like a cartoon doppelgänger glimpsed in the corner of one eye. His image sells magazines, books, compact discs, clothing, even sweat. Elvis impersonators turn up in movie after movie—*Aria, High Tide, Honeymoon in Vegas*. There's seemingly nothing left to sell. And still we want more. We won't let him rest. He's spotted in a mall in Spokane, his image projected on the side of buildings, at the FBI, in UFOs.

Since his death in August 1977 at age 42, he has become almost a religion. Fans really do worship at his grave, pay homage to his music. They want to believe. Graceland has become holy ground. They worship him with shrines in Baltimore and Seattle. They are willing to live an illusion by seeing Elvis impersonators. They want to believe they are still in his presence.

Many think that dying was a good career move for a man who had absolutely hit rock bottom in terms of his health and career. Bankrupted by drugs and poor diet, he got the break he'd craved all those years: no more performing, no more screaming women, no more long road trips, no bogus Las Vegas glitter; in fact none of the demands of fame, just the pure fame stuff itself—ad infinitum. It's a sort of immortality, I suppose, enough so that the Big E is surely more popular dead than he ever was alive.

This book is a compilation of Elvis dreams and desires. *Mondo Elvis* tracks the rise and fall of Elvis Presley. Some stories objectify Elvis the man, examine facets of the legend, try to return flesh and blood to his cold frame. Others ruminate over Elvis the idea, ponder the forks in the road, the life that might have been. Then there are the Dead Elvis stories, where his impact is felt from a distance of years by Elvis wanna-bes, the devout, the newly star struck. Or else we're left to contemplate the Night of the Living Dead Elvises and other horrors. (Some may not even be named Elvis—but are Elvis just the same.)

Did we say dead? Elvis never dies. He's remade and updated whenever we need him. Like King Arthur, Robin Hood, even James Bond. Because his life really was like a made-for-TV movie. Because inside every one of us there's a place where we live vicariously through others. Because Elvis got away with it. And split. And there's nothing left for us to do but love him or hate him. Nothing to do but be all shook up and sorry he's gone.

LUCINDA EBERSOLE
RICHARD PEABODY

Washington, D.C.
Summer 1992

TUPELO

Nick Cave

Looka yonder!
Looka yonder!
Looka yonder!
A big black cloud come!
O comes to Tupelo. Comes to Tupelo.

Yonder on the horizon
Stopped at the mighty river and
Sucked the damn thing dry
Tupelo-o-o, O Tupelo.
In a valley hides a town called Tupelo.

Distant thunder rumble
Rumble hungry like the Beast
The Beast it cometh, cometh down
Wo wo wo-o-o, Tupelo bound
Tupelo-o-o, yeah Tupelo
The Beast it cometh, Tupelo bound.

Why the hen won't lay no egg
Cain't get that cock to crow
The nag is spooked and crazy
O God help Tupelo, O God help Tupelo!

Ya can say these streets are rivers
Ya can call these rivers streets
Ya can tell yaself ya dreaming buddy
But no sleep runs this deep.
Women at their windows,

Rain crashing on the pane
Writing in the frost Tupelo's shame
Tupelo's shame
O God help Tupelo! O God help Tupelo!

O go to sleep lil children,
The sandman's on his way
O go to sleep lil children,
The sandman's on his way.
But the lil children know,
They listen to the beating of their blood

They listen to the beating of their blood
The sandman's mud!
The sandman's mud!
And the black rain come down.
Water water everywhere
Where no bird can fly no fish can swim
No fish can swim
Until the King is born!
Until the King is born!
In Tupelo! Tupelo-o-o!
Til the King is born in Tupelo!

In a clap-board shack with a roof of tin
Where the rain came down and leaked within
A young mother frozen on a concrete floor
With a bottle and a box and a cradle of straw
Tupelo-o-o! O Tupelo!
With a bundle and a box and a cradle of straw.

Well Saturday gives what Sunday steals
And a child is born on his brother's heels
Come Sunday morn the first-born's dead
In a shoe-box tied with a ribbon of red
Tupelo-o-o! Hey Tupelo!
In a shoe-box tied with a ribbon of red.

O mama rock your lil one slow,
O ma-ma rock your baby.
O ma-ma rock your lil one slow
O God help Tupelo! O God help Tupelo!

Mama rock your lil one slow
The lil one will walk on Tupelo
Tupelo-o-o! Yeah Tupelo!
And carry the burden of Tupelo
Tupelo-o-o! O Tupelo!
Yeah! The King will walk on Tupelo
Tupelo-o-o! O Tupelo!
He carried the burden outa Tupelo!
Tupelo-o-o! Hey Tupelo!
You will reap just what you sow.

FROM TENDER

Mark Childress

Leroy stayed in his room. No one could hurt him in his room. He had the radio.

White folks were not supposed to listen to WDIA, the Mother Station of the Negroes. Leroy discovered the station by accident when he slipped off a weak gospel signal and found himself in a torrent of chatter from a mile-a-minute wild colored man called Howlin' Wolf.

"Blessin' all the slick-back babes and their cool-cattin' beaus, we spinning a hot one this evening for Miss Doretha Watley from a most faithful secret admirer," the Wolf said in a guttery voice, and then: "Whoo, chillun! Hold on to who you hold on to, 'cause this is one sho-fo-real song! Call it Mr. Sam Davis, call it the 'Got No Home Blues'!"

Leroy bent over the Sound Star and whanged along. Sam Davis played the guitar with the side of his hand and began to wail:

> *I ain't got no home, baby*
> *Since you left and said good-bye*
> *Said I ain't got no no no no no home, bay-beh!*
> *Not since you went and said good-bye. . . .*

The radio was a cream colored Philco with a cigarette burn in the top. A whole new exotic world poured out through that little round speaker. Leroy couldn't get enough of it.

"Leroy," his mother called, "get up from there and come take out this garbage."

"Not now, Mama, I'm practicing."

Three chords would take you through every song on

the Mother Station, but the changes these colored folks worked on those chords! They moaned and shouted; they sang about real pain and leaving and good-bye and gone. John Lee Hooker and Lightnin' Hopkins! Tiny Bradshaw! Big Bill Broonzy! The songs shared a smoky-barroom feeling, but each singer had his own rhythm, his own kind of sound.

> *Get off your high horse, baby*
> *And come on back to town. . . .*

Leroy sang the words as he figured them out. The Five Keys! The Dominoes! The Diamonds! The Clovers! "Hmmmmm, babes and babies, don't that just set yo legbone to shakin!" the Wolf cried.

Leroy got off the bed to play harder. Jimmy McCracklin! Wynonie ("Mr. Blues") Harris! Riley B. King, the Beale Street Blues Boy himself, the smoothest blues guitarist on the planet Earth, and the host of "Sepia Swing Time." "Sixty Minute Man." "Rocket 88." Joe Turner's "Chains of Love." Pee Wee Crayton! Big Boy Crudup! The bump and the shuffle, the slow low-down blues.

These colored men must know they were a bad influence on boys like Leroy. They sang songs that might be dirty or might just be funny but were probably both. They knew the songs were loaded with sin; that's why they sang with such joyful enthusiasm. They said "rockin" when they meant "fuckin."

> *Come on and rock me Angelina*
> *Rock yo daddy all night long*

Lips touched the microphone. Voices sweated and wailed. People in the background coughed and dropped things.

"Leroy," Agnes called, "come to supper!"

"Not now, Mama!"

An irresistible beat started rackety-tacking along, and a joyous song came swinging out to banish all the sadness and meanness in Memphis to some other town down the road.

Have you heard the news? Mr. Blues shouted. *There's good rockin' tonight. . . .*

Leroy jumped up off the bed, shaking and beating his

guitar in time. Electricity shot down his legs, popped his fingers.

He danced over in front of the mirror. He was getting better-looking every day. For weeks he had avoided Ray's efforts to get him to a barbershop; his hair was nice and long, and his sideburns were looking very cool.

He put down the guitar. He poured a puddle of Vitalis in his palm and rubbed it all over his head. He combed and arranged his hair until the comb tracks stood out.

It was the same dirty blond as his father's hair. He wished it were wavy and blue-black, like Superman's, to set off his bedroom eyes. He practiced his insolent look: a curl of the lip, a rebellious half snarl.

He skipped supper and set out walking for the glow of downtown, trying to decide whether to be Tony Curtis or Marlon Brando for the evening.

It was Saturday night. Everyone in Memphis who owned or could borrow a car was out in it, driving around. The streets echoed with traffic and radios and front-porch conversations and kids pretending not to hear their mothers calling them to dinner. Half the radios in town were tuned to Arthur Godfrey, and half to the Mother Station.

Marlon Brando swaggered past the Peabody Hotel, through the electric daylight of Main Street and under the grand blinking marquee of the Loew's State Theater, announcing MARTIN LEWIS LAFF A MINUTE "AT WAR WITH THE ARMY" PLUS CARTOON SHORTS NEWS.

The Loew's giant arched entrance opened into a gallery of white columns and red carpets and velvet ropes. Brando approached the ticket booth, which resembled a giant gold jukebox. "One, please," he mumbled, putting down quarters.

The woman in the booth left off plaiting her hair to tear off a ticket. In the corner of the glass was a hand-lettered sign: HELP WANTED.

Well. Now. A job at the movies. That was an idea.

He pointed to the sign. "Who do I talk to about that?"

The ticket lady looked him over. "The manager, Mr. Faubus," she said. "In the projection room, upstairs."

Marlon Brando strode up the wide, curving staircase.

When he came back down fifteen minutes later, he was Leroy Kirby, movie usher, carrying an official usher's uniform on a hanger—black satin-striped pants, a gold braided vest, a red monkey jacket and cap. The short, bug-eyed Mr. Faubus had hired him on the spot. His head whirled. He would start tomorrow! A job at the movies! Twelve seventy-five a week! Oh, life was just fine.

He calmed down enough to remember that he'd already paid to see the picture. He entered the cavernous darkness of the theater and took a seat near the back.

Dean Martin was propped on a sofa in his fake army uniform with a drink in his hand and a lazy, arrogant look on his face—flashing eyes, that superior smirk. He was cool, cool, and Leroy was cool in the dark, breathing Dean's charm and his own hair oil and the rich smell of red velvet. Leroy was Dean Martin now, in his head. He was forty feet tall.

Leroy saw *At War with the Army* sixty-three times. He stood at the head of the main aisle in his monkey suit, wielding his Sculpto flashlight, directing kids to the bathroom and helping cranky old ladies find seats.

The insane giggle of Jerry Lewis haunted his waking hours. At night he dreamed of Dean Martin singing "You and Your Beautiful Eyes" to Miss Peavey, his algebra teacher. But it was the short subject, *Glacier Fishing*, that nearly drove him insane. Eskimos huddled around a hole. They speared a fish. They brought the fish up on the ice. They clubbed the fish to kill it. Leroy watched the same poor fish take it in the head three times a night, every night for five weeks. After a while he began to feel like that fish.

On the magic appointed afternoon Agnes drove him to the Highway Patrol station for his driver's license examination.

Leroy ran over the *Rules of the Road*. The little pamphlet was dog-eared from weeks of study. Leroy meant to pass this test. Once he had his license, he'd be able to drive around looking at life, checking out all the possibilities.

"If you studied half this hard for school, you'd have a perfect report card," his mother said.

"I can't flunk this test." He shook his head. "A girl at school flunked twice, and she has to wait six months before she can take it again."

"Six months isn't that long," Agnes said. "Sounds like she needed the practice."

The Highway Patrol station squatted beside the Nashville highway. Agnes pulled into a parking lot painted over with curves and arrows and stripes and squeezed the Plymouth into a tiny space.

Inside was a long line of kids waiting; Leroy remembered his first day of school, when the kids looked just this scared.

Agnes stood off with the other proud mothers and fathers.

Leroy whizzed through the written test. The questions came straight from the pamphlet. The test lady checked his score—92 of 100. He was halfway to freedom.

A tall, beak-nosed man came up and introduced himself as Weems. He was some sort of gym teacher, to judge from his skull-baring crew cut and his abrupt demeanor; he didn't say much except to direct Leroy behind the wheel of a Chevrolet sedan. "Start the car and drive out of the lot. Turn left."

The Chevrolet's brakes were grabbier than those on the Plymouth. Leroy screeched to a couple of abrupt halts before he learned how to apply subtle pressure.

Mr. Weems made a note in his ring binder. "Drive three blocks and turn right."

"This is a cool car," said Leroy. "Our car's a lot older."

"Pay attention to the road," said Mr. Weems.

Leroy flipped on the blinker and made a flawless right turn onto Davis Street.

"Now drive five blocks and turn left."

Driving was Leroy's best talent, after singing. He had no doubt he would be an excellent truck driver when he got his chance. He got to feeling so proud of his driving that he rolled right through a four-way stop at Ames Avenue without slowing down.

Mr. Weems said, "That looked like a stop sign to me."

"Yes sir, I think it was," said Leroy. What else could he say? He was guilty, guilty. He drove on, doing his best with the unfamiliar controls, sinking into the mortification of having blown the test outright.

"You always drive through a four-way stop without slowing down?" said Mr. Weems. "Turn left."

"No sir," he said. "I reckon I'm kind of nervous." He performed the turn with agonizing care. Blood throbbed in his temples.

"I make you nervous?" Weems barked.

"Yes sir, a little." They were almost back to the Highway Patrol station, which was just as well—no use going on with this.

"Hell, that's what everybody says. That's why I got out of the army," Weems said in a milder voice, almost to himself. "The recruits were all scared to death of me. I never did anything to 'em. I liked 'em. I don't know what it is. I guess I just look that way to people."

Leroy said, "Maybe you ought to let your hair grow out a little."

Mr. Weems smiled, made a mark in his book. "Hate to wind up as shaggy as you," he said. "Now turn into the lot and parallel park in that space over there."

Agnes watched anxiously from the sidewalk as Leroy maneuvered the car to a standstill, six inches from the curb.

Mr. Weems said, "You know, I have to fail you for a moving violation during the course of the test."

Leroy stared at his knees. "Yes, sir."

"I don't like to do it. I think you're a good driver. You practice and come back in two weeks and try it again."

"Yes sir," said Leroy. How could he face his mother?

Mr. Weems handed over a little green slip of paper. "You give that to the lady at the license desk next time you come, and you can skip the written part," he said. "Don't worry about it, son, lots of folks mess up the first time."

Leroy had only a few seconds to decide what to do. If his mother found out he had flunked this test, no telling when she'd let him try again.

He thanked Mr. Weems, walked to the Plymouth, waving the green paper, and climbed in. "I got it!" he declared.

"Oh honey, that's wonderful!"

"It was close, though." He stuffed the paper down in his pocket and laid his arm around her shoulder. "That man wasn't as mean as he looked."

That evening they all piled into the car with Leroy at the wheel. He drove down Winchester Avenue, steering with intense concentration along back streets to the river, the old cotton wharves. If a policeman stopped him without a license, he'd be sent off to the state pen.

He would sneak off somehow and take the test again, and nobody would ever have to know.

Dodger complimented his driving. Agnes said, "My baby's growing up."

They stopped at Murphy's Dairy Dream to celebrate. Ray ordered banana splits all around. Everything was happy until Ray started in on Leroy's hair, how dirty and shabby it looked.

Leroy threw his banana split in the garbage, went out to the Plymouth, and sulked.

The next day was Saturday. He took all the money he'd saved in his Folger's can and asked his mother for the car keys.

"Where are you going?" Agnes said.

"I don't know," he lied. "I just want to drive around by myself awhile. See what it feels like. I'll be careful."

"I know you will." She gave him the keys.

He climbed into the Plymouth, started the engine. The steering wheel tingled his hands.

Taking a deep breath, he inched away from the Lauderdale Court. When he turned onto Jackson Street, he laid into the gas pedal and felt the engine, a kick in the pants. He sailed past Humes High. This old car had life, once you quit treating it like a little old lady and put down your foot.

He zoomed up to a stoplight, slipped out of gear, and sat grinning at his luck: to be alive and sixteen and behind the wheel!

He traveled a roundabout way downtown. He parked out of sight of his immediate destination, the Mary Jane Beauty Salon.

He had cased the place for weeks and never spotted anyone he knew coming or going.

With his hands in his pockets, he sauntered down the sidewalk as if he might walk on by. At the last instant he ducked in the door.

A bell tinkled. The smell of hair chemicals stung his eyes. A young woman with tight blond curls peered up from a manicure table. "Well, hello."

"Hi," said Leroy. "I, uh, I want to get a haircut."

She smiled a bright lipstick smile. "Sweetie, this is a beauty parlor," she said. "You want Mr. Beebe's barbershop across the street."

"No ma'am," said Leroy. "I want you to do mine."

The woman whose nails were soaking said, "Go on, Deedee, do his hair," and laughed.

The manicurist looked him over. "Sure I will," she said. "Have a seat over there and I'll get Lorraine to wash you."

The salon was a quiet place, soft beige and warm. Four middle-aged women were in various stages of beautification: one with her head in a sink, where a colored woman scrubbed vigorously; two under gray dryer hoods; another wincing as a beautician installed pin curls.

Leroy took the folded-up magazine page from his hip pocket and smoothed out the creases. Tony Curtis grinned up, impossibly cool. That was the hair Leroy wanted. A pompadour, full and tall on the top, finished like steel on the sides, tapered to a DA at the neck—a duck's ass, an honest-to-God pointed tail. This haircut would make him the envy of Humes.

Lorraine, the shampoo girl, steered him to a sink with a smoothed-out hollow for his head and fastened a long bib around him. "Boy, what you doing in a lady parlor?" she said.

Leroy waved the picture.

Lorraine studied it a moment. "Hm. Well if that's what you want. Deedee can do it. You got enough hair."

She adjusted the water to a milky temperature and set to work with a wonderful energy. Her strong fingers caressed and dug into his scalp, scrubbing, tussling each hair at its root; the warm water streamed over. Leroy was glad for the long bib since the pleasure of her touch was making him hard in his pants.

Too soon, she was done. She sat him up, rubbed his head with a towel. "Good hair," she said.

The blond girl, Deedee, beckoned from a chair at the front. All the customers glanced up from their magazines to get a look at Leroy going by. No doubt one of them was the mother of somebody at Humes; Leroy would become notorious for all the wrong reasons.

But it was too late now. He lowered himself to a pneumatic chair and showed Deedee the picture of Tony Curtis.

Swiveling him to face the mirror, she grabbed up a hank of his hair. "That's what you want?"

"Sure."

"Keep the sideburns, too?" They reached to his earlobes.

"Yep."

"All right, then." She reached for a pair of scissors, tilted his head, started snipping around his collar. She trimmed and shaped the back, rolling the long swatches of hair around pink curlers. "This is what gives it the body so it can stand up like that."

Leroy watched gobs of hair falling onto his knees. Now and again he glanced at the mirror, trying to satisfy himself that the ridiculous spectacle of his head wadded in curlers would not turn him into something even more ridiculous.

. . . Why did they call it a *permanent* wave?

Deedee handed him a magazine and told him to quit worrying. She poured a cold, strong-smelling potion over the curlers, stretched a perforated shower cap over the whole mess, and positioned Leroy under a roaring steel dryer.

For forty-five minutes he baked in the chemical stink, deafened by the dryer motor, his hair singeing at the roots. He inspected the delicate drawings of ladies' underwear in *Woman's Day*. He began to consider what might happen if all his hair fell out.

The dryer shut off, leaving a thunderous silence. Leroy yawned, blinking tears. A poisonous sweat trickled down his brow. Deedee led him back to the chair, wiped his face with a towel. The cap came off, and the curlers, one at a time; the fronds of his hair had baked into coils.

What have I done. "Oh, it looks awful curly. . . . "

"No, you sit back. Wait'll we wash it and brush it out."

Lorraine repeated her magic at the shampoo sink, and then Deedee took up scissors and comb and a brush.

She snipped and tucked, rubbing in lots of Brylcreem, brushing, combing. Sure enough the curls relaxed into a soft flowing wave. She held up a mirror, angled so Leroy could see the back.

His hair was now full and wavy and smooth. A dramatic line swooped over his head to a V at his collar, sharp and shiny as a Cadillac's fin.

Deedee was an artist. "God, it looks great," he stammered.

She beamed. "I think so too. It looks just like the picture."

Oh cool. He was Tony Marlon Leroy tough guy, JD,

DA, a cool rockin' cat. He snarled for the mirror. Deedee laughed.

When she swept off the bib, shaking hair to the floor, Leroy saw that his plaid shirt and tan slacks were all wrong with his hair. He looked like Andy Hardy with a pompadour.

"That's three-fifty," said Deedee, "and you're supposed to give me a tip if you like how I did."

"How much?"

"Make it four dollars."

Leroy held out five. "You—really—I mean, I love it."

"Thanks, hon. And listen," she said, "that Brylcreem is not gonna shine it up the way you want. You get you some pomade."

"What's that?"

"They sell it at the Woolsworth. It comes in this little pink can, see? It's what the colored folks use. Gives you that shine."

Ignoring the smirks of the ladies, Leroy put on his jacket and turned up the collar. He went out to the Plymouth and sat for a while, contemplating his hair in the rearview mirror.

It rose in front to a lofty height. The oil darkened it and made the sides gleam.

There was no turning back from this hair. Deedee had told him the wave would be in there for weeks.

Leroy had new hair and the car keys and money. Now he needed clothes.

He knew where to go. Howlin' Wolf recommended the place every night around midnight: "Check out Irving Brothers, the pride of Beale Street, these brothers are a friend to you, brother, stop on in and give 'em your business. Dandy duds for the cool blue man inside of you."

Leroy drove over the hill on Beale. This was a street for fancied-up colored folks at night, but in the daytime it belonged to poor people of both races. Thin winter light bleached the sidewalk. Pool halls and seedy lounges stood open, nobody inside. A withered old man leaned in a doorway, sheltering a beer bottle against his chest. Three boys chased each other around a broken-down car.

The Irving Brothers' store was set in a block of old falling-in places: a pawnshop, a smoke shop, a shoe repair shop, a juke joint, then the Irvings' shiny plate glass and wide-open doors. Leroy parked carefully at the curb.

A balding white man in white shirt and tie lounged out front, talking in business off the street. "Hey, brother," he said as Leroy approached, "slick hair, my friend. Come on in and let us fix you up."

Leroy grinned. "I've got money today."

"Well that's what we like to hear, you just step right on in, let Myron take care of you—Myron? Young fellow's got money, and he wants you to make him look sharp."

Myron was a copy of his brother: squat, balding, with eager eyes behind rimless glasses. "Come on in here, my friend! Haven't I seen you before? What can we do for you today?"

"I need some clothes," Leroy said. "I listen to y'all's ads all the time on WDIA."

"Well that's fine there, son, that's fine—looking for anything in particular?"

Leroy gazed out over racks of brilliant clothing. This was where colored people came to buy their Saturday-night outfits, and famous hillbilly singers their spangly shirts. "I don't know," he said, "it all looks pretty good. Why don't you let me look around."

"You go right ahead," Myron said. He stood watching Leroy flip through the shirts. They were all loud, these shirts: some purple, some yellow, some with crazy paisley patterns, or Hawaiian, or gray with red and white cowboy trim. "You like that?" Myron kept saying. "You like that?"

The Irving Brothers had unusual taste. There were shirts with sequins, leather trim, rabbit-fur collars. Leroy loved them all.

He loitered for a long time at the leather jackets, but he'd have to spend a lot more time ushering movies before he could afford one of those.

He unearthed a pair of amazing balloon-legged pants, shiny black material with stark yellow lightning bolts zagging from the hip to the ankle—a blaze of electricity down both legs. The tag said eighteen dollars.

The pants would look cool with the black slinky pull-over shirt, woven with threads of what Myron said was Dutch gold. "Guaranteed not to rust," he said, "your wife can just throw it in with the rest of the wash."

Your wife! Leroy liked that. He felt like a big deal, picking through the clothes under Myron's watchful eye.

With a hot pink shirt, the lightning trousers, and a skinny yellow necktie added in, the bill came to forty-three dollars. That was two weeks of standing in the dark at the Loew's, but if everything fit, it was worth every minute. Leroy went to the tiny booth and changed in a hurry, taking care not to disturb his hair.

He stepped out from behind the curtain.

Myron whistled. "Would you look at that! Now *there* goes a man who believes in looking good."

Leroy found his way to the triple mirror.

What he saw stunned him.

The first thing was his hair. That was truly successful hair.

The slinky black shirt clung to his chest. The narrow-hipped pants flared out in the leg like something from a Valentino movie, with that flash of yellow electricity zagging up the legs.

He draped the yellow tie around his neck.

"Cool," he said.

"Cool? I'll say it's cool!" Myron exclaimed. "Ike! Come here! Take a look at this man!"

He was right. Leroy was beautiful. The hair made him older and sleek, and these clothes—yeah, cat, these were the clothes of a visible man.

He would look even better with his guitar.

Ike whistled, exactly as Myron had done. "Would you look at that," he said.

Myron spoke up: "You want me to wrap up your other stuff and you wear these home?"

"Sure, why not," Leroy said. "Let me get my money out of my pants."

He pulled himself away from the dazzling mirror and felt in his old limp pants pocket for his remaining bills.

"All right now," Myron was saying, "what else can we get you? Some socks? How about that green shirt you liked?"

Leroy handed over the money. "No, that's all for right now. Don't worry. I'll come back."

He took his change and his bag of old clothes and floated out into the light of Beale Street. He walked on new feet, with new hair and threads of gold on his skin. He walked like a star.

YOUNG ELVIS

Cornelius Eady

He's driving a truck, and we know
What he knows: His sweat
And hips move the wrong product.
In Memphis, behind a thick
Pane of glass, a stranger daydreams

Of a voice as tough as a Negro's,
But not a Negro's. A voice that
Slaps instead of *twangs*,
But not a Negro's. When it
Struts through the door
(Like he knows it will), and
Opens up, rides

The spiky strings of
The guitar, pushes
The bass line below the belt,
Reveals the drums
As cheap pimps,
In fact transforms the whole proceedings
Into a cat house, a lost night . . .

He wets his lips.
Already the young driver is imagining
A 20th century birthday present,
The one-shot lark of his recorded voice,
The awe he intends to
Shine through his mother's favorite
    hymns.

FROM ELVIS PRESLEY CALLS HIS MOTHER AFTER THE ED SULLIVAN SHOW

Samuel Charters

I was telling you about how the lights get so bright up there on the stage I sometimes can't see so good out in the theater. There was one time, Momma, before Colonel Parker started taking care of business for me, when Bill and Scotty and me got hired to play for a private party. I think it was down in Alabama someplace. We were going to play one of those shows in Louisiana—you know that Hay Ride Show we did—and we thought we could swing past this little town and do the job and get a little extra money.

It was one of those kind of places with lots of bright lights shining right in our eyes and we couldn't make out anything except that everybody seemed to have some kind of costume on. Okay, we said, it's going to be a costume party, and we can go out and do our show, just like always. We didn't let the crowd bother us none in those kind of places. Even with all the lights shining I could see people kind of crowding to get close when we started and I thought everything was going to be alright. But they didn't make much noise, even when I shook it up a little for them, and I figured, well, they got those costumes on and that must keep them dampered down a little. But when we finished the number and I went into my bow, there wasn't any kind of sound out of them. Everything was so quiet you couldn't tell they were breathing. Finally somebody said something in a loud voice right down in front. What he said was, "Boy, can't you do nothing but that nigger shit?"

Now the fellow that had hired us, he was standing off on the side of the stage, and when he heard that he jumped out there and he started in on the guy that said it. "You told me to get you something really hot, something that's really happening, and this is the boy out of Memphis who's got those records playing everywhere you go. This is Elvis Presley." And the other guy, who's still standing out there in the dark and we can't really get a look at him, he says, "What kind of a name is Elvis?" Then the fellow on the stage with us got upset and he started saying things and he was getting more and more answers from down in front, and finally, to calm everybody down, some of the public crawled up on the stage to get between them. We were still standing there, holding our instruments, and Bill had taken a couple of steps back so he could start running if the trouble got any worse, and then we got a look at their costumes. They were wearing sheets, and they had hoods that they'd pushed back so they could talk. They were white sheets they had on them. It was the Ku Klux Klan. That crazy guy had hired us to play a party for the Ku Klux Klan!

When we saw that, we started to go off the stage, but then the crowd started shouting and whistling. They'd paid their money to see the show and we were the only show they had. The guy down in front was a little quieter and the fellow that had hired us kind of backed up across the stage, coming toward us. He was smiling and waving his arm for everybody to be quiet, but when he got back close to us we could see him shaking. In that part of the country you don't mess around with the Klan. He stood there beside me waving his arms and he whispered out of the side of his mouth, "You know any other kind of numbers?"

We were just about as scared as he was, but when he said that we started in to some hillbilly number. I can't remember what it was. Something you and Daddy Vernon used to sing, and it was so simple we didn't have to rehearse it. This got everybody quieted down and we sang them every hillbilly number we could think of, but I could see we weren't going over. You know how I feel when I can't move around while I'm singing, and I didn't dare do anything that might get them started on us again. Finally I looked over at the guy at the edge of the stage and he gave us the sign that we'd been out there singing long enough to get our money.

Now you know I still didn't know what to expect when we did a show in those days, and I thought the way to end it was to try to get everybody on my side. What I did was start singing "The Star-Spangled Banner." I figures this would show them that we were good people, even if we did make a mistake with our first number. But right in the middle of it the noise started in again and I could see some of those boys in those white sheets starting to climb up on the stage again. Bill had more experience with this kind of show than I did, and when I stopped playing my guitar and turned around to ask the guys what I should do, Bill all of a sudden dragged his bass up to the microphone and started singing "Dixie" as loud as he could. When they heard this the boys climbing up on the stage started walking up and down like it was some kind of parade and we played "Dixie" over and over for them until we could get out of there.

That isn't the kind of thing that happens to me now, but I still don't know who's out there in the dark half of the time when I'm singing.

Just a minute, Momma. There's somebody who's just come in that I have to say hello to.

Where did you go off to, baby? When I told those girls to get out I wasn't thinking of you. I could tell by looking at them they weren't nice girls. You're different. You just sit down on the bed again and I'll be through talking to my mother and you and me will have all the time we want. Where do you go to school? You don't go to school anymore? You got some kind of job? You sell jewelry at Woolworth's? Woolworth's is a good place to be. One of those big companies you know they won't go out of business on you. Before I was doing this I had a job driving a truck. If nobody likes my movie and people get tired of rock and roll, I can always get my old job back.

I bet you have every one of my records. Well, if you don't have all the new ones you don't need to buy them. Before you leave I'll have one of the boys find all he can for you. But you're not thinking of leaving now. I wouldn't want to think about you going away just before we getting started. I can see you got on a fancy petticoat under that skirt you're wearing.

I see the little edge of it there, and it gets me wondering what you got on under that petticoat.

But you stay over on the bed there. I'll just lie back and look at you while I finish talking.

No, Momma, we didn't get cut off. I had my hand over the phone so you wouldn't have to listen to all those business things we have to talk about. No, you don't need to hang up. I can keep talking. I know you're just like me. It's as hard for you to get to sleep as it is for me. You taking your pill? I don't like to take too many pills. Oh, I take them if I have to sleep real bad. I hate it when I lie there and I don't feel like sleeping and I'm too tired to get out of bed and do something else. When I stay up so late it isn't so bad. If it gets to be nine or ten o'clock in the morning then I can sleep.

I had to use the pills when I was out in Hollywood. I had to get up early so I could go to work on the picture. That was the way they did it out there. If I was going to get up and not look like I was a hundred years old, then I had to get to sleep on time. But I don't like to use them. You take yours now, and I'll keep talking until you feel like you want to lie down. It isn't my place to ever say anything about how God made the world, but sometimes I wish He'd made it just a little bit easier to sleep.

Just a minute, Momma.

Miss, if you like everybody else around this crazy place you probably feeling tired. You're not? Honey, I know why that is. You're thinking about what's coming next. You just keep lying there and let me look at those pretty legs of yours.

No, Momma, we didn't get cut off this time either. I just had something to discuss with the boys. You know, like you told me to do, I always have Gene or Junior sleeping in the room with me in case I start to walking around in my sleep, and I had to tell them to wait a little. I wouldn't let them cut off the connection while you still are waiting to get to sleep. Anyway, I know I won't walk off anywhere in my sleep tonight. After all that dancing they made me do in those rehearsals— and then after I got all ready they didn't show it anyway! You know how those people are. I'm telling you the truth, just like the preacher tells the congregation when he wants to let them know they're hearing the word. Listen to this, Momma, what you are hearing is the truth, it's God's truth, it's the one hundred and ten percent truth—and the truth is, when I get into my bed tonight, I'm going to stay right in it and not get up for one minute. And you know I mean every word I'm saying.

Who am I talking to? I'm just talking to you, Momma. And one of the boys—he's still here. Somebody's always watching me so I don't get in any trouble.

WORDS AND PICTURES

♪♪

Rachel Salazar

When did you first meet J? How did you happen to get together?

Oh, I think we have to begin with the shoe on the other foot, to tie the ribbon in a different way. . . . It was ages ago when a photographer took me to the Club 82 to pose with J for fan photographs for the magazine Confidential. *They wanted to take some photos but somehow they were missing a woman, like parsley or a slice of lemon. They called my agency and told them that Vera was just what they needed. I had just done a movie, and my name was around then. So it was arranged that we would go to the Club 82 together with a photographer and a PR man.* (A pinkish photograph, as they all are, of a sign that reads Club 82—diagonal as if on a stairway—with an arrow pointing upward.) *Yes, that must be it. The wallpaper was gold, I remember, with these designs— balloons and polka dots—flying all over it.*

Was J alone?

He came with his two fat, nasty bodyguards—yes, it's them exactly. (A double portrait: on the left, a blond guy with freckles, maybe a redhead—skinny actually—hair slicked back, curly on top, mean-looking, thin upper lip all but swallowed by the lower, chin dimpled from compression, he's looking up slightly, whites showing underneath the iris, shiny checked shirt, tie askew, buttons missing, striped elbow on the table; the other, his cauliflower ear visible, light eyes sizing up the viewer, fat jowly face, lips tucked into a small prim smile, rumpled shirt open at the neck over a white T-shirt, tweed jacket with a shawl collar; an empty Coca-Cola bottle before him, another half-full beside it.) *I can't remember their names . . . They were standing around him like walls, and I have to say they were really ordinary, with belching and farting and everything that belongs to it.* (A close-up, just sleeves, tweed and stripes, Coke tumblers lifted in a toast. Next page: a blond woman in a black dress cut like a slip sitting with the fat bodyguard in a booth. Her heavy ringed fingers reaching under his lapel, she leans against him, his hand clasped around her ribs, thumb delicately lifted, so that it does not touch her breast. His cauliflower ear is facing the viewer. Then, the two bodyguards with J. They're both laughing, while he seems doubled over, as if he's been punched in the stomach.)

How did you and J get along?

It's hard to say—I mean, he was a very nice kid, polite, soft-spoken, a crease in his pants, a real hick, in fact. At first, we didn't say much to each other. (The two-page spread shows J and Vera sitting next to each other, turned away from one another. J exhibits his straight profile, his eyebrow is straight too, over a smoky eyelid, black hair long on top but shaved at the sides and back, white shirt, dark suit, narrow tie, a white rose in a vase before him. A man is speaking to him, but J seems not to be listening, attention elsewhere, over the man's shoulder.) *This other guy was from Texas, a good old boy, but sharp. He was trying to get J to put money into some deal he was cooking up—a chain of motels he wanted to call J's Hound Dog Motor Inns. A real sleaze—every time I leaned over, he'd look down my dress.*

Your dress was very décolleté. . . . (Vera, at a three-quarter angle, lips parted, fresh-faced, bangs damp on her forehead, hair pulled back, a white rose at the crown. Slavic face, high cheekbones, upturned eyes with black wings, the quizzical eyebrows of the late fifties, spaghetti straps, straight low-cut bodice, natural cleavage, although her arms pressed against her

body and arched shoulders may contribute to the effect.)
What can you remember about Club 82?

It was like any other club—there was music. On stage was a
band, and after we came, they kept playing J's songs—I guess
they were hoping he'd sing. (The photograph—slightly out of
focus—a band: a light-skinned black man, hair conked, in a
pale, speckled jacket, holding the neck of his guitar; the drummer seated, smiling under his pencilled mustache; the saxo-
phonist, fingers on keys, holds out his other hand to J, who is
recognizable from the back. Shiny pompadour, thick neck, he
mounts the stage. A few pages later, the musicians have re-
arranged themselves around J. The drummer standing by a
grand piano, hanging over its side; the black guitarist snapping his fingers, laughing; J at center, hair mussed, knees
apart, one hand on his thigh, the other between his legs, baby-
faced, mouth pulled up on one side—the familiar sneer.) *He*
got up on stage, like in the picture, and he began to sing. One
of his bodyguards said he should stop, he should know he
wasn't allowed to sing, against the rules, breaking contract,
or something. Then J was singing at the table, and that wasn't
allowed either, so he beat time with his fingers, and they
stopped that too. It was awful.

Was J a heavy drinker? (J, head to one side, is waving, hand
foreshortened, probably for a waiter. His face is puffy, coarse-
featured, nostrils flared, lips curled. The bodyguards and the
Texan watch the camera. Vera seems to be saying something
to the PR man, who has a paunch, and wears thick glasses
and a three-piece plaid suit.)

No, actually, although he ordered champagne and it was ex-
pensive too—the real stuff, not André Cold Duck or any-
thing—his bodyguards wouldn't let him touch it. We were all
raising our glasses to toast the release of J's new record when
the blond guy reached out and took J's glass, telling him to
keep his mitts off the hard stuff and order himself some V-8.
They kept him on a leash like a dog. Well, he just hung his
head and said, Yessir. No balls, that guy. . . .

Did they tell him to do other things? The bodyguards, I mean.

Like I said, they were really awful. They bullied him. I remember one of them threw a comb across the table at J, and said his hair was a mess and he'd better spruce himself up. J jumped like a rabbit and did like he was told. He didn't say anything for himself—just smiled like he wanted to do what he was supposed to. Even when J went to the toilet, one of them went with him. I was pretty upset when I saw that, so I asked the other guy why J couldn't go by himself, and he answered that they had so many contracts for J that if some crazy broad got the idea to throw some hydrochloric acid in his face or some other flipped-out stuff, it would be all over. There was too much money on him to take any chances.

You and J seem a bit friendlier here? (J and Vera have moved closer together, although they still aren't looking at each other. His arm is behind her back, around her shoulder, but the hand is open, fingers dangling not touching her, although it appears as if his thumb is resting against her skin. His timid dazed expression may be a response to the move, surprise at his own boldness. Above Vera, the upholstered wall; four stuffed sections meet in a shiny button—a navel, an eye.)

After his first tomato juice, he relaxed a little, still didn't talk to me but his arm kept on sneaking along, like a mouse against a baseboard, from his lap, to the back of my chair, to my shoulder. When I suddenly turned around, he flushed very red and said, Excuse me, but he didn't pull away. (Close-up of the previous photograph: the texture grainy, light reflected in J's hair, on Vera's lower lip—her perfect teeth!—a point of light caught in both their eyes. The symmetry of his face: horizontal lines of eyes, brows, mouth; vertical, nose, ears, hair; the upper lip curled slightly, a suggestion of the famous sneer. Vera's face, though pretty, is irregular: one eye higher than the other, lopsided smile, eyebrows don't match. Her eyes meet the viewer's. She seems to know whatever it is that frightens J, maybe that she herself is the cause of his fear.)

How did the people at the club respond to J? Were they excited by his presence? After all, he was at the peak of his popularity then.

Well, everyone wanted to pose with him—hugging him, kissing him, and so on. It was really silly—J squeezing the cook, cuddling with the waitresses, the barmaids, dancers, strippers. Even the men wanted to touch him, to have their pictures taken with him. (J between two men, each one with his arm linked through J's, one in a bow tie and white waiter's jacket; the other, a kitchen worker in an open shirt, wiping his hand on his apron. J's own hands are clenched before him like a fighter protecting his body.)

And the women?

You should have seen the way they carried on! A lot of them were real trash, like this one. (A shiny blonde, appliquéd daisies incongruous at the neckline of her dark sheath, between J and the skinny bodyguard, an arm over each man's shoulder, her hand clasping J's, fingers interlocking, an intimate gesture, smug possessiveness in her dark eyes and wide mouth.) *This girl was really common. She would have gone with anyone, even the bodyguards—with both of them at once! She should have taken her daisies to 42nd Street.*

Who is this? (J is not in this photograph. A naked woman standing, arms raised, holding a light-colored satin cape behind her like a curtain. Her body is beautiful: flat belly, graceful arms, round breasts—a black crude-looking patch over her pubis; her face is pretty: a joyful smile showing gums, heavily drawn theatrical eyebrows, sparkling drop earrings, a white plume in her short dark hair. Right below her patch, a man's head—he's smiling too.)

She was a stripper. What a funny photo! No, she was much nicer. I know for sure she was the picture of beauty. (Another photograph of the same woman, this time with clothes on and this time with J. They are facing each other. Her eyes are closed, chin lifted, tongue out. His fingers dig into her shoulder, tangled in the fringe of her dress. His mouth is open too, and his eyes are on her tongue. The next shot, taken from further back, her lovely arms are around his neck, one hand over the other, a cigarette dangling from her fingers. His hands rest on her hips, her close-fitting dress showing her tight little bottom. Noses touching, their lips are puckered in a playful, closed-mouth kiss.) *I remember when she did her act—I already thought she was a knockout—but when she finally dropped her last stitch of clothes, I sort of gasped because— well, you can see for yourself the body she had. I was looking over at J out of the corner of my eye, and he was staring at the tablecloth and stirring his tomato juice with a cocktail straw. The bodyguards were snickering and coughing and making all kinds of stupid cracks.*

Things got pretty wild as the night went on, didn't they?

It depends on what you call wild. I guess I was kind of surprised at the time. There were these two twins—dancers— who just jumped all over him. You have pictures of them too? (J between two young women, virtually identical, pert teenagers, slim-hipped in satin haltered costumes, which cover their girlish breasts but plunge open to the waist. They wear fishnet stockings and long satin mitts elasticized above the elbow. J holds one of them tightly, his skin dull against the shiny cloth. The other girl reaches for a banister; J's hand, barely visible, clasps her from behind.) *They were very young—maybe seventeen or eighteen—younger than I was at the time—real flirts. They came up to our table asking for autographs, then wanted to have their picture taken with him.* (J between the two girls seems isolated, not connected to them, or to the rest of the scene. Neck tilted slightly, mouth slack but hinting at an amiable diffidence, his sincere gaze focuses on the viewer. The thin end of his tie hangs below the wider part. Painted nails, which could belong to either girl, clutch his shoulder.)

It all seems rather innocent—good, clean fun, and all that.

*You've got to be kidding! Those girls knew a thing or two.
They squealed and giggled a lot, but when it came down to
business, they could tell apples from oranges. Tell me these
tootsies are Girl Scouts?* (Another photograph: J is embracing
one of the twins, who now wears a satin skirt over her costume.
His nose squashed against her face, lips fixed like a suction
cup on the corner of her mouth, while she faces the camera,
wide smile, a large circular birthmark or discoloration on her
cheek. One of his hands holds her bare back; the other hovers
oddly in mid-air. Her twin stands behind him, pushing against
him, hand on his arm closed, except her extended index finger,
as if pointing out the naughty pair. Her lips are pursed, eyebrows raised in mock surprise, long stockinged thighs thrust
at the camera.) *These girls just couldn't keep their hands to
themselves. They ate him up!* (Facing page: J has turned
around and has the girl with the long thighs in his arms. His
lower face is hidden, his eyes on her. She leans away from
him—a small smile of vanity—light glinting on her bobby pin
and on the rhinestone barrette in her hair. She holds on to
the banister with one hand, while the twin with the skirt pulls
at him from behind, open mouth showing teeth. Below the
three figures, as if sitting or kneeling, is a clown, his head
thrown back, tongue curled between painted cupid's bow lips,
the white around his eyes and mouth giving him an expression
of vacuous hilarity. Balloons float over the wallpaper.)

These photographs show J with a lot of different women. Were
these just publicity shots?

*Well, like I told you, the whole thing was a publicity stunt,
but these photos never got into* Confidential. . . . *I remember
he did really like one woman. I think her name was Angie—
yes, that's her.* (J and a woman, clearly older than he—probably in her mid-thirties—her head against his cheek. Although
he is looking away, he seems intent on her, his mouth soft,
tender. There is an almost matronly dignity, which has its own
allure, in her smooth well-made-up face, eyes carefully outlined in black—top and bottom—light lipstick, painted beauty
marks at the corner of her left eye and on her right cheek.
She wears a white tailored blouse, a round medallion on a fine
chain resting on her full bosom. In the next photograph, which

looks as if it had been taken a moment later, J's right hand holds her, his face pressed into her hair, dark lids closed, a moment of concentrated feeling.) *He was really knocked out by her—she was obviously in a different league than the others. By the end of the evening, she was parked at our table. I was sitting on one side of him and she was on the other, and when Mike Dunn, the PR guy, said it was late and he had to get me home—I was living with my mother then—J looked at her and said, I'm staying here tonight.*

Did he stay at Club 82 for the rest of the evening?

I don't know, but the next day, he came to my house to take me out for breakfast at one of the big hotels—the Pierre, I think it was—and he had bits of tinsel everywhere—in his hair, his eyebrows, sticking out of his pockets. He looked like a Christmas tree in a window display. I asked him what happened, and he just said, I stayed there.

How did you like that evening? What did it mean for you?

The interviewer adjusts the volume of his tape recorder, watching Vera struggle, perplexed by the question, her attempts at guile unsuccessful, as she visibly agonizes over her answer. It is late summer, a warm night in the city. She is wearing a cotton sun dress, which, although not revealing, bares her arms and collarbone. She must be close to forty, but her skin has a kind of freshness to it.

"Is that a difficult question?" He lays a hand, meant to reassure, on her forearm.

Her crooked smile is demure. Still those lovely teeth!

"A kind of disappointment?" He raises his eyebrows, giving his voice a tone of encouragement that usually overcomes hesitation. He covers her hand with his own.

Her forehead creases faintly with, what he reads as, annoyance at the accuracy of his observation. Her hand underneath his trembles slightly.

ELVIS CUTS LOOSE

Eleanor Earle
Crockett

Pillows of flesh tumbled like ice loaded with mercury inside blue silk pajamas sticky with sweat as Elvis rolled toward the nightstand in those last few frames of drug-induced sleep. "Take these," a doctor held out a prescription to him, hand gloved in a rainbow mist that kept spreading 'til Elvis felt its breath enveloping him like the cold sweat he was waking in. "You'll never worry about falling asleep again."

Slowly the heavy eyelids parted, slowly closed, rose again conscious of waking . . . "never worry . . . never worry . . ." the doctor's voice faded under Elvis' own, much more famous, voice inside his brain, manly protesting, "What, me worry? You got that all wrong, mister, I ain't ever worried 'bout *anything!* Not since you four-eyed mutha-suckin' sonsabitches give me a solid gold medal for doin' absolutely *nothin'* in Viet Nam . . . rat-fuckin', toe-suckin' . . . so now what d'ya want me *not* to do?"

Head hung, chin pinned to his collarbone, Elvis was sitting up now, gazing down at ten lined-up, close-ranked faces flat and blank as little boxes on an application form. They seemed to be curling up like claws growing in his direction, like some chick's long, imitation plastic fingernails held too close to the flame of a cigarette lighter. His stomach rumbled deep inside, so he looked further up the sticky blue silk pajama legs to his heavy belly and felt hunger, not in the belly but in his throat.

Elvis lifted his bulk up from the mattress, ignoring the

runaway toenails, and made for the medicine chest he'd had installed in the room. It was refrigerated. Opening the door, he stood gazing into it. "Ham sandwich" flashed before his eyes. He reached into the cabinet, chose a bottle from the assortment, snapped off the lid and shook three or four sandwiches into a cupped hand.

"It was that dickface Cap'n 'r *Colonel*, that's who it was, always orderin' whatever he wanted for supper and makin' me eat ham sandwiches. That must be why these suckers taste so bad. Man, the worst ham sandwiches I ever tasted, that's what they are. Get rid of 'em, Colonel!" He then poured out the bottle into a cup, carried it the few yards between cabinet and toilet, fiddled in his pajamas for his member, then proceeded to take potshots at the pills as he dribbled them one by one into the toilet. "Pow! Pow!" he spoke aloud, "Pow! Pow!" The pills sank under contact, then surfaced again contentedly until gradually they melted, speckling the yellow water with little green pools.

"Like some Jell-O with your ham sandwich, soldier? I said I ain't a soldier, you . . . geezus, where am I anyway. . . looks like a fancy hotel." Elvis raised his big arms, grabbed the collar of his blue silk pajama shirt and ripped it up over his head. "Ten million is what he promised them, ten million clams pissin' all over *me*." No way was he taking any more of those pills. "Nossir, no way, *sir!*" He saluted the camouflaged water. He wanted a salad, and a steak. "So they got twenty instead."

"Knock knock" at the white French doors drove Elvis back to the bed. He hastily messed with the covers, looking for the underwear he knew was hiding somewhere among their blue silk ripples. "Jus' a minute, I'm getting dressed."

"Knock knock knock," someone rattled the huge doors on their flimsy hinges. "Jus' a minute, I said, I'm comin', I'm comin'," the words massaged his lungs. Need a microphone, where's the mike . . . he found a pair of white silk boxer shorts, pulled off the pajama pants and slipped one leg into the shorts, plopping onto the edge of the bed to wrangle his other long, rumbling leg into the elusive opening. Snapping himself into the waistband, he stood. "Come in!" he shouted at the medicine cabinet. The door rattled impatiently, then ceased.

Elvis padded to the door, turned the deadbolt and

jerked it wide open. A silver breakfast tray lay at his feet. "Good timing, fellah," he told it. Lifting a silver coffeepot from the tray, he carried it to the coffee table, then returned for cup and sugar, carried those objects also to the table and arranged them in a pleasant motif. When he was satisfied with the composition, he donned the blue silk pajama shirt, flipped up the collar and studied his tousled image in the gigantic mirror of the Hollywood blond armoire.

"Hey-hey, welcome, sir, to the USA," Elvis saluted himself in the mirror, clicked his bare heels together, pivoted and goose-stepped to the settee on one side of the coffee table, then abruptly sat down to tea. To his left, the whole of Hollywood gazed up at the glass wall of the penthouse boudoir jailhouse rock upon which Elvis sat sipping coffee from a Louis XIV gold-rimmed cup. He lifted a ringed pinky, focused both eyes on its tip and snorted in mock glee. "Time for our bath, son," he thought. His arm extended the teacup out and up in a silent toast, swung smoothly to the right, tilted voluntarily and dumped the warm, dark liquid in a steady stream down, down into the thick beige carpet. "Sorry, sir, let me pour you another cup." He set the cup on the rapidly disappearing carpet stain, grasped the ornate silver pot by the handle and emptied the remaining contents into and around the tiny cup, miles below him on the floor. "Pennies from Maryland," he crooned. "Oops, better save some for the reporters." He stopped pouring and set the urn back on the table. The phone on the nightstand rang twice, then was silent.

"Guess they got lost." Elvis retrieved his teacup, transferred an inch or so from the gold rim to the overflowed saucer, added an ounce of sugar and resumed sipping.

The phone began again, this time insistently. It kept on ringing while Elvis poured coffee from the saucer into his cup and placed it all on the table, before reaching for the receiver. It was a long reach, but he accomplished it and spoke into it. "King Kong, Avon calling."

"Good, you sound awake. Are you?" It was the Colonel.

"With your permission, sir."

"Cut the crap. Have you finished breakfast?"

"It's suppertime, man, I feel like a steak."

"I'll send it up. T-bone okay?"

"Yeah, but make it three, well-done, none o' that *pink*

stuff, y'hear? Make it charbroil. I hate that panfryin' thang they do, tastes like my mom's. Charbroil, that means *crisp*. And some spuds, like in the Army, that's somethin' they do right anyhow. And cloverleaf yeast rolls, you know what that is? Send a dozen. I'm famished, man. I'm out o' smokes."

"You quit smokin' over two years ago, remember? You *don't smoke*. I'll send the chow, though."

"Okay, hurry it up. Man, I'm famished," he repeated.

"I'm sending the barber for a shave."

"Send the manicurist too, my toenails are crawlin' up my thighs."

"Awright. Take your pills?"

"Yeah, *all* of 'em. I hate the slimy mothers. What about the tour?"

"Reporters on their way. Eat your T-bones and cut the profanity. Be there at 3:00. Be *dressed*." He hung up.

"Fuckin' tongue-suckin' muthafucker," said Elvis to empty space. "I'll dress you." He tossed the receiver toward the stand. "*Man*euver, fuckin' *man*euvers. *Man*icurist, fuckin' *man*icurist. Reporters, fuckin' potatoes. T-bones, fuckin' talent. No, pills, fuckin' talent. No talent, fuckin' image. No profanity, fuckin' . . . fuckin' . . . *talent*."

He shut off that tape, the same tape kept playing over and over, and inhaled deep. He stood up, enjoying it, the sensation of air flooding to his brain, into the muscles of his legs. Several more luxurious, deep breaths. "No cough," he thought, "quit smoking, tha's good." He performed a few deep knee bends, breathing ever more deeply, long and slow breaths, becoming elated.

"Fuckin' profanity is *no* profanity. Tha's takin' the Lord's name in vain an' I *never* did that, never. Who'd ever want to fuck the Lord . . . be fuckin' dangerous, man, very risky. Fuckin' is fuckin', has nothing whatsoever to do with God, whoever that is, though I'm sure he's hangin' around somewhere. Oh yes, dear God, and we all thank you, standin' around in our shorts waitin' on T-bone steaks an' a *man*icurist an' . . . geez, I wonder if he's listenin' . . . maybe this is just a prayer, from me to you, dear O Lord, who, thank the Lord, praise the Lord, is not Elvis, King of Rock n' Roll . . . so they say . . . so somebody says, is not me, not I, not Elvis fuckin' Prezley standin' here breathin' your name O Lord and Jesus Christ, Son of God the Father, no not I who is the son

33

of man, that is, the son of one human being who is, or was, my own daddy, mine and only mine, at least I was until the fuckin' Colonel put hisself in the picture . . . or was I? Can't remember, too long ago, long long ago, before I ever even thought of ever bein' a man . . . "

By now Elvis was starting to feel a gnawing sense of hunger someplace other than, but in addition to, his belly and his throat. It was creeping through his brain, stirring deeply slumbering nerves or synapses or sexual chemicals, and starting to flow down into his backbone and float around his genitals and down his legbones all the way down to his curling toenails. He stopped listening to the words spoken in his own voice inside his ears and brain, and started listening to another soft, whisper of a voice, not the preaching voice which may or may not be his own, which indeed did somewhat resemble the voice of a preacher he once heard, from his childhood, a voice blended with his own quieter, smoother voice.

Whispers in the night when he was scared of what might be happening outside in the dark, shadowy, moonlit woods. His mama's voice hushed and low with interrupted sleep, telling him not to worry, the dogs just found a raccoon or a possum, telling him how sleepy he was feeling and it was okay for him to close his eyes and go to sleep. It would all be over in the mornin', everything would be just fine, not to worry now . . . and go to dreamland . . . and outside in full moonlight the niggers, uh-uh, bad word, used to be called darkies, but anyway then they were called niggers . . . croonin' to themselves an' their babies to make them go to sleep . . . make them forget the . . . tellin' them their own daydreams of dancing and mockingbirds and Chevrolets and diamond rings.

Elvis crooned low to himself one of those tunes he remembered hearing the mammies sing. He started getting into it, his knees started shivering and his shoulders shaking 'til he was flinging his head from side to side like a chickensnake, then he was chicken-walking fast on tiptoe from wall to wall and jumping onto the bed, bending low to watch himself in the Hollywood mirror movie screen and making the whole room shiver and shake with his childhood daydream and nightmare memories, watching the movie inside reflected in fragments of himself in the mirror and flashing on the niggers flinging themselves all over the dance floor of little backroad beer and barbeque and juke joints, and other niggers flinging themselves all over the pews and aisles of little backwoods churches, and realizing they were the very same niggers and he was one of them, only they were on the inside and his overgrown ten-year-old body was on the outside looking in, marveling at how black folks getting beat up and shot in their balls and swung by the neck until purple with pain, and their kids dragged through the fields and their women raped and their clothes ripped to shreds, just marveling at how they could dance and carry on like wild beasts and seem to be having such a good time getting drunk on their ass in the face of such torture and murder and terror and shame being done to them.

So then he quit shivering and writhing in the mirror and threw his body down on the king-size mattress, flat on his back and just lay there squirming and slapping his body all over, fully awake now and feeling like the full-grown angel of God that he knew he was, his voice quivering and moaning to itself—and he noticed the room had stopped spinning.

"Aw, geezus crist, now the man's gonna come an' probably trim my sideburns, an' the reporters," but remembering T-bones and Johnnie Walker Red, he hurled himself off the mattress and stomped into the bath for a quick, hot shower before they all got there.

"Mr. Prezley, I got your clean sheets and your towels here." It was the new maid, a voluptuous little girl the hotel had just hired to help out because Elvis was such a good-paying customer and also such a big problem for the staff with his night schedule and unusual demands. "I brought the razor you wanted, though Mrs. Thompson told me not to. Mr. Prezley?"

He stepped into the boudoir from the bath with a towel held around his hips because he knew that's what she wanted him to do. "Okay, okay, honey, lay 'em there on the bed an' come over here. Why don't you shut the door there, too, while you're at it. I got company comin' soon, we don't want to scare anyone."

The maid lay down her duties and pleasantly wandered toward the door. "I just wanted to look at you this time, that's all," she said softly, "I didn't have anything else in mind."

"Oh, I know ya didn't, honey," Elvis said.

"I see you left the tray again out in the hallway, but I moved it. Want me to bring it in? You ought to eat your breakfast, Mr. Prezley, it just goes to waste out there." She sounded serious, but it didn't bother him much.

"I thought someone else might want it, tha's all. It looks real good. You want it? Bring it in here, then. Maybe I'll take a few bites of it when I'm through showerin'. Lock the door too, do you mind?"

"Oh no, I don't mind." She fetched in the tray, turned the bolt and walked over to the coffee table and set it down there. "It's squishy here, did you spill somethin'?"

"Oh yes, I did, sorry. Don't worry about it."

"Okay," said the maid, removing her apron.

"Leave that on, if you don't mind. Wha's your name again?" Elvis whipped off his cover-up and popped it at her before returning to the steaming bathroom. She came toward him across the carpet. "Missy."

"Oh yeah, Missy. Very nice name. I like it a lot."

"I know. Remember what we talked about yesterday?"

" 'Bout what?"

"About going together somewhere?" Missy stood in the doorway, removing the rest of her clothes. Then she walked through the doorway into the bath and slid a foot beneath the shower curtain before easing her body through after it. Elvis felt her coming and reached an arm over her shoulder, pulling her ever so gently nearer his own wet skin. "Feel this water, babe, ain't it hot, ain't it wet?" He leaned down, cupping her sweet, round buttocks in his strong, tender hands, and raised her up to his lips. "Mm hmm," she answered. They were going together somewhere.

"But I cain't, 'til after this interview. Then I'm on my own," he said later. She stood in the doorway loaded with the silver tray, now empty of food. "Check back with me in a couple of hours." He looked under his lowered eyebrows at her, like in the movies, and thought to himself, "But nobody, nobody ever told me to do that, it's just how I do it, it's how I am," as he slipped his right hand into a solid gold watch-band. "That'll make it, say, seven o'clock, they'll be gone by then. We have to get some tickets or something someplace, that'll take even more time."

"I got us some tickets, see?" She pulled an envelope from the pocket of her apron.

"Well, all right then. We're on our way. See ya later, sport. And bring along that white lace thing."

"Oh, you like that?"

"Yeah, I like it. Now, scat!" He tossed yesterday's boxer shorts at her and she left, laughing at him.

"Leave 'em laughin', tha's what I always say," he said to himself. "Only not this time, folks, sorry to be gone so soon, jus' when the party's gettin' started, or almost, only not quite in my direction—but tha's life, I guess, ain't it, Colonel? Tha's life. Hero today, zero tomorrow . . . about twelve of 'em in fact." His eyelashes fluttered, calculating all the zeros.

The telephone rang. He answered it. "Send 'em on up, I'm ready," he said, and hung up.

"There is trenches, and there is ruts, man, and I am in one," would be his first words to them. It was going to be hard to convince them his future was still in their hands, considering his new plans. He'd done it plenty of times before, while keeping his personal life out of it, he could convince them he was theirs, he knew he could. Best to forget about it 'til Missy was in his arms. Only a few short hours to freedom. "I hope it's someplace in Italy," that voice deep in the flaming heart of Elvis said. They could have all their money, except what he had comin' to him for the work he'd just done. There was plenty to last him and Missy, however long it lasted, or until the new person inside him decided it was time to go back to work, until that man could make it on his own, with no help from reporters or lawyers or those awful, really awful, little pills. It wouldn't be so tough, he'd been Elvis before, he could be Elvis again.

Amid this simple train of ideas, Elvis was rearranging the furniture. He picked up the settee and placed it directly in front of the big Hollywood mirror, facing it. He climbed into bed naked and pulled the sheets over his hefty frame. "Come in," he grumbled at the first knock. "It's open." He watched in the mirror as a bevy of reporters and photographers tried pressing into the room simultaneously.

"You fellas come in two at a time, that's all," he addressed the mirror. "You and you, if you don't mind. The Colonel will be along soon and help you decide who's next. I haven't had my dinner, it should've been here before now but as you see, it ain't, an' I didn't order enough for ever'body. Hell, I ain't even dressed yet."

The two men hesitated, then came into the room. "Shut the door there, Charlie, that's your name ain't it? Have a seat there on the settee. I got it all arranged like I want it, see, so we'll do it thisaway. I'm prepared to answer any and all questions, so load 'em up and start shootin'.''

The phone jangled. The reporters looked uneasy, but settled themselves and their paraphernalia on the settee and stared at their images in the mirror with Elvis spread out on the bed behind them, and behind that, the open sky through plate glass. "Yes, it's about time, send 'em on up. And then send up a batch of coffee with about a dozen cups. We're havin' a pressure party. Thanks a lot.''

He set the phone back in its cradle and grinned into the mirror, avoiding all three sets of eyeballs reflected there.

''Kind o' disturbin', ain't it? Jus' relax and get comfortable, though, I promise no cameras back there 'r anything. You get used to it after a while. Me an' the Colonel got this welcome home gig all laid out. Lemme tell you about it. It's gonna be a real nightmare.'' He set all the switches on automatic to repeat everything he and the Colonel had discussed to date concerning the tour. As he talked, he felt the air growing cooler around him, the air growing thinner as behind his eyes he saw himself floating above the Alps in a hot air balloon. They were dressed in those kind of costumes like the little dolls on cuckoo clocks wear. Then they were floating over Fujiyama, gazing down at rolling mountainside farms with little people hauling wooden carts loaded with panda bears and mockingbirds and Chevrolets. He saw the big Cadillac his mama and daddy were driving now weaving in and out of the carts, and thousands of schoolkids climbing a tall ladder of their schoolmates trying to reach the balloon where Elvis and Missy were, all laughing and waving at them to come down closer. Then they were scuba diving off the coast of Borneo, looking for sunken treasure, and the water was deep purple shot with shimmering gold tiger stripes, and all these hopes and dreams Elvis was enjoying behind his lowered eyelids were the fuel he used to cut loose the tragic future which the Colonel and the media and the government of his own country, at least part of it, were planning for him. Vaguely, he wondered who they'd find to take his place.

BLUE SUEDE SHOES

Diane Wakoski

The blond whose skin was translucent as a glass slipper,
   whose small-boned frame allowed silk to drape
   as if underwater crenellating fans of sea anemone
   were breathing when she walked,
wore a sapphire blue maternity dress
and sat in the living room of The Home for Unwed
   Mothers
playing cards with her less-glamorous enciente friends.

I on the sofa, reading Shakespeare's love sonnets, or was it
TESS OF THE D'URBERVILLES? 1956. Pasadena,
   California.
Most of us there are teenagers.
Though she's the beauty;
I'm the book-worm brain. And I heard her say,
   that blond, the girl who'd been to a party with a
   college fraternity boy and wound up here,
   as ashamed as all the rest of us
         the nurse who found out she was going to have
         the hydrocephalic baby,
         the fourteen year old raped by her father,
         and lots of girls like me whose boyfriends loved
            us
         (we thought),
         but were not ready to be fathers,
she who wore a diamond on one of her sea cucumber
pale fingers and always had a cool
remark on her witty red tongue, said

"This baby will probably be born with blue
        suede shoes."
I imagined her blond baby boy,
      a princeling, with royal
            Cupid lips and his mother's
                  nose, straight as a golden pin;
                  he'd be a blue blood,
                        I thought. A "king" in baby shoes.
My literary ear recognized a title, though I knew little else,
listening to Beethoven or Chopin as I did,
not even the Beach Boys, now such a classic sound to me,
      representing the Orange County of my youth,
      of beach parties, and parked cars, and
      high school class rings.
I hadn't heard of Carl Perkins who wrote the song before
   Elvis
recorded it, though I knew
      where Memphis was; hadn't heard of
            Sun Studios, or "The King"/
the Sun King, I thought; Incas, blood sacrifices, virgins
having their hearts cut out over jungle pyramids.
      I knew that royalty was in my blood,
my swollen belly, and I knew that my love,
      like that love alluded to in the sonnet,
was the kind
that was so great
I'd "scorn to trade it" for a kingdom.

I felt the martyrdom of adolescence, but savored the
irony,
that I was the brain,
she, the woman with
      the delicate princess face
            who fantasized that her
                  taboo baby might be born with little blue
                  suede Elvis-shoes on his little
blond feet, was the beauty,
and Chance had us both sitting here in the same parlor,
glass slippers shattered,
      bare foot and pregnant,

No, no, no,
that wasn't us!

There *were* shoes. If not for us
    Cinderella's crystal slipper. Or Dorothy,
    innocent Dorothy, drug addict Dorothy's ruby
    slippers of Oz,
                        then there were
for our sons,
those swinging blue suede shoes;
and we would be left with music,
music in our heads, both of us,
she listening to Elvis
and I to the dissonant sounds of late Beethoven.
She with her skin translucent as a glass slipper
and I with my shy-girl skin, blushing, blushed ruby-slipper
   red,
both of us dancing, bare footed, just dancing,
in our ruby slippers or glass slippers or blue suede shoes,
dancing hard to survive our shame.

JUNGLE MUSIC
The All-Time All-Star 1950s Rock 'n' Roll Movie

Greil Marcus

STARRING

Elvis Presley
as the Good Boy Gone Wrong

Gene Vincent
as the Bad Boy Gone Wrong

Fats Domino
as The Old Con

Pat Boone
as The Prison Guard

Little Richard
as The Chaplain

Chuck Berry
as The Warden

Jerry Lee Lewis
as The Leader of the Pack

*Frankie Lymon, Ritchie Valens, Dion, the Del-
Vikings, the Everly Brothers, and Many Others*
as Members of the Pack

Buddy Holly
as The Leader of the Laundromat

*Carl Perkins, Rod McKuen, Frankie Avalon,
Frankie Sardo, the Platters. the Three Chuckles,
and Many Others*
as Members of the Laundromat

Bo Diddley
as The Dean of High Hopes High School

Fabian
as The Dope Pusher

Dick Clark
as Mr. Big

Eddie Cochran
as The Undercover Agent

Natalie Wood
as The Girl

and featuring
Alan Freed
as President of the United States

FADE IN on a crowded country music bar. Alone on the
bandstand, Elvis Presley is singing "Don't Be Cruel." Halfway through the number a drunk staggers to the stage and
vomits on Presley's blue suede shoes. Elvis smashes the man
with his guitar; suddenly the room is in chaos. Several goons
jump Elvis; the lights go out. We can barely make out Gene
Vincent, dressed in black from head to foot, as he flicks open a
knife and plants it square in the back of one of Elvis's assail-
ants. As the crowd scatters, the lights go up; the police arrive.
No one is left in the bar but Presley, Vincent, and the corpse.
The police handcuff the two young men and lead them away.

High Hopes High School. On the soundtrack: "High School
Confidential." The Pack, led by Jerry Lee Lewis, and the rival
Laundromat, led by Buddy Holly, are in the midst of a lunch-

time face-off over Natalie Wood, the only girl in school. The Pack make quick work of the Laundromat and are moving in on Wood when Dean of Boys Bo Diddley appears on the scene. "More small potatoes," Bo sneers at Jerry Lee. "I always said the Pack ain't got no class." Nettled, Jerry Lee rolls Holly's unconscious body down a flight of stairs. "How's that, Dean Diddley?" Jerry Lee asks politely. "That's *class*, man!" smiles the Dean; Natalie Wood takes Jerry Lee's arm and gazes at him adoringly. Soundtrack: "I Only Have Eyes for You."

The State Prison. Warden Chuck Berry is at his desk. "Thirty years, thirty years," he sings to himself. "Gonna take you thirty years to get back home." Guard Pat Boone enters. "Time to sign out Fabian," Boone reports. "The Parole Board ordered him freed today." " 'Bout time," snaps Berry. "Payoff came through from Mr. Big months ago. I'se beginning to worry we was gonna have to give it *back*."

The prison exercise yard. Soundtrack: "Rock Around the Rockpile." "Dadgummit!" Vincent whines. "Why'd that creep Fabian get sprung?" "I'm sure I don't know," says Elvis. "Must be God's will."

"God's will, my aunt," says Vincent. "He's out, we're *in*. I'm going nuts in here! I'm gonna blow! We'll never get out! Never!"

"Ain't that a shame," calls a voice; Elvis and Vincent turn to see Fats Domino lumbering across the yard. "Who're *you*?" Vincent growls.

"They call me the Fat Man," Domino says, " 'cause I weigh two hundred pounds. All the boys love me 'cause I know my way around, and I know why Fabian's on the street. Mr. Big's slipping *payola* to Warden Berry, that's why. Mr. Big's sending Fabian down to High Hopes High School to hook the whole student body on dope, and everybody from the Warden to the High Hopes Dean got a piece of the action!"

"That's *terrible*," says Elvis. "I figured that Fabian for a ringer ever since I heard him sing 'Hound Dog Man' at the prison variety show. We gotta save those kids—and maybe get ourselves a pardon in the bargain."

"Reet petit, King," Vincent says. "I suppose we just ask Buck Cherry for a pass and waltz on out, so's we can queer his scam?"

"God will show the way," Elvis says.

"Darn straight," says the Fat Man. "You know crazy Richard, the chaplain? Well, he's always looking for converts, and he's blackmailed the Warden into letting a couple out each month for a night so he can take 'em up to his Holiness church and get 'em born again. But—you gotta learn how to speak in tongues."

"I already know how," Elvis says.

"*Fine*," says the Fat Man. "You just stay cool. Wait til Richard gets into his stuff and the place is going wild, sneak out, double back to High Hopes High. It's a cinch. But remember, you gotta act *devout*. That Richard may be crazy, but he can tell the wheat from the chaff like Mr. Big can tell horse from sugar."

A small wooden church filled with a screaming mob. Richard stands at the pulpit chanting, picking up momentum by the second. "TUTTI FRUTTI!" he shouts. "ALL ROOTIE! I'M READY! I'M READY READY READY TO ROCK 'N' ROLL RIGHT INTO THE ARMS OF THE LORD! I DON'T WANT NO UNCLE JOHNS JUMPIN' BACK IN THE ALLEY TO-*NIGHT*! I DON'T WANT NO LONG TALL SALLY, I DON'T WANT NO MISS ANN! I WANT—"

Elvis and Vincent stand facing the pulpit, draped in white. The congregation begins to sanctify; then lightning strikes the church and plunges it into darkness. "Now!" whispers Vincent. He and Elvis turn to escape, but a huge blue flame materializes behind Richard; he raises his arms toward the roof and begins to scream. Elvis, his face bathed in the blue light, is transfixed.

Shifty, Vincent says, "For heaven's sake, nobody's looking now, let's make our break!"

Elvis smiles and says, "Nix, nix. I gotta—"

"NOW I'M REALLY READY!" Richard howls. Vincent knocks Elvis over the head with a hymnal and drags him from the church as the worshippers go into hysterics. "I'M READY READY READY READY READY . . . "

Quick cuts of Fabian, Elvis, Vincent, and a new face we recognize as Eddie Cochran, all registering as transfer students at High Hopes High. Soundtrack: "School Is In."

The screen reads TWO WEEKS LATER. Study Hall. The

Laundromat, with Fabian in their midst, are nodding off, falling over, and laughing madly. Fabian has made his first connection. At the other end of the room sit the Pack, with new members Elvis, Vincent, and Cochran. "What's *happening?*" says Jerry Lee to his boys. "I know," says Elvis brightly. "It's that little Fabian who—"

"*Cool it!*" Cochran hisses. "Meet me after school. We gotta talk. But *cool it.*"

Cochran, Elvis, and Vincent are huddled in a booth in the Soda Shop. "All right," snaps Eddie. "I got something to spill. I wasn't supposed to cop, but I gotta if I'm gonna keep you guys in line. *I'm not really a student here.*"

"Well, kiss the moon," sneers Vincent.

"We're not *either*," glows Elvis. "We're here to nab Fabian and Mr. Big and save the kids!"

"And *us*," Vincent adds.

"That's really *something else*," says Eddie, flashing a badge. "I'm Treasury. What's your outfit?"

"Uh, freelance," says Vincent.

"As it happens," Cochran says, "I don't care what your cover is. But here's the story so far. We can't move on Fabian til we flush Mr. Big into the open, and by that time he's gonna have the whole school on the needle. We don't even know who he is. We need a plan."

Elvis notices Vincent and Cochran tapping their fingers to "Race with the Devil," playing on the jukebox. "Do you dig the Rock?" Elvis asks. " 'Cause if you do, we just might form a band—everyone knows musicians are junkies—and Mr. Big will come to *us*. And even if he doesn't, we can pick up some bread playing the prom. You go for it?"

Vincent and Cochran look to Elvis with stunned admiration. "We need a name," Eddie says after a long moment. " 'The Go-Valeers'?"

" 'The Plume Gods'?"

" 'The Wrong Way'?"

" 'The Vacant Lot'?"

" 'The Last Period'?"

Elvis gets a gleam in his eye. "How 'bout—'The Rolling Stones'?"

"I like it," says Vincent. "I like it *a lot*. It *says* something."

"What?" says Elvis.

"OK. Stones!" Eddie cries. "Let's shake it!"

Prom night at the High Hopes gym. Students wander the room in a daze, not even bothering to hide the works in their pockets. Off to one side the Pack and the Laundromat are taking on Natalie Wood one by one, while Dean Diddley administers injection after injection to the nearly comatose girl. "Help me, Jerry Lee," she moans; he giggles like a moron. Fabian snakes through the crowd, keeping the supply up, occasionally snorting from a glassine envelope. The Pack and the Laundromat turn Natalie over to Dean Diddley while passing a dirty needle from hand to hand, splattering each other's clothes with junk. Elvis, Eddie, and Vincent gather backstage.

"*Great* idea, King," Vincent mutters. "We got the band, we got the gig, we ain't got Mr. Big, and any minute people are gonna start wondering why we're the only ones in school without tracks on our arms." "Keep your sleeves rolled down and your head straight," Elvis says; they hit the stage. They run through three furious tunes—"Hound Dog," "Summertime Blues," and "Be-Bop-a-Lula." Not one High Hoper pays the slightest attention; Mr. Big is nowhere to be seen. The plan has failed. Broken, the Stones head backstage.

There, waiting for them, is Dick Clark.

"Hi, I'm the world's oldest teenager," he says. "I've heard about you boys. I like your sound. We can go places. I can make you."

The Stones forget their mission. Fabian, Mr. Big, prison. They see records, stardom, money, girls: the American dream.

"We're ready," says Elvis.

"We want the big time," says Vincent.

"Where do we sign?" says Cochran.

"Great," says Clark. "Let's shoot on it."

Immediately it hits them. This is Mr. Big. The whole school has gone under and only they are left. Today, High Hopes—tomorrow, High School U.S.A. *Dope School U.S.A.* Their dreams of glory fade on their faces; they have no choice. One wink between them and they take Mr. Big without a struggle.

With Fabian, Dick Clark, and Dean Diddley in chains, and the students entering the first stages of cold turkey, Eddie puts in a call to Washington. "We got him, Chief," he says to President Alan Freed. "But I'm through. I want a pardon for my friends, and then we're going on the road. I want a clean life, sir—I'm tired of messing with scum. From now on, it's rock 'n' roll for me."

"Congratulations, son," says the President. "I know the kids just love that jungle music. Good luck—you'll need it." Then his voice grows hard. "But you better remember one thing, and that goes double for your pals."

"What's that, President Freed?" asks Eddie.

"I had half a mil tied up with Mr. Big, you little twerp, and you blew it for me, you and your bopcat buddies. I never dreamed you'd turn down his offer. So go on, rock around the clock, slop til you drop, shake til you break. I could care less. But you make sure my office gets half of every gig, and every cent of your publishing—or the only groove you'll get into will be six feet in the ground."

The phone clicks dead. Elvis and Vincent look hopefully at Eddie, anxious to hear the results of the call. Slowly, Cochran turns toward them.

A look of incredible horror is on his face.

FADE OUT

THE END

IKE AT THE MIKE

Howard Waldrop

Ambassador Pratt leaned over toward Senator Presley.
"My mother's ancestors don't like to admit it,"
he said, "but they all came to the island from the Car-
pathians two centuries ago. Their name then was something like Karloff." He smiled, then laughed through his silver
mustache.

"Hell," said Presley, with the tinge of the drawl which
came to his speech when he was excited, as he was tonight.
"My folks been dirt farmers all the way back to Adam. They
don't even remember coming from anywhere. That don't
mean they ain't wonderful folks, though."

"Of course not," said Pratt. "My father was a shop-
keeper. He worked to send all my older brothers into the Foreign Service. But when my time came, I thought I had another
choice. I wanted to run off to Canada or Australia, perhaps
try my hand at acting. (I was in several local dramatic clubs,
you know?) My father took me aside before my service exams.
The day before, I remember quite distinctly. He said, 'William' (he was the only member of the family who used my full
name), 'William,' he said, 'actors do not get paid the last
workday of each and every month.' Well, I thought about
it awhile, and next day passed my exams with absolute top
grades."

Pratt smiled once more an ingratiating smile. There
was something a little scary about it, thought Presley, sort of
like Raymond Massey's smile in *Arsenic and Old Lace*. But
the smile had gotten Pratt through sixty years of government
service. It had been a smile which made the leaders of small

49

countries grin back as Kings George, number after number, took yet more of their lands. It was a good smile; it made everyone remember his grandfather. Even Presley.

"Folks is funny," said Presley. "God knows I used to get up at barn dances and sing myself silly. I was just a kid, playing around."

"My childhood is so far behind me," said Ambassador Pratt. "I hardly remember it. I was small, then I had the talk with my father, and went to Service school, then found myself in Turkey. Which at that time owned a large portion of the globe. The Sick Man of Europe, it was called. You know I met Lawrence, of Arabia, don't you? Before the Great War. He was an archaeologist then. Came to us to get the Ottomans to give him permission to dig up Petra. They thought him to be a fool. Wanted the standard 90 percent share of everything, just the same."

"You've seen a lot of the world change," said Senator E. Aaron Presley. He took a sip of wine. "I've had trouble enough keeping up with it since I was elected congressman six years ago. I almost lost touch during my senatorial campaign, and I'll be damned if everything hadn't changed again by the time I got back here."

Pratt laughed. He was eighty years old, far past retirement age, still bouncing around like a man of sixty. He had alternately retired and had every British P.M. since Churchill call him out of seclusion to patch up relations with this or that nation.

Presley was thirty-three, the youngest senator in the country for a long time. The U.S. was in bad shape, and he was one of the symbols of the new hope. There was talk of revolution, several cities had been burned, there was a war on in South America (again). Social change, lifestyle readjustment, call it what they would. The people of Mississippi had elected Presley senator after five years as representative, as a sign of renewed hope. At the same time they had passed a tough new wiretap act, and had turned out for massive Christian revivalist meetings.

1968 looked to be the toughest year yet for America.

But there were still things that made it all worth living. Nights like tonight. A huge appreciation dinner, with the absolute top of Washington society turned out in its gaudiness.

Most of Congress, President Kennedy, Vice President Shriver. Plus the usual hangers-on.

Presley watched them. Old Dick Nixon, once a senator from California. He came back to Washington to be near the action, though he'd lost his last election in '58.

The President was there, of course, looking as young as he had when he was reelected in 1964, the first two-term president since Huey "Kingfish" Long, Jr., thought Presley. He was a hell of a good man in his Yankee way. His three young brothers were in the audience somewhere, representatives from two states.

Waiters hustled in and out of the huge banquet room. Presley watched the sequined gowns and the feathers on the women; the spectacular pumpkin-blaze of a neon orange suit of some hotshot Washington lawyer. The lady across the table had engaged Pratt in conversation about Wales. The ambassador was explaining that he had seen Wales once, back in 1923 on holiday, but that he didn't think it had changed much since then.

E. Aaron studied the table where the guests of honor sat—The President and First Lady, the veep and his wife, and Armstrong and Eisenhower, with their spouses.

Armstrong and Eisenhower. Two of the finest citizens of the land. Armstrong, the younger, in his sixty-eighth year, getting a little jowly. Born with the century, thought Presley. Symbol of his race and of his time. A man deserving of honor and respect.

But Eisenhower. Eisenhower was Presley's man. The senator had read all the biographies, reread all the old newspaper files, listened to him every chance he got.

If Presley had an ideal, it was Eisenhower. As both a leader and a person. A little too liberal, maybe, in his personal opinions, but that was the only possible drawback the man had. When it came time for action, Eisenhower, the "Ike" of the popular press, came through.

Senator Presley tried to catch his eye. He was only three tables away, and could see Ike through the hazy pall of smoke from after-dinner cigarettes and pipes. It was no use, though.

Eisenhower looked worried, distracted. He wasn't used to testimonials. He'd come out of semiretirement to attend, only because Armstrong had convinced him to do it. They were both getting presidential medals.

But it wasn't for the awards that all the other people were here, or the speeches that would follow, it . . .

Pratt turned to him.

"I've noticed his preoccupation, too," he said.

Presley was a little taken aback. But Pratt is a sharp old cookie, and he'd been around god knows how many people through wars, floods, conference tables. He'd probably drank enough tea in his life to float the Battleship *Kropotkin*.

"Quite a man," said Presley, afraid to let his true misty-eyed feelings show themselves. "Pretty much man of the century, far as I'm concerned."

"I've been with Churchill, and Lenin and Chiang," said Ambassador Pratt, "but they were just cagey, politicians, movers of men and material, as far as I'm concerned. I saw him once before, early on, must have been '38. Nineteen thirty-eight. I was very, very impressed then. Time has done nothing to change that."

"He's just not used to this kind of thing," said Presley.

"Perhaps it was that Patton fellow."

"Wild George? That who you mean?"

"Oh, didn't you hear?" asked Pratt, eyes all concern.

"I was in committee most of the week. If it wasn't about the new drug bill, I didn't hear about it."

"Oh. Of course. This Patton fellow died a few days ago, it seems. Circumstances rather sad, I think. Eisenhower and Mr. Armstrong just returned from his funeral this afternoon."

"Gee, that's too bad. You know they worked together, Patton and Ike, for thirty years or so—"

The toastmaster, one of those boisterous, bald-headed, abrasive California types, rose. People began to applaud and stub out their cigarettes. Waiters disappeared as if a magic wand had been waved.

Well, thought Presley, an hour of pure boredom coming up, as he and Pratt applauded also. Some jokes, the President, the awarding of the medals, the obligatory standing ovation (though all of the senator's feelings were going to be in his part of it, anyway). Then the entertainment.

Ah, thought Presley. The thing everybody has come for.

Because, after the ceremony, they were going to bring out the band, Armstrong's band. Not just the one he toured with, but what was left of the old guys. *The* Armstrong Band, and they were going to rip the joint.

But also, also . . .

For the first time in twenty years, since Presley had been a boy, a kid in his teens . . .

Eisenhower was going to break his vow. Eisenhower was going to dust off that clarinet.

For two hours, Ike was going to play with Armstrong, just like in the old days.

"Cheer up," said gravelly-voiced Pops, while the President was making his way to the rostrum. Armstrong smiled at Eisenhower. "You're gonna blow 'em right outta the grooves."

"All reet," said Ike.

The thunderous applause was dying down. Backstage, Ike handed the box with the Presidential medal to his wife of twenty years, Helen Forrest, the singer. "Here goes, honey," he said. "Come out when you feel like it."

They were in the outer hall back of the platform set up behind the head tables. Some group of young folksingers, very nervous but very good, were out there killing time while Armstrong's band set up.

"Hey hey," said Pops. He'd pinned the Presidential medal, ribbon and all, to the front of his jacket through the boutonniere hole. "Wouldn't old Jelly Roll like to have seen me now?"

"Hey hey," yelled some of the band right back.

"Quiet, quiet!" yelled Pops. "Let them kids out there sing. They're good. Listen to 'em. Reminds me of me when I was young."

Ike had been licking his reed and doing tongue exercises. "You never were young, Pops," he said. "You were born older than me."

"That's a lie!" said Pops. "You could be my father."

"Maybe he is!" yelled Perkins, the guitar man.

Ike nearly swallowed his mouthpiece. The drummer did a paradiddle.

"Hush, hush, you clowns!" yelled Pops.

Ike smiled and looked up at the drummer, a young kid. But he'd been with Pops's new band for a couple of years, so he must be all right.

Eisenhower heaved a sigh when no one was looking. He had to get the tightness out of his chest. It had started at George S.'s funeral, a pain crying did not relieve. No one but he and Helen knew that he had had two mild heart attacks in the last six years. Hell, he thought, I'm almost eighty years old. I'm entitled to a few heart attacks. But not here, not tonight.

They dimmed the work lights. Pops had run into the back kitchen and blown a few screaming notes which they had heard through two concrete walls. He was ready.

"When you gonna quit playing, Pops?" asked Ike.

"Man, I ain't ever gonna quit. They're gonna have to dig me up three weeks after I die and break this horn to stop the noise comin' outta the ground." He looked at the lights. "Ease on off to the left there, Ike. Let us get them all ready for you. Come in on the chorus of the third song."

"Which one's that?" asked Ike, looking for his play sheet.

"You'll know it when you hear it," said Pops. He took out his handkerchief. "You taught it to me."

Ike went into the wings.

The crowd was tasteful, expectant.

The band hit the music hard, from the opening, and Armstrong led off with the "King Porter Stomp." His horn was flashing sparks, and the medal on his jacket front caught the spotlight like a big golden eye.

Then they launched into "Basin Street Blues," the horn sweet and slow and mellow, the band doing nothing but carrying a light line behind. Armstrong was totally in his music, staring not at the audience but down and at his horn.

He had come a long way since he used to hawk coal from the back of a wagon; since he was thrown in the Colored Waifs Home in New Orleans for firing off a pistol on New Year's Eve, 1913. One noise more or less shouldn't have mattered on that night, but it did, and the cops caught him. It was those music lessons at the Home that started him on the way, through New Orleans and Memphis and Chicago to the world beyond.

Armstrong might have been a criminal, he might have been a bum, he might have been killed unknown and unmourned in some war somewhere. But he wasn't: He was born to play that music. It wouldn't have mattered what world he would have been born into. As soon as his fingers closed around the cornet, music was changed forever.

The audience applauded wildly, but they weren't there just for Armstrong. They were waiting. And they got him.

The band hit up something that began nondescriptly—a slow blues beginning with the drummer heavy on his brushes.

The tune began to change, and as it changed, a pure sweet clarinet began to play above the other instruments, and Ike walked onstage playing his theme song, "Don't You Know What It Means to Miss New Orleans?"

His clarinet soared above the audience. Presley wasn't the only one who got chill bumps all the way down the backs of his ankles.

Ike and Armstrong traded off slow pure verses of the song; Ike's the sweet music of a craftsman, Armstrong's the heartfelt remembrance of things as they were. Ike never saw Storyville; Armstrong had to leave it when the Navy closed it down.

Together they built to a moving finale, and descended into a silence like the dimming of lights, with Ike's clarinet the last one to wink out.

The cream of Washington betrayed its origins with applause.

And before they knew what to do, the tune was the opening screech of "Mississippi Mud."

Ike and Armstrong traded licks, running on and off the melody. Pops wiped his face with his handkerchief; his face seemed all teeth and sweat. Ike's bald head shone, the freckles standing out above the wisps of white hair on his temples.

They played and played.

Ike's boyhood had been on the flat pan of Kansas, small-town church America at the turn of the century. A town full of laborers and businessmen, barbershops, milliners and ice-cream parlors.

He had done all the usual things—swum naked in the creek, run through town finding things to build up or tear down. He had hunted and fished and gone to services on Sunday; he had camped out overnight or for days at a time with his brothers, made fun of his girl cousins, stolen watermelons.

He first heard recorded music on an old Edison cylinder machine at the age of eight, long-hair music and opera his aunt collected.

There was a firehouse band which played each Wednesday night in the park across the street from the station. There were real band concerts on Sunday, mostly military music, marches and the instrumental parts of ballads, on the courthouse lawn.

Eisenhower heard it all. Music was part of his background, and he didn't think much of it. His brother had taken piano lessons for a while, but gave it up as, in his words, "sissy."

So Ike grew up in Kansas, where the music was as flat as the land.

Daniel Louis Armstrong was rared back, tooting out some wild lines of "Night and Day." In the old days it didn't matter how well you played; it was the angle of your back and the tilt of your horn. The band was really tight; they were playing for their lives.

The trombone player came out of his seat, jumped down onto the stage on his knees and matched Armstrong for a few bars.

The audience yelled.

Eisenhower tapped his foot and smiled, watching Armstrong and the trombone man.

The drummer was giving a lot of rim shots. The whole ballroom sounded like the overtaxed heart of a bird ready to fly away to meet Jesus.

Ike took off his coat and unknotted his tie down to the first button.

The crowd went wild.

Late August 1908.

The train was late. Young Dwight David Eisenhower hurried across the endless steel grid of the Kansas City rail yards. He was catching the train to New York City. There he would board another bound for West Point.

He carried his admission papers, a congratulatory letter from his congressman (gotten after some complicated negotiations—it looked for a while like he would be Midshipman

Eisenhower), his train ticket and twenty-one dollars emergency money in his jacket.

He'd asked the porter for the track number. It was next to the station proper. A spur track confused him. He looked down the tracks, couldn't see a number (trains waited all around, ready to hurl themselves toward distant cities . . .) and went to the station entrance.

Four black men, ragged of dress, were smiling and playing near the door. What they played young David had never heard before—it was syncopated music, but not like a rag, not a march, something in between, something like nothing else. He had never heard polyrhythms like them before— they stopped him dead.

The four had a banjo, a cornet, a violin, and a clarinet. They played, smiled, danced a little for the two or three people watching them. A hat lay on the ground before them. In it were a few dimes, pennies, and a single new half-dime.

They finished the song. A couple of people said, "Very nice, very nice" and added a few cents to the hat. They walked away.

The four men started to talk among themselves.

"What was that song?" asked young David.

The man with the cornet looked at him through large horn-rimmed spectacles. "That song was called 'Struttin' with Some Barbecue,' young sir," he said.

Dwight David reached into his pocket and took out a shiny one-dollar gold piece.

"Play it again," he said.

They nearly killed themselves this time, running through it. It was great art, it was on the street, and they were getting a whole dollar for it. David watched them, especially the clarinet player, who made his instrument soar above the others. They finished the number and all tipped their hats to him.

"Is that hard to learn to play?" he asked the man of the clarinet.

"For some it is," he answered.

"Could you teach me?" asked David.

The black man looked at the others, who looked away; they were no help at all. "Let me see your fingers," he said.

Eisenhower held out his hands, wrists up, then down.

"I could probably teach you to play in six weeks," he

said. "I don't know if I could teach you to play like that. You've got to feel that music." He was trying not to say that Eisenhower was white.

"Wait right here," said Ike.

He went inside the depot and cashed in his ticket. He sent two telegrams, one home and one to the Army. He was back outside in fifteen minutes, with thirty-three dollars in his pocket, total.

"Let's go find me a clarinet," he said to the black man.

He knew he would not sleep well that night, and neither would anybody back on the farm. He probably wouldn't sleep good for weeks. But he sure knew what he wanted.

Armstrong smiled, wiped his face and blew the opening notes of "When It's Sleepy Time Down South."

Ike joined in.

Then they went into "Just a Closer Walk with Thee," quiet, restrained, the horn and clarinet becoming one instrument for a while, then Ike bent his notes around Armstrong's, then Pops lifted Eisenhower up, then the instruments walked arm in arm toward Heaven.

Ike listened to the drummer as he played. He sure missed Wild George.

The first time they had met, Ike was the new kid in town, just another guy with a clarinet that some gangster had hired to fill in with a band, sometime in 1911.

Ike didn't say much. He was working his way south from KC, toward Memphis, toward New Orleans (which he would never see until after New Orleans didn't mean the same anymore).

Ike could cook anyone with his clarinet—horn player, banjo man, even drummers. They might make more noise but when they ran out of things to do, Ike was just starting. He'd begun at the saloon filling in, but the bandleader soon had sense enough to put him out front. They took breaks, leaving just him and the drummer up there, and the crowds never noticed. Ike was hot before there was hot music.

Till one night a guy came in—a new drummer. He was a crazy man. "My name is Wild George S. Patton," he said before the first set.

"What's the S. stand for?" asked Ike.

"Shitkicker!" said the drummer.

Ike didn't say anything.

That night they tried to cut each other, chop each other off the stage. Patton was doing two-hand cymbal shots, paradiddles, and flails. His bass foot never stopped. Ike wasn't a show-off, but this guy drove him to it. He blew notes that killed mice for three square blocks. Patton ended up by kicking a hole through the bass drum and ramming his sticks through his snare like he was opening a can of beans with them.

The bandleader fired Patton on the spot and threatened to call the cops. The crowd nearly lynched the manager for it.

As soon as the hubbub died, Patton said to Ike, "The S. stands for Smith," and shook his hand.

He and Ike took off that night to start up their own band.

And were together for almost thirty years.

Armstrong blew "Dry Bones."

Ike did "St. Louis Blues."

They had never done either better. This Washington audience loved them.

So had another, long ago.

The first time he and Armstrong had met had been in Washington, too. A hot bleak July day in 1932.

The Bonus Army had come to the capital, asking their congressmen and their nation for some relief in this third year of the Depression. President Al Smith was powerless; he had a Republican Congress under him.

The bill granting the veterans of the Great War their bonus, due in 1945, had been passed back in the twenties. All the vets wanted was it to be paid immediately. It had been sitting in the Treasury, gaining interest, and was already part of the budget. The vote was coming up soon.

Thousands, dubbed the B.E.F., had poured into Washington, camping on Anacostia Flats, in tin boxes, towns of shanties dubbed "Smithvilles," or under the rain and stars.

Homeless men who had slogged through the mud of Europe, been gassed and shelled, and who had lived with rats in the trenches for democracy, now they found themselves back in the mud again.

This time they were out of money, out of work, out of luck.

The faces of the men were tired. Soup kitchens had been set up. They tried to keep their humor. It was all they had left. May dragged by, then June, then July. The vote was taken in Congress on the twelfth.

Congress said no.

They accused the Bonus Marchers of being Reds. They said they were armed rabble. Rumors ran wild. Such financial largesse, said Congress, could not be afforded.

Twenty thousand of the thirty thousand men tried to find some way back home, out of the city, back to No Place, U.S.A.

Ten thousand stayed, hoping for something to happen. Anything.

Ike went down to play for them. So did Armstrong. They ran into each other in town, got together their bands and equipment. They set up a stage in the middle of the Smithville, now a forlorn-looking bunch of mud-strewn shacks.

About five thousand of the jobless men came to hear them play. They were in a holiday mood. They sat on the ground, in the mud. They didn't much care anymore.

Armstrong and Ike had begun to play that day. Half the band, including Wild George, had hangovers. They had drunk with the Bonus Marchers the night before, and well into the morning before the noon concert.

They played great jazz that day anyway. A cloud of smoke had risen up from some of the abandoned warehouses the veterans had been living in, just before the music began. There was some commotion from over toward the Potomac. The band just played louder and wilder.

The marchers clapped along. Wild George smiled a bleary-eyed smile toward the crowd. They were doing half his job.

Automatic rifle fire rang out, causing heads to turn.

The Army was coming. Sons and nephews of some of the Bonus Marchers there were coming toward them on orders from Douglas MacArthur, the Chief of Staff. He had orders to clear them out.

The men came to their feet, picking up rocks and bottles.

Marching lines of soldiers came into view, bayonets

fixed. Small two-man tanks, armed with machine guns, rolled between the soldiers. The lines stopped. The soldiers put on gas masks.

The Bonus Marchers, who remembered phosgene and the trenches, drew back.

"Keep playing!" said Ike.

"Keep goin'. Let it roll!" said Armstrong.

Tear gas grenades flew toward the Bonus Marchers. Rocks and bottles sailed toward the soldiers in the masks. There was a real explosion a block away.

The troops came on.

The gas rolled toward the marchers. Some picked up the spewing canisters to throw them back, fell coughing to the ground, overcome.

The tanks and bayonets came forward in a line.

The marchers broke and ran.

Their shacks and tents were set afire by chemical corpsmen behind the tanks.

"Let it roll! Let it roll!" said Armstrong, and they played "Didn't He Ramble" and the gas cloud hit them, and the music died in chokes and vomiting.

That night the Bonus Marchers were loaded on Army trucks, taken fifty miles due west and let out on the sides of the roads.

Ike and Louis went up before the Washington magistrate, paid ten dollars each fine for them and their band members, and took trains to New York City.

The last time he had seen Wild George alive was two years ago. Patton had been found by somebody who'd known him in the old days.

He'd been in four bad marriages, his only kid had died in the taking of the Japanese Home Islands in early '47, and he'd lost one of his arms in a car wreck in '55. He had been in a flophouse when the guy found him. They'd put him in a nursing home and paid the bills.

Ike had gone to visit. The last time they had seen each other in those intervening twenty-odd years had been the day of the fistfight in 1943, just before the Second World War broke out. Patton had joined the Miller band for a while, but was too much for them. He'd gone from band to band and marriage to marriage to oblivion.

He was old, old. Wild George was only five years older than Ike. He looked a hundred. One eye was almost gone. He had no teeth. He was drying out in the nursing home, turning brittle as last winter's leaves.

"Hello, George," said Ike, shaking his only hand.

"I knew you'd come first," said Patton.

"You should have let somebody know."

"What's to know? One old musician lives, another one dies."

"George, I'm sorry. The way things have turned out."

"I've been thinking it over, about that fight we had." Patton stopped to cough up some bloody spittle into a basin Ike held for him.

"God, oh, jees. If I could only have a drink." He stared into Ike's eyes. Then he said:

"About that fight. You were still wrong."

Then he coughed some more.

Ike was crying as they went into the final number. He stepped forward to the mike Helen had used when she came out to sing with them for the last three numbers.

"This song is for the memory of George Smith Patton," he said.

They played "The Old, Rugged Cross." Ike, nor anybody else, had ever played it just like that before.

Ike broke down halfway through. He waved to the crowd, took his mouthpiece off, and walked into the wings.

Pops kept playing. He tried to motion Ike back. Helen was hugging him. He waved and brushed the tears away.

Armstrong finished the song.

The audience tore the place apart. They were on their feet and stamping, screaming, applauding.

Presley, out there, sat in his chair.

He was crying too, but quickly stood up and cheered.

Then the whole thing was over.

At home, later, in Georgetown, Senator Presley was lying in bed beside his wife Muffy. They had made love. They had both been excited. It had been terrific.

Now Muffy was asleep.

Presley got up and went to the bathroom. Then he went

to the kitchen, poured himself a Scotch, and stood with his naked butt against the countertop.

It was a cold night. Through the half curtains on the window he saw stars over the city. If you could call this a city.

He went into the den. The servants would be asleep.

He turned the power on the stereo, took down four or five of his Eisenhower records, looked through them. He put on *Ike at the Mike*, a four-record set made for RCA in 1947, toward the end of the last war.

Ike was playing "No Love, No Nothing," a song his wife had made famous three years before. She wasn't on this record, though. This was all Ike and his band.

Presley got the bottle from the kitchen, sat back down, poured himself another drink. Tomorrow was more hearings. And the day after.

Someday, he thought, someday, E. Aaron Presley will be President of these here United States. Serves them right.

Ike was playing "All God's Chillun Got Shoes."

I didn't even get to shake his hand, thought Presley.

I'd give it all away to be like him, he thought.

He went to sleep sitting up.

FROM COUSINS

Judy Vernon

The year is 1935, and the Great Depression is in full swing. The aristocracy of the North (the old monied aristocracy, not the landed) is taking a beating. Quite a few old barons up there are wondering what hit them. They feel as lost as some Confederate colonels did on coming home from the Civil War. Wall Street has the air of Peachtree Street in Atlanta in 1864. Modern-day Yankee Scarlett O'Hara's are singing the blues.

Dimes are scarce, dollars scarcer, credit almost nonexistent. "Depression" is something other than a psychological state now.

Down in Mississippi hardly anyone notices. Affluence is a thing few have had here in a very long time—most people never. There is a perverse glee, too, in the little additional suffering the depression is causing locally, because the North is finally getting its comeuppance. For many white Southerners, the Civil War never ended, and was certainly *not* lost. Like Ester and Rubell and Francis, they are discovering that some things aren't easily forgotten.

Joker Fleming is the happiest man in Union County, Mississippi, perhaps the happiest man in the country. He is not rich, but he is handsome, in a sleazy sort of way. Women find him attractive, devastatingly so. And Joker does not have to work as a tenant farmer anymore, for he has a talent: he can make a flat-top guitar do whatever he wants it to.

Joker also has a wife who adores him and who works full-time. She, Ester, cuts off the heads of chickens all day long at the local poultry processing plant, one of the few businesses in New Albany that is still thriving. Ester is as good at her job as Joker is at his—when he works. Joker does not apologize for not working, because he can make as much money playing his flat-top guitar in one night as Ester can earn in a week.

He saves himself for other and better things than daily labor. He spends his days with other men's wives, women he usually meets at roadhouses and country juke-joints where he plays on Friday and Saturday nights. Joker, blond hair lightly oiled, fingernails well-manicured, shirt collar turned up, has only one rule where women are concerned: they must be married. Contraceptives are loathsome, and bastard children are an unnecessary complication.

"I understand jist three things," Joker often boasted to his cronies, "a guitar, a dollar sign, and women."

He was quite disinterested in money, though, after he had earned it. He conscientiously gave every dollar he earned to Ester, and asked only that his chalkstripe suit be clean and wellpressed at all times. Except for his notorious philandering, he had no bad habits. He didn't drink, didn't smoke, didn't gamble. He consequently had the pearly white teeth and manly build of a twenty-five-year-old until he was well into his fifties.

Ester considered herself a lucky woman. She knew of Joker's weakness for women, and vice versa. She never mentioned it to anyone, however, or chastised Joker for it. She demanded only two things of her handsome husband: that he devote himself totally to *her* when she was not working, and that he not sleep with other women in *her* bed. Joker gladly complied.

All things considered, they had a perfect marriage. That is, they had a perfect marriage until 1935, the year Ester found herself pregnant. She had to be off work for several months, and the money situation became tight. And though she demanded the almost constant attendance of Joker during those months, she considered him less and less adorable as the days and weeks and months passed. He was a terrible housekeeper, nurse, and companion, downright disgusting in his sexual demands, and did not at all understand why Ester should be so sickly, bitchy, and unaffectionate. Then the boy was born, and Joker could never afterwards declare that he understood women without mentally noting that there was one exception: his wife, Ester.

The child was called Trinity, after a river Ester once

crossed in Texas and thought beautiful. Joker silently lamented the name, but consoled himself by thinking that at least the boy could be called "Trent" for short. But after a while, he began to regret the fact of the child as much as its name, for Trinity was obviously the sole object of his mother's affections and attention.

Ester worshipped the child with a reverence most people reserve for God and country. She bathed him, oiled him, suckled him, coddled him her every waking minute. She fondled him, brushed his coal-black hair, stared into his wide blue eyes as if hypnotized.

When the boy was two months old, she said absent-mindedly to Joker one day: "I'm not going back to work until Trinity starts to school. You'll have to make do."

"Make do," in this context, meant, "Get your ass out and find a *real* job."

Joker, whose real name was James, was dumbfounded, all the more so because Ester refused—from Trinity's birth onward—to sleep with her husband without the careful and bothersome use of contraceptives, *plural*. Thus did Joker's comfortable and enjoyable existence draw temporarily to a close.

He rented fifty acres of bottom land and went back to doing the only kind of work he had ever done: farming. He held the handles of a mule-drawn, single-bladed plow in the spring, guided mule and plow through the reddish-brown earth twelve hours a day. Then came the planting, the weeding, done with half-moon shaped hoes wielded by Joker and the black family of four which lived in a shack on Joker's rented land. Then came the back-breaking harvest, the dragging of long and heavy sacks down the narrow rows.

The Fleming home, though two rooms larger than the Negro shack, was almost as dilapidated. Ester covered the bare plank walls with newspapers and then wallpaper. She built shelves and cupboards, even a small closet, out of scrap lumber. She sewed clothes for herself and her darling boy from cheap bolts of cloth, and made quilt tops from the scraps. She planted, weeded, and harvested a large garden, canned dozens of jars of tomatoes, cucumbers, kraut, and peas. She did the laundry in a huge iron washpot heated over an open fire in the back yard. She used home-made lye soap in this last operation.

She made a couch out of an old Studebaker carseat. The couch, a rocker, two straight-back chairs, and Joker's old flat-top guitar constituted her parlor furnishings. The house was warmed by a small coal-burning fireplace in the living room, and a pot-bellied stove in the kitchen. Red papier-mâché shades were suspended from the light bulbs in each of the house's four rooms.

Joker's calloused palms and thick fingers no longer elicited sweet music from the guitar. Joker's blond hair was thinning, and he no longer looked like the local dandy, except on Saturday nights. He wore his chalkstripe suit then, and sometimes even found a willing woman. On such occasions, he usually didn't make it back to the farm until late Sunday evening. Ester would fix him a hearty meal then, so that he would be able to go back to the cotton fields on Monday morning.

No matter what Ester thought, she said nothing. Never was there less communication between two people residing in the same household. Even on those rare occasions when she and Joker coupled, she let him know that she wasn't enjoying it. And she began to put on weight, let her hair and facial features grow frowsy, so that he wouldn't enjoy it either.

Trinity had a bedroom of his own and wasn't aware that his parents weren't particularly genial toward each other. He wasn't aware of very many things, to tell the truth. He was still his mother's darling boy, and the things he was most aware of were her smiles and frowns. He would go to any lengths to please her and keep from displeasing her. Otherwise, he didn't notice or give a damn about much.

He went to church, since Ester often sang there. When she sang, her blowsy features took on a blurred, angelic look, as if Ester had temporarily and partially been translated into light. Her strong alto voice only partly explained this. Her voice did express some intense sorrow and joy for which there was no religious basis, it seemed. Trinity believed for a long time that her songs were praises, prayers, and supplications of and to *him* instead of God, and in a way this was true. Ester lived in the light of her son's blue eyes always.

Joker, in retaliation, began to teach the boy chords on the old flat-top guitar at night. Trinity, his fingers sensitive and agile, unused to any hard work, learned quickly. By the time he was ten, he could play that instrument as well as Joker ever had. Even Ester was pleased, and she insisted that Joker pay a music teacher to teach the boy how to read music, something Joker himself could not do. For the first time in ten years, Mr. and Mrs. Fleming agreed on something. Trinity learned to read music and play the piano, though he would never play it well. The shiny old guitar now rested atop a used piano in the parlor.

Trinity won his first talent contest when he was thirteen years old. The contest was a local thing, a high school thing. Trinity won it by singing a spirited rendition of "An Uncloudy Day," one of Ester's favorite hymns. In fact, she sang the song much better than the boy, whose voice was reedy and uncertain. The emotion, the sense of suffering, *were* there in Trinity's song, however, though it might be hard for an objective observer of his life to explain why. Trinity Fleming never suffered anything. He was big for his age, very good-looking, and casually stupid. His several teachers, past and present, were astounded that he could memorize the words of a song, much less sing one with anything approximating sincere feeling.

Ester went back to work in the chicken processing plant that year, and the family moved back to town. Trinity began to learn fewer religious songs and to accompany his father to roadhouses and juke-joints and gin-mills. Now the son, not the father, was the musical attraction—and the sexual attraction.

Trinity had his first woman at the age of fourteen in the backseat of an Oldsmobile. The woman was twice his age, but he made up in ardour what he lacked in experience. Joker was having his own fling in the backseat of another car in the same roadhouse parking lot, but Trinity didn't know that, or care.

Music and sex were forever afterwards linked in his mind. Music was the foreplay, the inducement, the prayer; sex was the reward for the music.

"There are as many songs as there are women," Trinity told his cronies. "And I mean to sing and screw them all."

The Flemings moved to Memphis, Tennessee, when Trinity was in his last year of school. They apparently meant to give the boy a chance to make good on at least one-half of that boast. But his dark good looks (he looked remarkably like an Indian), his polite manners, his music insured that he would never be lacking in female admirers.

To his credit, he was as serious about the music as he

was about the sex. He wrote his own songs, pastiches of the rhythm and blues and rocking spirituals of his youth. He went to several black clubs in Memphis, listened intently, found the white heat and movement of the black music exciting beyond words. All this became part of his music.

He discovered himself. He walked into a sound studio and paid ten dollars to cut his own record. The song, sung to the accompaniment of his guitar, was "Frisco Train."

> Frisco train,
> Leaving Springfield Station way behind.
> Where it's going when it's gone
> Ain't no concern of mine.
> When it's gone at midnight
> I'll be moving, too—
> Riding that Frisco train
> Into the morning blue.

He all but physically forced the owner of Planetarium Records to listen to the record. The owner, Jonah Clements, wasn't quite sure what he had heard, but it sounded hot. He signed Trinity Fleming to a three-year contract, re-cut the song with a four-piece band (lead guitar, bass guitar, piano, and drums), and released it. Within two months, it had sold a million copies.

Trinity Fleming was graduated from high school and built his parents a colonial mansion in his eighteenth year. He hung the diploma in the game room of the mansion beside the dart-board. There was a red plush carpet on the room's floor. Black leather sofas faced the fireplace, pool table, and piano. Full-length mirrors at one end of the room sometimes reflected Trinity eating pizza or hamburgers, drinking Coke, and composing his songs.

But for the most part he wasn't at home; he was on the road, performing in cities that had nothing and everything in common with Memphis. His audiences, mostly female, were hysterically worshipful. Trinity quickly discovered that there were *more* women than there were songs, more women than there were nights to seduce them in. It both helped and hurt that he could multiply his voice (and later, his image) a million times. Even working a double or triple shift, he could not handle all those women.

At age twenty-five, Trinity had sold eleven million single records, and six million albums. He had starred in half-a-dozen movies. The colonial mansion in Memphis now had a swimming pool, a tennis court, and garage space for seven Lincolns, one Corvette, eleven motorcycles, and a GMC pickup. Ester called the Lincolns "Abrahams." This was the only joke anyone ever heard her make.

By that time, Trinity had discovered amphetamines, barbiturates, and boys. He was usually tired. He was especially tired of playing the polite gentleman pursuer, even for five minutes at a time. Golden and hairy young men relieved him of that burden, serviced him as worshipfully as golden and unhairy young girls had done for the last ten years of his life. Trinity compensated for his excesses by cutting an album of hymns and a Christmas record, and by continuing to adore his mother.

Both compensation and adoration were very real. Trinity never brought his female or male groupies to "Ester's house"; that would have been sacrilege. And he possessed a maudlin kind of awe at his own dumb luck. Somebody upstairs must love him, Trinity concluded. The least he could do was record a few hymns every now and then to show that he appreciated God's being so thoughtful of his comfort and pleasure.

In 1962, at the age of twenty-seven, Trinity decided to give up sex and get married. His new wife Wanda, a beautiful girl seven years his junior, didn't appreciate the order in which those resolutions fell. It was not a happy marriage.

Many people were unhappy in 1962. Discontent was almost fashionable, and terrifically sane. Many Americans were becoming "aware" of something. It was a drug-fed, media-fed, federally funded awareness, but none the less real for all of that. Blacks were discovering that whites had been using blacks as slaves and pseudo-slaves for two centuries, had been stealing black labor, music, and women for generations. Teenagers were discovering that Eisenhower and parents were bad news. John Kennedy was discovering that there were Russian missiles in the Western Hemisphere. Women were discovering that husbands and boyfriends didn't *naturally* take household and child-rearing duties upon themselves just because women were working. Eighteen to twenty-one-year old men were discovering that there was a war going on in a little Asian country called South Vietnam. Everyone between the ages of twelve and ninety was discovering that sex was as enjoyable a hobby as golf, Ping-Pong, chess, poker, or dominoes. Lo and behold, all this awareness, all these discoveries boded ill for the nation, made white, middle-class American males over forty very nervous.

White, middle-class American males over forty *were* the nation in the 1950's. This was not the case in the 1960's. Everybody wanted a piece of the action. And got it.

Back at the colonial mansion in Memphis, Trinity Fleming popped another diet pill into his mouth and chased it down with a diet soda. He was getting fat. His music no longer contained its original fire; his songs, no longer written by himself, were putridly sweet ballads and ditties. His movies were all the same; only the settings and leading ladies changed. His mother was ill; diet pills and liquor were killing her. His sweet wife Wanda hated him, threatened to divorce him every other day. Joker was five states away, having a good time, as always. Trinity hadn't had an erection in six months.

He set his diet soda down and wrapped his old bathrobe more tightly about him. Rings, seventy-thousand dollars worth, glittered on his pudgy fingers.

"Wanda," he said, for she was in the room, "we can't go on like this."

"No, we can't," she nodded sagely.

"How did we ever come to be like this?" he asked, and threw up his hands in dismay.

"I don't know," she said unhappily, and waited for Trinity to explain it all to her. She is waiting still.

W.C.W. WATCHING PRESLEY'S SECOND APPEARANCE ON "THE ED SULLIVAN SHOW":
Mercy Hospital, Newark, 1956

D a v i d W o j a h n

The Tube
    like the sonnet,
        is a fascist form.
I read they refused
    to show this kid's
        wriggling bum.
"The pure products
    of America . . ."
        etc.
From Mississippi!
    Tupelo,
        a name like a flower
you wouldn't want
    beside you
        in a room
like this,
    where the smells hold you
        a goddamn
hostage to yourself,
    where talk's
        no longer cheap.
Missed connections,
    missed connections—
        a junk heap

blazing there in
          Ironbound,
                    a couple kids
beside it,
          juiced on the
                    cheapest wine. Mid-
thought. Midwinter,
          and stalled
                    between the TV screen
and window. . . .
          This pomped-up kid
                    who preens
and tells us
          "Don't Be Cruel."
                    Kid, forget it.
You don't know
          a fucking thing
                    about cruelty yet.

THE ASSASSINATION OF ROBERT GOULET, AS PERFORMED BY ELVIS PRESLEY:
Memphis, 1968

D a v i d   W o j a h n

—"That jerk's got no heart."—E. P.

He dies vicariously on "Carol Burnett,"
Exploding to glass and tubes while singing "Camelot."

Arms outstretched, he dies Las Vegas-ed in a tux,
As the King, frenzied in his Graceland den, untucks

His .38 and pumps a bullet in the set.
(There are *three* on his wall, placed side by side.)

The room goes dark with the shot, but he gets the Boys
To change the fuses. By candlelight he toys

With his pearl-handled beauty. Lights back on,
But Goulet's vanished, replaced by downtown Saigon:

Satellite footage, the Tet offensive,
Bodies strewn along Ky's palace fences.

Above a boy whose head he's calmly blown apart,
An ARVN colonel smokes a cigarette.

NIXON NAMES ELVIS HONORARY FEDERAL NARCOTICS AGENT AT OVAL OFFICE CEREMONY, 1973

David Wojahn

The King is thinking Tricia's got nice tits,
Of Grace Slick at Tricia's wedding, trying to spike
The punch with acid (orange sunshine, 300 hits).
While the bubblegum Turtles churned out their schlock,
And the Ehrlichmans danced the Funky Chicken.
Grace Slick named her baby *God*, a moniker,
He thinks, almost as good as *Elvis Aaron*—
Who's today shaking hands with the Chief, his mind
    a blur
Of dexies and reds, but scored with an M.D.'s
    prescription.
Pompadour, karate *ghee*, and cape,
Twenty pounds of rhinestones, a corset to tuck
    the paunch in:
Late model Elvis. His hands shake as he takes the plaque.
Explaining the hieroglyphic on his ring, he laughs.
"It means, sir, *Taking Care of Business with a Flash*."

ELVIS MOVING A SMALL CLOUD:

The Desert Near Las Vegas, 1976

David Wojahn

—after the painting by Susan Baker

"Stop this motherfucking Limo," says the King,
And the Caddie, halting, raises fins of dust
Into a landscape made of creosote,
Lizards, dismembered tires. The King's been reading

Again—*Mind Over Matter: Yogic Texts
On Spiritual Renewal by Doctor Krishna
Majunukta, A Guide on How to Tap the
Boundless Mental Powers of the Ancients.*

Bodyguards and hangers-on pile out.
His Highness, shades off, scans the east horizon.
"Boys, today I'm gonna show you somethin'
You can tell your grandchildren about."

He aims a finger at Nevada's only cloud.
"Lo! Behold! Now watch that fucker *move!*"

AT GRACELAND WITH A
SIX YEAR OLD, 1985

David Wojahn

It's any kid's most exquisite fantasy,
To have his name
         emblazoned on a private jet.

So Josh stares through the cockpit of
                The Lisa Marie,
Its wings cemented to the Graceland parking lot.
The kitsch?
      All lost on him, the gold records and cars,
Dazzling as the grave's eternal flame.
And I read him the epitaph's Gothic characters.
"A gift from God . . ." etc. Daddy Presley's wretched poem.
Colonel Parker was asked, after Elvis's death,
What he'd do now to occupy his time:
                    "Ah guess
Ah'll jus' keep awn managin' him." He's really *Dutch*.
The accent, like the colonel tag, is a ruse,

Like the living room's wall of mirrors—rigged immensity,
Pipsqueak Versailles,
        where Josh makes faces, grinning
        at me.

PHARAOH'S PALACE

Memphis, 1988

David Wojahn

Last week a half-crazed Mormon woman in a blue-white
   bouffant claimed
miraculous healing at the grave, hurling away her crutches
   to walk
a few unsteady feet, until a gang of courteous
   uniformed

guards restored her to her braces,
   and dispatched
her in a golf cart to the entrance. She wept in ecstasy
   or sorrow
as the iron sixteenth notes of the gate
   clattered shut.

Labor Day weekend: the day's final tour. Above us,
   the shuttered
room where the overdose took place, although
   the guards claim
heart attack. Around us in the living room,
   row upon row.

of phony potted daisies, his favorite flower,
   and we walk
the arena of the dining room, its behemoth TV, the ceiling
   still patched
where the chandelier, a ton of crystal
   in the form

of a guitar, crashed last year to the table,
    a formal
setting for sixteen. In the basement snack bar
    we shudder
at the color scheme, the three TV sets side by side.
    Our guide, an incongruous patch

on her eye, tells us he "watched three stations *at once!*"
    Mirrors climb
walls and ceiling, TVs in infinite recession. Mirrors
    line the walkway
to his "Jungle Den," waterfalls cascading from
    imitation stones. The Pharaoh,

he claimed, of rock and roll. The gift shop girl
    looks up from a row
of souvenir glasses and posters. In his late-phase
    karate uniform,
rhinestones and white leather, he poses sulking
    wherever we walk.

I think of how his crooked Greek physician shot him up,
    the shut-in,
pacing his bedroom, rolling up his silk kimono
    sleeves, exclaiming
like a child when the methedrine surged in, and how
    he once dispatched

his private jet from Memphis to Las Vegas—the gleaming
    Beechcraft *Apache*—
to ferry back peanut butter and jelly sandwiches
    from some skid row
deli he remembered. But he was a *nice boy*, always,
    and claimed

his needs were simple: nymphets in white panties,
    the snow that formed
on each TV screen after "The Star-Spangled Banner"
    played, and the stations shut off

and he'd stare awhile at nothing. We weave
    down the sidewalk

to the grave, the clumsy epitaph his Daddy wrote.
   A woman walks off
sobbing to herself. Her husband in cowboy boots,
   face a patch
of oily sores, follows her shaking his fist, slaps her twice
   and tells her *Godamn you, shut up.*

He drags her off by the arm, but still she's
   wailing, sorrowfully
crouched on a bench. On the parking lot loudspeaker
   he's performing
"Young and Beautiful." On the two-lane headed home,
   we stop at a house claimed

by kudzu and grass, barn and house collapsed,
   wood a uniform gray,
   windows shuttered.
Evening coming on: we walk a path to a family plot,
   a hornet's nest patching
a single marker proclaiming no name, only HERE US
   O LORD IN R SORROW.

FROM STARK RAVING ELVIS

William McCranor Henderson

Byron met Elvis Aron Presley face-to-face in the summer of 1976, at a Boston Garden concert. A distant cousin of Larry McCann's (the same Fat Larry) was working for Elvis, one of the black belts on his security crew. He ushered Byron through the cavernous back corridors of the Garden and slipped him into Elvis's dressing room. It was full of preshow hangers-on. The air was heavy with the smell of sweat. Byron felt suddenly sick—a jangling in his head, a taste of metal in his mouth. The thought of backing out flickered through his mind, but the door had been locked behind him.

The area where Elvis sat glowed as if they had lit it with a spotlight. Elvis looked puffy and tired, in a bulging white jumpsuit with gold and blue trim. He was reading aloud from a book called *The Golden Voice of Ra*. His face was dripping with sweat and his eyes had a dull polyurethane glaze. There was a gun strapped around his paunch.

"And the mountains shall split asunder to make way for the coming of the Final Spirit, the Fire-Lighter of History, the igniter of the Universe . . . "

His eyes wandered toward the door. He noticed Byron immediately.

"C'mon over here, son," he said.

Byron steered himself into the light and shook hands

with the King. Then he looked, close up, and what he saw almost made him choke.

Elvis seemed stuck to the jumpsuit, as if it had melted and hardened, a poisonous second skin, tightening its grip on his tired flesh, draining the life out of it, killing him slowly. Sickness seeped through the hooded eyes. Byron tried to shake the image of death out of his head.

The boys from Memphis were fluttering around Elvis, cracking a stream of dumb jokes and snickering nervously at each other. They seemed to want to pull the boss's attention away from Byron.

"Elvis! Hey, Elvis—!" they were calling. Elvis this, Elvis that. Byron had no sense of time. The moment seemed to spin in an endless circle, as he and Elvis exchanged a few words.

"Y'know. Somebody's been trying to kill me," Elvis said in a soft monotone. "I thought for half a second it was gonna be you."

Byron laughed uncomfortably and shoved his hands in his pockets. He couldn't look Elvis in the eye.

"Nah . . . not me. Not me, man."

"You carry a gun?"

"Nah."

"Y'ought to. This ain't a world for gentle people. I got a damn Browning Automatic Rifle."

Then somebody took Byron by the arm and moved him gently toward the door.

"Stop right there—" said Elvis suddenly. He stared oddly at Byron from across the room and then removed the .22 Savage revolver from his bulging waist, belt, holster and all. He folded it and held it out to Byron.

"TCB, my friend," he said, with a nod. *Take Care of Business*, read the belt. "TCB" was tooled all over it, with lightning bolts in ornate clusters.

And then Byron found himself out in the hall, cradling the cold weight of Elvis's own gun in his hands.

TCB. There had been something uncanny, a special tone in the way Elvis had said it. A glint of recognition had gone back and forth between them. It struck Byron that this was more than just a casual exchange. Something enormous had happened here. Elvis had given him a secret message and it clearly said: I am surrounded by assholes—but Brother, I know you and you know me. We *know* each other in a secret way. We are fated. Like father, like son, like brothers, like lovers.

He had said: You've got to finish it for me, man. I'm too far gone to be what I was. Go out and do it! Byron had seen it in that look as clearly as if it had been written across Elvis's face in magic marker. In that moment, Byron understood. It was like a picture in his mind: Elvis, weakened; Prince Byron, strong and ready, standing over the suffering king, receiving his potency, the full force of his earthly mission. And then, if there were any doubts, in front of those gobbling turkeys, Elvis had silenced them by passing on his gun. There was the final answer: Byron would be King, it was only a matter of time. Amen.

Except that now, over a fucking year later, Elvis was still out on the road, struggling and thrashing like a weary old dray horse, embarrassing himself in front of the whole damn world, while Byron simply hung in the wind, his vision deadened by forty desolate hours a week at Cavanaugh Pump Works. Month by month, the promise was running dry. But he kept the gun shining, the leather rich and soft. He practiced quick draws in front of the mirror, over and over, dropping to one knee and fanning the Savage like a gunfighter.

"How 'bout it, man?" Byron would plead with the face on his T-shirt. "How long are we gonna play this game?"

FROM THE GIRL WHO LOVED ELVIS

Susie Mee

Both newspapers and almanacs are predicting that the summer of '57 will be one of the hottest on record. From the way it feels already—and it not even June—I'm thinking they may be right. My whole upper body has a tickling sensation from perspiration drops rolling down and bunching at my waist in one big sweat band. For this reason, I stop wearing a belt and choose my loosest dresses to work in. Folks seem unable to talk about anything but the heat.

" 'Nother scorcher today, ain't it?" Marvin says in the canteen, wiping his brow.

"Yep," Tessie says. "They say tomorrow's gonna be worse."

"No!"

"What they say."

Or, "Hey, Boley, is it hot enough for ya?"

"It's drying me out. My insides are rattling around like butterbeans."

"That's just your brain y'hear."

Or—this from Dot—"If I sweat much more, ain't gonna be nothing left of me but a pinch of salt."

As always in hot weather, my appetite goes, and when I sit down at the table, I'm only able to eat a few small bites.

"Eat up now," mama says, laying out piles of meat

loaf, mashed potatoes, fried okra, tomatoes, and cantaloupe.

And I do try, really *try*, taking a bite of this, a bite of that, before setting down my fork. "Mama, it's too *warm* for hot food!" I protest when she urges me on to more helpings.

"That's exactly when you need it most."

"What? *Why?*"

"Because it gets the boiler stoked so you can perspire. Keeping all the sweat inside is what causes the trouble. Same as wearing a black cloth over your head."

"I don't understand."

"It's not a question of *understanding*, just take my word for it."

After dinner, she moves the parakeet out to the porch where it's cooler. Then she hauls out a chair for herself from the living room and sits there trying to teach it to talk. If I drag out a chair, too, or make any noise at all, mama hushes me. Sometimes I get up in a huff and go over to the Inn to visit Dot. Other times I just sit, wondering how my mother can be so stupid.

Then one day towards the end of the summer, it happens. By mama's reaction, you'd think the heavens'd opened up and fourteen angels had floated through.

Mama's just called me into the kitchen. "Everything's on the table," she says. "Sit down and start buttering your cornbread." She pulls out a chair herself. "Nothing in this world worse than lukewarm cornbread." Then she passes the pinto beans, straight from the stove and bubbling still, and the potatoes, barely browned and shaped like tiny bridges with scads of grease dripping off the ends.

"Eat up now," mama says.

But I can only pick around, dabbing my fork in and spearing a bean or two, then sticking it into my mouth and going back for two more, and all the while mama getting more and more impatient.

"Eat up," she says again, this time frowning.

But I can't. I just can't. I sit there, piling the food into a mound and stabbing it in the middle in order to watch the beans scoot across the plate.

And next to me, on the cabinet, the parakeet crackles away, though I don't pay much attention, thinking instead about how I'm going to get down to the Tooga to see *Lovin' You* without having to go in Bub's Taxi. Without looking directly at her, I sense mama stiffen.

"Shhhh," she hisses, putting a hand up.

"I didn't say anything."

"I *said* shhhhhh!"

For a second everything's quiet. I look at mama who's staring at Pretty Boy. I turn. The dumb bird's sitting on its perch the same as always. "Is something wrong?"

"Shhhh!" This time her shush is sharp and quick. Her head's tilted back and her hand raised, as if it's frozen in mid-air. "Did you hear that, or am I going crazy?"

"Hear what?"

"Shhh. . . ."

The parakeet's squawking again, and this time I sit up because anybody listening hard can pick out a definite sound. Poor imitation of a human voice, maybe, but a sound all the same. Saying . . . what is it? "Eat . . . eat up now." And again, "Eat up now." Like mama speaking over a radio that's lost one of its tubes.

Letting out a yelp, she runs over and kneels in front of the cage.

"My God!" she says, pressing her mouth against the bars. "My Pretty Boy can talk good as anybody, yetz he can." Opening the door, she pours half a box of millet seeds into the feed dish until it overflows. "There. That's for him being so smart." She whistles and purses her lips.

"Can't eat no more." I march my full plate over to the garbage pail and rake it out.

"Mmmmmm," mama murmurs, listening only to the bird.

"Going to work now." At the door I turn and say real loud, "Don't worry about my not taking any supper. I'll share Dot's and Tessie's."

Normally mama would've thrown a fit at this news. Now she merely nods.

Reaching the Grey Mill early, I wait on the steps for the others to arrive. Grady Fay comes over by way of the Grey Mill sign and the little group that's always gathered around it. I can hear them exchanging a joke or two about the Fall harvest on Sand Mountain.

"Hear y'got enough corn to feed the whole state."

"Hear y'got watermelons big around as the moon."

He takes it all in good humor, answering, "Yeah, yea," to each one until he reaches the steps. "So," he flings himself down. "What's new?"

My usual answer to this question is "Nothing much." But now, two things are on my mind. "Mama's bird talked today. For the first time. She thinks it's a miracle." Pausing, I sit there wiggling my toes inside my white sandals. "Reckon you know that *Lovin' You* is coming to the Tooga next week?"

"*Lovin' You?*" Grady Fay crooks his bad arm and rotates the elbow round and round. I'm so used to counting for him that I can hardly stop myself from doing it now.

"The new Elvis movie."

"Oh yeah." Reversing his motions, he circles backwards. "You going?"

I smile. "You have to ask?"

"Wanna go with me?"

This is exactly what I'd hoped to hear. "I don't mind."

"What time does it start?"

"Seven-thirty, I think. But we oughta get there early. Sure to be a big crowd."

"Pick you up at seven."

"Quarter till. And I'll be at the Inn." This is so I don't catch any flack from you-know-who.

So, quarter till it is.

Or is it?

I'm sitting in the lobby of the Inn, glancing up at the clock. It's now almost seven. Doesn't he understand how important it is to be early? Dot and Troy—promising to save us seats if they can—left fifteen minutes ago.

Struggling out of the leather armchair, I pace back and forth, only stopping to pick up a *T.V. DIGEST* from the magazine rack in the corner and thumb through it, skipping the story on Gisele MacKenzie's bachelor apartment to glance at the latest Arthur Godfrey gossip so I can tell mama. Finally I throw it down. Maybe Grady Fay's forgotten and gone to my house by mistake.

I walk over to the pay phone to call, but think better of it. How can someone be so unreliable? A horn sounds. Racing to the window, I see his truck.

"Where you been?" I ask as I climb in. "We'll be lucky to get a ticket."

He nods toward the door. "Be sure you slam it good."

Isn't it just like him not to apologize for turning me into a bundle of nerves! Wish he'd drive faster. "O, please help us get a seat, Lord," I pray silently.

In the long run, though, it's more Dot's doing than the Lord's. In spite of people making all kinds of nasty comments, she's stubbornly held on to two empty seats in a middle row. Me and Grady Fay slip in just as the picture's starting.

The story line is close to Elvis's own life, at least the rise-to-fame bit. He's such a natural singer that after he wins the talent contest, Tex asks him to join the band. Every time Elvis opens his mouth, the girls go wild. He makes everything look so easy. My daddy made things look easy, too. Wonder if Grady Fay can feel—through the spot where our legs touch—the nerve ends crawling beneath my skin.

Out the corner of my eye, I see Dot all scrunched up next to Troy. Every now and then, he turns her face in his direction and gives her a soul-searching kiss that sometimes lasts so long people behind yell, "Down in front, down in front!"

Glenda, Tex's ex-wife, is always making up to Elvis, even though she's old enough to be his mama. Anyway, I'm rooting for Susan, the girl singer.

And all the time I keep waiting for Grady Fay to take my hand or something. But he doesn't. It stays on my lap, prim as a paper napkin.

The white convertible gives Elvis extra dash. Susan sits beside him, her hair blowing in the wind. Wish I looked like Susan. From the way they gaze into each other's eyes, you can tell they're dying to kiss.

Once in a while I glance over in Dot's direction to see how she and Troy're making out. Actually they're pretty quiet now. Troy's big knuckles rest right over Dot's crotch. Mama was shocked once to see them sitting like that on a bench in front of the store. "His hand . . . right *there*," she said. "In front of everybody. That's what I call cheap!"

Then things get a little tangled up. Poor Susan pining away, and Elvis driving like a demon. I cover my eyes so I won't see the car crash. It's Grady Fay who leans over and whispers, "He's okay." First words he's spoken since the picture started.

Then a turn for the better. A winning streak. Elvis looks Susan in the eye and tells her in that deep voice of his how much he loves her. It clinches everything. Elvis and Susan, Tex and Glenda. No loose strings.

When the house lights come on, I blink. After the bright technicolor, everything seems so drab.

"Wanna go to Hookey's for a hamburger?" Dot asks.

Grady Fay shrugs as if he's leaving the answer up to me. I shake my head. "Didn't you love it?" I whisper to Dot.

She looks at Troy and grins. "Sure did."

Dot and Troy go off arm in arm. Grady Fay and me stand there a few minutes, then he leads the way to the Western Auto store where his truck's parked.

Driving back, I roll down the window to let in some air. The second it hits my face, I feel weightless. I glance over at Grady Fay. He's even quieter than usual. "If we were in a convertible right now, we could look up at the sky. Imagine."

"Then you'd complain about being cold."

The wind sweeps my hair away from my face. Raising my arms, I take a deep breath and lean back against the seat. Wish this road would stretch on forever. Wish we could drive straight to Memphis.

Instead, we drive straight to Smoky Road.

Surely, *surely* he doesn't intend to simply pull up in front of my house and let me out. Doesn't he have *any* imagination? The truck begins to slow down.

"I'd . . . like to ride around a little bit. Would you?"

"Where do you want to go? Not far, I hope. I don't have that much gas."

"How about up to the golf course?"

"The golf course! Nobody's there now." But I notice he puts his foot back on the accelerator.

"We can sit and talk. And if we want some music, we can always turn on the radio."

"Radio doesn't work."

"Well, then, I can sing." I begin humming, then singing, the tune from the movie. After a second or two, he joins in.

I listen to his voice, surprised at how deep it goes, at

the way it slides up and down the scale. At the end, I'm silent for a second. "That was wonderful! You should join our church choir."

"Aw . . . " He turns into the dead-end road that leads to the golf course and, beyond that, to the river.

"I mean it."

"Better be careful."

"Why?"

"You'll turn my head." He turns and grins at me, but keeps both hands fastened on the wheel. If it was Elvis sitting there, he'd reach out and pull me over next to him, close enough for me to feel the thud of his heartbeat through his shirt. And if I made the slightest move to draw away, he'd hold me real tight, and then, first chance he got, he'd turn my face around and graze my lips with his.

At the clubhouse, Grady Fay slows down. "Wanna stop here and walk around?"

Walk around? I shudder. "No. Let's go on."

The road down to the water's so narrow that branches whip the sides of the truck, making me roll my window up.

"Hope none of the paint's getting scratched off," Grady Fay says.

We twist along the narrow ruts until the road abruptly opens up into a clearing by the river's edge. Grady Fay stops the truck and turns off the motor. "Hope I can get back outta here," he mutters, glancing behind him.

But I'm looking straight ahead. "This used to be the place where they'd bring in cotton bales by boat. My daddy told me. That was before they built the big dam."

"Really?"

"And before that, it was a Cherokee campground."

"You know a lot," he says.

"Well, I've lived here all my life. And my daddy lived here, and *his* daddy. My granddaddy Grubbs, he's dead now, but he used to drive one of the Allgood wagons down to the Rome depot and back. That's where they shipped the cloth from. He told me a story about him getting home late one Christmas because one of his old mules took sick and he had to walk to the nearest farm for a replacement. He didn't reach Trion till after midnight. Sang Christmas carols to himself to keep up his spirits. Granddaddy had a wonderful voice. He was songleader and main soloist at the Baptist Church for over

40 years. Mama said some folks wouldn't know they's dead without him singing 'Asleep in Jesus' over their caskets. My daddy had a good voice, too.''

Then I stop. Don't know what's got into me. Never, in all my life, have I talked so much about myself at one time.

"Wanna get out of the car?" Grady Fay asks.

"Okay. Wish we had a blanket. Then we could spread it out and sit down."

We walk to the water's edge. Except for the silvery curls made by the tiny ripples, it's completely black. I stand very still.

He comes toward me. I'm prepared for him to kiss me the way he kissed Susan in the movie, mouth puckered against mouth. But this is different. Tracing the outlines of my lips with his tongue, he digs the tip inside. And what that tongue does cannot be described in the pages of TRUE CONFESSIONS. *It swims in like a fish into a tank, wiggling through my teeth, squirming against my own tongue.*

Suddenly I get goosebumps and rub my arms up and down.

"You're not cold, are you?" Grady Fay asks.

"No."

Picking up a stone, he throws it into the distance. Then he tries it with his bad arm. A second later, we hear a distinct plunk. "Wish I could get it all the way across," he says.

I bend and grope around, too. "When I was little, some of us girls had a game we used to play."

"What's that?" Grunting, he throws again, this time harder.

"We'd get different-shaped sticks and toss them into the river. Then we'd watch them float all the way downstream. The one whose stick went the furtherest without getting stuck would be the one who'd get married first."

"Did your stick float all the way?"

"Sometimes."

A hand pushes up my skirt, fingers brushing against my panties, groping inside.

"Did you hear anything?" Grady Fay asks.

"What?"

"Did you hear my stone hit the water?"

"No."

"Then maybe I did it. I'm gonna try again."

I hear him take a deep breath. And all the time I'm staring at the water. It's so dark. So dark. "Something real sad happened here once. It just came to mind."

"What?"

"A little boy—well, he was older than me, but then I hadn't started to school yet—was drowned here. In this very spot. I still remember his name . . . Frankie . . . Frankie Teems. He was swimming across with some friends and the current got too much for him and he couldn't make it. It took them the longest time to find his body and pull him out. Because of the dyes. My daddy was the one who embalmed him. Said his lips were still green, and there wasn't a thing in this world he could do about it. I sure would hate to die with green wouldn't you?"

"Yeah."

"Hope I didn't depress you. Don't know what got me started on that."

"You didn't."

"I'm glad because I didn't mean to."

"No," I whisper. "No, don't do that."

"I have to, sugar, I have to. Watching you, I just itch to be there, right there. Does it feel good to you?" I hesitate. "Tell me. I wanna hear you say it. Say it, baby."

"It feels . . . oh, I can't!"

"Tell me, baby. Tell me." "I can't. . . ."

"Want me to do it more?" I nod. "Then say it, baby, say you never want me to stop. Say it."

"I don't. . . ."

"Say it."

"I never want you to stop. Oh, God," I moan.

Grady Fay turns to me. "Are you about ready to get back in the truck?"

"Guess so." I trip over a rock and almost stumble, but he catches my arm.

. . . and all the time me thinking that I'll be punished for letting myself go in a second of weakness, a fallen woman, like Eve, like Mary Magdalene, like the young girls in TRUE CONFESSIONS. "One false step and that's it," mama's always saying. A slip as good as a mile. The devil on the mountaintop. The snake in the grass. How can the Lord have made it plainer?

We climb back in the truck. "This is going to be really hard," Grady Fay says, starting the motor.

I see him struggling with his pants, taking them off, flinging them aside. . . .

"What?"

Grady Fay has opened his door and is peering out. "I said, would you help me look on that side, so we don't hit so many branches?"

"You're okay. Just go on back."

"Relax now. Relax." As he bends over me, I try to speak. He puts a finger to my lips. "Shhh, baby, shhh. I won't hurt you." His face comes closer. In the half-dark his eyes are enormous. The nose flares in and out. Raising my body slightly, he begins pushing into me.

"I'll never drive in here again, tell you that," Grady Fay says. "Too hard to get out of." He passes the clubhouse, then we're back on the main road.

At first I shut my eyes, but then as he keeps thrusting, I open them wide and look into his. When I scream, my voice seems to soar right out the window.

"You're awfully quiet," Grady Fay says, turning to me.

"Just thinking."

. . . and he answers with a final plunge.

"Anything the matter?" he asks as I take a deep breath and lean my head against the seat.

"Just tired, I guess."

"Hope I didn't keep you out too late."

"No."

Pulling up to the curb in front of my house, he starts to get out but I hold up a hand like a traffic cop. "You don't have to do that. Anyway we might wake up mama."

"Oh. Right."

"Thank you." I press down the handle. "I really enjoyed the movie."

"LaVonne . . . I have something I been meaning to tell you." He stares down at his fingers gripping the wheel.

"What?" I step back and wait. Maybe he'll ask me to go steady. Maybe he'll say that I look just like a movie star.

"You're . . . a . . . real nice girl."

Before I have the chance to answer, he's already shifted gears and is chugging off. Both taillights on the truck have holes in the middle as if somebody shot a BB gun at them. Remind me of two bloodshot eyes disappearing into the night.

ELVIS, AXL, AND ME

Janice Eidus

I met Elvis for the first time in the deli across the street from the elevated line on White Plains Road and Pelham Parkway in the Bronx. Elvis was the only other customer besides me. He was sitting at the next table. I could tell it was him right away, even though he was dressed up as a Hasidic Jew. He was wearing a yarmulke on top of his head, and a lopsided, shiny black wig with long *payes* on the sides that drooped past his chin, a fake-looking beard to his collarbone, and a shapeless black coat, which didn't hide his paunch, even sitting down. His skin was as white as flour, and his eyes looked glazed, as though he spent far too much time indoors.

"I'll have that soup there, with the round balls floatin' in it," he said to the elderly waiter. He pointed at a large vat of matzoh ball soup. Elvis' Yiddish accent was so bad he might as well have held up a sign saying, "Hey, it's me, Elvis Presley, the Hillbilly Hasid, and I ain't dead at all!" But the waiter, who was wearing a huge hearing aid, just nodded, not appearing to notice anything unusual about his customer.

Sipping my coffee, I stared surreptitiously at Elvis, amazed that he was alive and pretending to be a Hasidic Jew on Pelham Parkway. Unlike all those Elvis-obsessed women who made annual pilgrimages to Graceland and who'd voted on the Elvis Postage Stamp, I'd never particularly had a thing for Elvis. Elvis just wasn't my type. He was too goody-goody for me. Even back when I was a little girl and I'd watched him swiveling his hips on "The Ed Sullivan Show," I could tell that, underneath, he was just an All-American Kid.

My type, on the other hand, is Axl Rose, the tattooed

bad boy lead singer of the heavy metal band Guns n' Roses, whom I'd recently had a *very* minor nervous breakdown over. Although I've never met Axl Rose in the flesh, and although he's quite a bit younger than I am, I know that, somehow, somewhere, I *will* meet him one day, because I also know that he's destined to be the great love of my life.

Still, even though Elvis is a lot older, tamer, and fatter than Axl, he *is* the King of Rock n' Roll, and that's nothing to scoff at. Even Axl himself would have to be impressed by Elvis.

I waited until Elvis' soup had arrived before going over to him. Boldly, I sat right down at his table. "Hey, Elvis," I said, "it's nice to see you."

He looked at me with surprise, nervously twirling one of his fake *payes*. And then he blushed, a long, slow blush, and I could tell two things: one, he liked my looks, and two, he wasn't at all sorry that I'd recognized him.

"Why, hon," he said, in his charming, sleepy-sounding voice, "you're the prettiest darn thing I've seen here on Pelham Parkway in a hound dog's age. You're also the first person who's ever really spotted me. All those other Elvis sightings, at Disneyland and shopping malls in New Jersey, you know, they're all bogus as three-dollar bills. I've been right here on Pelham Parkway the whole darned time."

"Tell me *all* about it, Elvis." I leaned forward on my elbows, feeling very flirtatious, the way I used to when I was still living downtown in the East Village. That was before I'd moved back here to Pelham Parkway, where I grew up. The reason I moved back was because, the year before, I inherited my parents' two-bedroom apartment on Holland Avenue, after their tragic death when the chartered bus taking them to Atlantic City had crashed into a Mack truck. During my East Village days, though, I'd had lots of flirtations, as well as lots and lots of dramatic and tortured affairs with angry-looking, spike-haired poets and painters. But all that was before I discovered Axl Rose, of course, and before I had my *very* minor nervous breakdown over him. I mean, my breakdown was so minor I didn't do anything crazy at all. I didn't stand in the middle of the street directing traffic, or jump off the Brooklyn Bridge, or anything like that. Mostly I just had a wonderful time fantasizing about what it would be like to make love to him, what it would be like to bite his sexy pierced nipple, to run my fingers through his long, sleek blond hair and all over his many tattoos, and to stick my hand inside his skintight, nearly see-through, white lycra biking shorts. In the meantime, though, since I had happily bid good-riddance to the spike-haired poets and painters, and since Axl Rose wasn't anywhere around, I figured I might as well do some flirting with Elvis.

"Okay," Elvis smiled, almost shyly, "I'll tell you the truth." His teeth were glistening white and perfectly capped, definitely not the teeth of a Hasidic Jew. "And the truth, little girl, is that I'd gotten mighty burned out."

I liked hearing him call me that—*little girl*. Mindy, the social worker assigned to my case at the hospital after my breakdown, used to say, "Nancy, you're not a little girl any longer. You're too old for Axl Rose, not that you have any chance of meeting him in the first place. Do you really think— I'll be brutal and honest here, it's for your own good—that if, somehow, you actually were to run into Axl Rose on the street, he would even look your way? I mean, you're thirty-five years old, Nancy!" Mindy was a big believer in a branch of therapy called "Reality Therapy," which I'd overheard some of the other social workers calling "Pseudo-Reality Therapy" behind her back. Mindy also was only twenty-three, and she'd actually had the nerve to laugh in my face when I tried to explain to her that, in fact, all over the world there were gorgeous young men who desired older women, and that, ultimately, it would be my older woman's sophisticated and knowing mind that would make Axl go wild with uncontrollable lust, the kind of lust no vacuous twenty-three-year-old bimbo-like social worker could ever evoke in a man. Axl and I were destined for each other precisely *because* we were so different, and together we would create a kind of magic sensuality unequaled in the history of the world. But she'd stopped listening to me. So after that, I changed my strategy. I kept agreeing with her, instead. "You're right, Mindy," I would declare emphatically, "Axl Rose is *much* too young for me, and besides, he's a rock n' roll superstar, and there's no way our paths are ever going to cross. I'm not obsessed with him anymore. You can sign my release papers now."

"Little girl," Elvis repeated that first day in the deli, maybe sensing how much I liked hearing him say those words,

"I ain't gonna go into all the grizzly details. You've read the newspapers and seen those soppy t.v. movies, right?"

I nodded.

"I figured you had," he sighed, stirring his soup. "Everyone has. There ain't been no stone left unturned—even the way I had to wear diapers after a while," he blushed again, "and the way I used my gun like a spoiled brat, shooting out the t.v. set, and all that other stuff I did, and how the pressures of being The King, the greatest rock n' roll singer in the world, led me to booze, drugs, compulsive overeatin', and impotence. . . . "

I nodded again, charmed by the way he pronounced it impotence with the accent in the middle. My heart went out to him, because he looked so sad and yet so proud of himself at the same time. And I really, really liked that he'd called me *little girl* twice.

"Want some of this here soup?" he offered. "I ain't never had none better."

I shook my head. "Go on, Elvis," I said. "Tell me more." I was really enjoying myself. True, he wasn't Axl, but he *was* The King.

"Well," he said, taking a big bite out of the larger of the two matzoh balls left in his bowl, "what I decided to do, see, was to fake my own death and then spend the rest of my life hiding out, somewhere where nobody would ever think to look, somewhere where I could lead a clean, sober, and pious life." He flirtatiously wiggled his fake *payes* at me. "And little girl, that's when I remembered an article I'd read, about how the Bronx is called 'The Forgotten Borough,' because nobody, but *nobody*, with any power or money, ever comes up here."

"I can vouch for that," I agreed, sadly. "I grew up here."

"And, hon, I did it. I cleaned myself up. I ain't a drug and booze addict no more. As for the overeatin', well, even the Good Lord must have one or two vices, is the way I see it." He smiled.

I smiled back, reminding myself that, after all, not everyone can be as wiry and trim as a tattooed rock n' roll singer at the height of his career.

"And I ain't im*po*tent no more," Elvis added, leering suggestively at me.

Of course, he completely won me over. I invited him

home with me after he'd finished his soup and the two slices of honey cake he'd ordered for dessert. When we got back to my parents' apartment, he grew hungry again. I went into the kitchen and cooked some *kreplach* for him. My obese *Bubba* Sadie had taught me how to make *kreplach* when I was ten years old, although, before meeting Elvis, I hadn't ever made it on my own.

"Little girl, I just love Jewish food," Elvis told me sincerely, spearing a *kreplach* with his fork. "I'm so honored that you whipped this up on my humble account."

Elvis ate three servings of my *kreplach*. He smacked his lips. "Better than my own momma's fried chicken," he said, which I knew was a heapful of praise coming from him, since, according to the newspapers and t.v. movies, Elvis had an unresolved thing for his mother. It was my turn to blush. And then he stood up and, looking deeply and romantically into my eyes, sang, "Love Me Tender." And although his voice showed the signs of age, and the wear and tear of booze and drugs, it was still a beautiful voice, and tears came to my eyes.

After that, we cleared the table, and we went to bed. He wasn't a bad lover, despite his girth. "One thing I do know," he said, again sounding simultaneously humble and proud, "is how to pleasure a woman."

That night, as we lay side by side together, I decided never to tell Elvis about my obsessive love for Axl Rose. He would just get jealous, and what good would that do? Besides, since then I've learned that Elvis has no respect at all for contemporary rock 'n' roll singers. "Pretty boy wussies with hair," he describes them. He always grabs the t.v. remote away from me and changes the channel when I'm going around the stations and happen to land on MTV. Once, before he was able to change the channel, we caught a quick glimpse together of Axl, strutting in front of the mike in his sexy black leather kilt and singing his pretty heart out about some cruel woman who'd hurt him and who he intended to hurt back. I held my breath, hoping that Elvis, sitting next to me on my mother's pink brocade sofa, wouldn't hear how rapidly my heart was beating, wouldn't see that my skin was turning almost as pink as the sofa.

"What a momma's boy and wussey *that* skinny li'l wanna-be rock 'n' roller is," Elvis merely sneered, exaggerating his own drawl and grabbing the remote out of my hand. He switched to HBO, which was showing an old Burt Reynolds movie. "Hot dawg," Elvis said, settling back on the sofa, "a Burt flick!"

Still, sometimes when we're in bed, I make a mistake and call him Axl. And he blinks and looks at me and says, "Huh? What'd you say, little girl?" "Oh, Elvis, darling," I always answer without missing a beat, "I just said *Ask. Ask* me to do anything for you, anything at all, and I'll do it. Just *ask*." And really, I've grown so fond of him, and we have such fun together, that I mean it. I *would* do anything for Elvis. It isn't his fault that Axl Rose, who captured my heart first, is my destiny.

Elvis and I lead a simple, sweet life together. He comes over three or four times every week in his disguise— the yarmulke, the fake beard and *payes*, and the shapeless black coat—and we take little strolls together through Bronx Park. Then, when he grows tired, we head back to my parents' apartment, and I cook dinner for him. In addition to my *kreplach*, he's crazy about my blintzes and noodle *kugel*.

After dinner, we go to bed, where he pleasures me, and I fantasize about Axl. Later, we put our clothes back on, and we sit side by side on my mother's sofa and watch Burt Reynolds movies. Sometimes we watch Elvis' old movies, too. His favorites are *Jailhouse Rock* and *Viva Las Vegas*. But they always make him weepy and sad, which breaks my heart, so I prefer Burt Reynolds.

And Elvis is content just to keep on dating. He never pressures me to move in with him, or to get married, which— as much as I care for him—is fine with me. "Little girl," Elvis always says, "I love you with all my country boy's heart and soul, more than I ever loved Priscilla, I swear I do, and there ain't a selfish bone in my body, but my rent-controlled apartment on a tree-lined block, well, it's a once-in-a-lifetime deal, so I just can't give it up and move into your parents' apartment with you."

"Hey, Elvis, no sweat," I reply, sweetly. And I tell him that, much as I love him, I can't move in with him, either, because *his* apartment—a studio with kitchenette—is just too small for both of us.

"I understand, little girl," he says, hugging me. "I

really do. You've got some of that feisty women's libber inside of you, and you need your own space.''

But the truth is, it's not my space I care about so much. It's that I've got long range plans, which don't include Elvis. The way I figure it, is this: down the road, when Axl, like Elvis before him, burns out—and it's inevitable that he will, given the way that boy is going—when he's finally driven, like Elvis, to fake his own death in order to escape the pressures of rock 'n' roll superstardom, and when he goes into hiding under an assumed identity, well, then, I think the odds are pretty good he'll end up living right here on Pelham Parkway. After all, Axl and I *are* bound to meet up someday—since destiny is destiny, and there's no way around it.

I'm not saying it *will* happen just that way, mind you. All I'm saying is that, if Elvis Presley is alive and well and masquerading as a Hasidic Jew in the Bronx, well, then, anything is possible, and I do mean *anything*. And anything includes me and Axl, right here on Pelham Parkway, pleasuring each other night and day. It's not that I want to hurt Elvis, believe me. But I figure he probably won't last long enough to see it happen, anyway, considering how overweight he is, and all.

The way I picture it is this: Axl holding me in his tattooed, wiry arms and telling me that all his life he's been waiting to find me, even though he hardly dared dream that I existed in the flesh, the perfect older woman, a woman who can make *kreplach* and *blintzes* and noodle *kugel*, a woman who was the last—and best—lover of Elvis Presley, the King of Rock 'n' Roll himself. It *could* happen. That's all I'm saying.

ELVIS P. AND EMMA B.

Elizabeth Ash

Bear with me:
Memphis is not far
from Yonville-L'Abbaye,
and would you have guessed
at the cornfields, blond,
set against a tidy French sky
and a wilder Tennessee one?

Elvis and Emma
went in for spending
were Philistines
were suckers
for gilt and glitz
were wracked and ruined
by Romance.

Monsieur Lheureux and
Colonel Parker
were fat and happy.

We knew from the beginning
that the Hotel-de-Boulogne,
as well as any Hilton,
was full of heartbreak.

FROM ELVIS PRESLEY BOULEVARD

Mark Winegardner

On the west side of Elvis Presley Boulevard, across from Graceland itself, the parking lot borders a dozen giftshops and a fenced-in compound containing Elvis's tour bus and his two airplanes. On the tail of the larger one, a jet, underneath a parallelogram-shaped American flag decal, was a logo in gold letters: TCB with a lightning bolt underneath.

Next to the compound was the loading area for the white raised-ceiling vans that transport twenty tourists at a time to the front porch of Elvis Presley's home. Though tours didn't start until nine, and it couldn't have been long after that, we were assigned to tour group D, which meant there were a few hundred folks ahead of us. Bob raised an eyebrow and affected a pained look when he saw the tour would cost us six bucks. He'd known about this trip for months, I thought, and besides, he'd just inherited a little money. I wasn't sure I could take three more weeks of his whining about money.

Bob finally paid and, while we waited in the adjacent gift shop, he considered paying even more. "Isn't this great? An Elvis ashtray. I think I'll buy it. For bad taste, pink flamingoes don't have a leg up on Elvis ashtrays."

"Well, wait until after the tour," I said. I wanted to buy a piece of Elvisobilia myself. "We're up next, and you aren't going to carry that around all day."

Bob laughed and set it down. "Okay, we'll come back. Right after the tour."

The van's eight-track tape player treated us to "Rock-a-Hula Baby" as the driver welcomed us to Graceland, shuttled us across the street, and told us we were among the 6,000 visitors who tour the mansion each of the 360 days that it's open. Six thousand people. Over two million a year.

The front of the house is not gaudy, and the house itself is of the minimum size necessary to qualify as a "mansion." Its architecture is neither Antebellum Southern nor Hollywood glitz; in fact, with its gray stone walls, black shutters and four modest white columns, Graceland could easily be mistaken for a dormitory at a Midwestern women's college. It could, except for the steel bars covering all the windows.

On the front porch our lovely tour guide Kelly—wearing, like all Graceland employees, a blue pinstriped shirt, navy chinos and perfect hair—told us that in 1957, at the age of twenty-two, Elvis purchased Graceland and the 13.8 surrounding acres from Dr. and Mrs. Thomas Moore "for one hundred thousand dollars cash." That was a good year for Elvis. For precisely half of 1957, he had the #1 record in America: first "Too Much" (three weeks), then "All Shook Up" (nine), "Teddy Bear" (seven), and "Jailhouse Rock" (seven). I found it hard to imagine: I was now the same age that he was then, and I was living in a Chevy.

"There is still a family member living in the house today, Miss Delta Mae Presley Biggs," said our guide. "That is Elvis's aunt, on his father's side. She's been living here since 1967, when she became a widow, and according to the . . . um, er . . . at the invitation of the estate, she is welcome to live here as long as she pleases." She was a bit flustered by her flub of the canned speech, but few of our group noticed. Most of us were consumed by frantic gawking, irrationally expecting—on cue—an appearance by this frail old woman returning home from Piggly Wiggly.

Our group didn't seem significantly different from a random sampling of twenty tourists plucked from the World's Fair or Ruby Falls. They wore shorts, mostly, and a few middle-aged men embarrassed their families by sporting dark socks and street shoes. I suppose I expected people to be carrying red roses to lay across Elvis's grave and boxes of tissues to sop up the tears they planned to shed.

Kelly explained that no flash photography would be allowed inside, due to its deleterious cumulative effect on drapes and upholstery. No movie cameras or tape recorders, either. "We also ask that you refrain from sitting, leaning or touching anything in the home. It is still a private residence, and we'd like you to show the same respect as you would in any other private home."

As a few thousand more people would do that day, we filed solemnly into Elvis Presley's private home.

We acquired a new tour guide in the dining room—a Kelly-clone with a singsong delivery that sounded remarkably unlike human speech. We learned that the dining-room table, built for six, usually accommodated a dozen guests at each meal; dinner tended to be served between 9 and 10 P.M. The pattern of Elvis's everyday china was Buckingham. "Elvis always sat there at the head of the table, not because he considered himself the man of the family, but because that chair gave him the best view of the TV set you can find in your left-hand corner. Now, we do believe that Elvis was an avid TV watcher, and this is just one of fourteen sets located throughout the home."

In the living room we saw a custom-built 15-foot sofa and 10-foot coffee table and framed photographs of certain family members that were said to be favorites of certain other family members. Beyond the couch were stained-glass partitions decorated with peacocks, Elvis's favorite bird. "At one time here at Graceland, Elvis had about fourteen of these peacocks running around, until they scraped the paint off Elvis's Rolls Royce. Then Elvis gave them to the Memphis city zoo."

A short, pretty, sixtyish woman next to me chuckled. "Fourteen televisions, fourteen peacocks." She elbowed me in the hip. "That's some kind of coincidence for you, isn't it?"

I agreed.

At the far end of the room was a concert grand piano, "twenty-four-carat gold leaf, inside and out," an anniversary gift from then wife Priscilla.

"Why, that piano's worth more than the whole neighborhood Elvis grew up in," the woman said. "Don't you think you'd lose your grasp on reality if you had a piano like that?"

Again I agreed.

She introduced herself and shook hands with Bob and me. "I'm an Elvis fan from way back, you know," Chloe said. "My students told me about him back in 1955. I was teaching in Minnesota then. Microbiology."

Except for the mirrors in the entry hall and along the staircases—installed in 1974, "when Elvis's decorator, Mr. Bill Eubanks, said that they gave the home a more spacious look"—the first rooms were fairly subdued: whites and grays, forgivable flourishes of royal blue and gold.

At the bottom of the stairs a new escort told us that "tourists do not go into the upstairs area due to personal family reasons, but I can tell you what is located there. Elvis's bedroom—above the living room/music room area—Lisa Marie's bedroom, dressing rooms, bathrooms, and also Elvis's office."

"Upstairs," Chloe interjected. "That's where Elvis—"

"Passed on," interrupted the guide. "Yes, ma'am."

"What room was that in?"

"We don't know for sure. None of us has ever been up there. No one really goes up there anymore. Miss Delta Biggs lives downstairs, through that door over there."

"So," Chloe persisted, "you don't know what it looks like up there?"

"No ma'am. Almost no one does. I'm sure you can understand."

In the basement we saw further work of "Mr. Bill Eubanks." The TV Room was done in bright yellow and blue—the exact shades used on Cub Scout uniforms. Displayed on one wall was the TCB symbol we'd seen on the tail of the jet; this was Elvis's personal logo, which stood for "Taking Care of Business in a Flash." The room also contained a wet bar, a jukebox, several televisions, and an eclectic record collection, a mixture of gospel, blues, rock 'n' roll and Dean Martin, who the guide cited as Elvis's favorite singer. We also learned that the televisions were almost always in use simultaneously.

"Dean Martin?" Chloe said. "I could never *abide* Dean Martin."

The Pool Room featured 750 yards of pleated fabric, affixed to the walls and ceiling to resemble mutant wainscoting. We were assured that the rip on the pool table was not made by Elvis—"a good pool player whose favorite games were eight ball and rotation"—but by a friend attempting to execute a trick shot. Above our head was one of several surveillance cameras installed throughout Graceland in the early '70s.

Sources say the basement was the King's favorite portion of his castle.

Nicole welcomed us at our next stop: "The den, or Jungle Room." Added to the house in 1965, this was the only room Elvis decorated himself—and it fulfilled my worst fears with a (now broken) waterfall, rampant ferns, sofas and chairs covered with pseudo-animal hide and supported by arms and backrests into which animal faces and paws were carved. Because the ceiling and walls were carpeted with mottled green shag, the acoustics were good enough to allow two lackluster albums—*Moody Blue* and *Live from Elvis Presley Boulevard*—to be recorded here. Elvis also ate his breakfast here in the Jungle Room, at a polished cypress coffee table.

When Lisa Marie, Elvis's daughter, was a toddler, she enjoyed napping in a huge, barrel-shaped chair in the corner. "Lisa Marie," Nicole said, "is now sixteen. According to her father's will, when she reaches the age of twenty-five, she will inherit this estate in its en-*tire*-ty. It's all being held in a trust fund until then."

On our way outside Chloe asked me what I'd do if I were Lisa Marie.

"It'd be great, I guess, to have the whole world love your dad so much. But I think I'd boot the tourists."

She agreed. "You're right, though. It would be flattering. People in my hometown hated my father. He was a traffic judge."

Somewhere, Lisa Marie might've already made her decision. In 1993, we'll all find out. Then, perhaps, two million people a year will have to wander through someone else's private home.

Outside in the carport we saw a portion of the Presley motorpool: motorcycles, a Dino Ferrari, two Stutz Bearcats and a 1955 pink Cadillac—a gift his mother never used because she didn't know how to drive. We tourists could have our pictures taken in a fringe-topped pink Jeep (which Elvis drove in *Blue Hawaii*) or on one of Elvis's snowmobiles. Because of the lack of snow in Memphis, Elvis had the skis removed and go-cart wheels installed. On the snowmobile I leaned to the left to imitate a severely banked curve, then Bob and I asked Chloe to take our picture in the Jeep. She snapped two, as we took turns driving.

"Do you want your picture taken, too?" Bob offered.

"No thank you," she said. "I find it just a bit ghoulish, to be honest, sitting on vehicles only because Elvis might've once sat on them." She handed me my camera. "But I do suppose they'll make a good souvenir for you boys."

The Trophy Room had been forged out of a garage-sized building in which Elvis housed his sprawling slot-car track. Now it's a museum. The building's former pastime is represented only by six slot cars and four pieces of track.

In the first of three rooms, memorabilia was arranged chronologically to create a timeline of Elvis's life, starting with photos of him growing up in Tupelo and recording his first singles with Sun Records, continuing through his draft notice, a pile of his movie scripts, three Grammies and paintings of his favorite horses, concluding with a large Lucite box stuffed with telegrams received on the occasion of his death. "Thank heaven," Chloe muttered, "there's none of the drug material." Several of us nodded in agreement.

The second room was devoted to his gold and platinum records, of which there are hundreds. I'd expected this to be more interesting than it was, but gold and platinum albums all look about the same, even when some of them are Brazilian and Norwegian.

In the third room: miscellany. Here we learned that Elvis was six-four in his stocking feet and wore a size 12D shoe. Here we saw a replica of his wedding cake, his acoustic and electric guitars, and several pounds of jewelry, including solid-gold car keys and a gigantic TCB ring. Display cases were packed with trophies, medals, keys to cities, and letters from fan clubs, martial-arts instructors and politicos (including Richard Nixon, Jimmy Carter and J. Edgar Hoover). One case contained ten of Elvis's guns and forty-four of his honorary law-enforcement badges, most of which were awarded for narcotics enforcement.

But the clothing is the soul of the room. The first suit displayed is the black leather affair a svelte, dangerous Elvis had worn in the famous 1971 Singer TV special that had been a reaffirmation of his mammoth talent. The suits after that marked a descent into beads, buckskin and bell-bottoms. Fringe was a favorite accessory, until its excess began to promote Elvis's entanglement in microphone wire. Rhinestones gained favor next, reaching a peak with an enormous, bejeweled cape—never used because it weighed too much for Elvis to lift.

Alongside the exit is an unfinished jumpsuit, the color of the deep end at a municipal swimming pool. Elvis was scheduled to wear it onstage August 17, 1977, but he died the day before. I looked past it, back toward his snazzy wedding tux, his leather jacket and his platinum record for "Suspicious Minds," then across the room to his guns and his slot cars. The contrast between what the man achieved and what he'd come to be was so stark and so immediate that I knew I could never again consider Elvis Presley's death in any way premature.

We walked into the sun and out to the memorial garden, where we joined a few lingering tour groups at the graves of Elvis, his stillborn twin, his mother, his father and his grandmother—all arranged in a semicircle, with Elvis in the center. Flowers were strewn across the bronze tablets marking the final resting place of each Presley, though the graves of Elvis and his mother boasted more arrangements than the others. Few cried or made any sort of noise. People studied and photographed the inscriptions on the tablets. As she walked away from all this, Chloe shook her head and spoke to no one.

The van dropped us off back at the airplane holding pen, where I convinced Bob that despite the extra $3 admission, his trip to Memphis wouldn't be complete without the adjunct tour through Elvis Presley's private plane, the *Lisa Marie*.

This tour had its own gift shop, a smaller version of the one we'd already been in. Framed flight documents filled the walls—Elvis's first flight, his last, various flights to and from noteworthy concert appearances.

"God, then it must be real," Bob said, pointing to one of the frames.

"What must be real," I asked.

"This." Bob laughed and shook his head. "I just thought this was one of those apocryphal celebrity legends," he said. "You know, like George Washington and the cherry tree."

But there they were, the flight papers from a twisted journey Elvis commissioned on Groundhog Day of 1976, when he converted a mere hankering into an act that provided the world with a working definition for obscene wealth. Late that night, the King piled his entourage onto a jet and flew them to Denver, Colorado, for peanut-butter-and-banana sandwiches.

When the *Lisa Marie* touched down, it was greeted by a long, black limousine. A man got out, bearing big silver trays full of food readily available in every Memphis supermarket. Elvis and his lackeys snatched up the sandwiches and taxied down the runway. If we read the flight document correctly, the entire trip took fewer than five hours and required 42,000 gallons of fuel.

"He died almost exactly a year-and-a-half later," Bob said. "I'm guessing this is the sort of thing one might have to answer for."

A film we were shown before our trip through the *Lisa Marie* featured Elwood David, the pilot on that Denver excursion and part of the four-man flight crew that Elvis had on call at all times. David seemed tentative as he told the story of his most famous flight, relating the facts as if he were giving an affidavit that would imprison his King. "Sure enough, they were peanut-butter sandwiches and, um, Elvis insisted that the crew have some of his famous peanut-butter sandwiches,"

David stammered. "And, um, I'm not much one for peanut-butter sandwiches, but acourse I had to say it was the best peanut-butter sandwich I ever had."

Over strains of Presley's gospel music, our tour guide explained that Elvis had purchased the *Lisa Marie*—for nearly $1 million—to conquer his fear of flying, which had sentenced him to barnstorming in a converted bus like any number of Country and Western smalltimers. This speech was shorter than most of the ones in the mansion, though just as canned.

The plane was decorated in '70s velour and featured gold-flaked bathroom fixtures. Some of this we should perhaps forgive—few people in the 1970s wore or decorated with material that does not now seem embarrassing. So, to be fair, the plane wasn't half bad. The beds, sofas, recliners, wetbars and cardtables were arranged comfortably, and anyone who imagines some new carpet and upholstery can't help but covet the thing.

We poked around until the rest of our group had filed out. "I have a question," I asked the guide.

"Glad to answer it." She had beauty-pageant hair, coated with enough hairspray to stay curly even on this hot Memphis summer day. She couldn't have been much older than sixteen.

"I mean—how do you listen to this music pumped in here every day? Isn't there times you get up in the morning and think you'd rather die than listen to Elvis?"

"Actually . . . no." She smiled, right at home on this plane. She would make a great stewardess. "You'd think that, but it grows on you. You start listenin' to it on your spare time, too."

"Oh, come on. You listen to Elvis in your *spare time?*" I consider myself a fan, but this hardly seemed plausible. And even if it *were* somehow plausible, it was incontrovertibly deranged.

"Really," she insisted. "You know, not all the time. But a lot of times you do. It's real easy to get all . . . hyped up. Like I said, it becomes . . . I mean, it grows on you."

Just out of earshot, Bob examined the King's VCR. I

could hardly wait to tell him about this. "Don't be offended, but that's strange. You know, not what you'd think. Is that, uh, common among the guides?"

She nodded, though her hair stayed put. "It's that way with everybody. Even if you weren't an Elvis fan when you started workin' here, you start likin' it a whole lot more."

I almost asked her how long she'd been coached to answer that question. Instead, I chose a friendlier tack. "Do people ask that question a lot?"

"Yeah. We get asked everything, just about."

I caught up with Bob, who was teetering on the railing of the rear stairs, attempting to photograph the TCB logo on the tail. "Get this," I said, then told him about our conversation.

Bob snapped the shutter. "You know, I bet they have to go to classes. I bet it takes months to learn."

At an outdoor information booth we found a Graceland employee who was a little less doctrinaire. Ann, at least, lacked the glazed-over eyes and the sing-song voice of many of her co-workers. So I asked her. "There's a script, isn't there?"

She burst out laughing. "Well. . . . "

"How long is it?"

"Ninety-two pages," she confessed. "We all have to learn it." Everyone, she said, knew the speeches for every room, for the *Lisa Marie* and the memorial gardens, the works.

"So if I asked you the speech for the Jungle Room—"

"In my *sleep*," she said.

We talked for a while, introducing ourselves, bemoaning the heat, flirting. She was a student at Memphis State— major undecided—and for her this was just a summer job.

"Would this be a good place to work," Bob asked. "See, we're English majors, so we have to look into any employment option."

Ann laughed. She laughed easily—a good audience. "It's, well, a job, let me leave it at that." Bob must've looked disappointed, because she added, "Well, the thing is, a lot of these people take it too seriously. And a whole lot were groupies and they just naturally gravitated to these jobs."

I told her about the stewardess.

"Yeah, we have a lot like her too. Terminally perky."

"Well," Bob asked, "do *you* listen to Elvis at home?"

She scrunched up her face. "Get serious. I don't even listen to him *here*."

Past the booth walked two middle-aged parents who had suited up their little boy in a satin facsimile of one of Elvis' thunderbird-embroidered jumpsuits.

"Good lord," I said. "I hope that's not a common sight."

"It is," she said. "I think it's sort of mean, but we see a couple of those a week."

"Yeah." Bob fumbled with the camera, but couldn't get it focused in time to get a snapshot of the kid. "I believe you can be declared an unfit parent for that. It could at least provoke a mighty ugly custody battle."

We made small talk for a few more minutes, during which we learned that the blue-and-white-striped oxford shirts that all Graceland employees wear are purchased from the company for $9 apiece. Because Bob told her, she learned that Bob purchased his for a quarter at a thrift shop in Middletown, Ohio.

"Oh, now I know what I was going to ask you," I said as we were getting ready to leave. "Nobody ever gets to go upstairs no matter what, right?"

"Right."

"Nobody who works here, not even when you get started, as a part of orientation? Or, for a twenty-five-year pin, do they take you up and show you a closet? Nothing?"

"Not a thing."

"Curious?"

"Oh, yeah. Yeah. Real curious. All they tell us is what's up there. I don't even know exactly which room is located where, but I do know that Elvis's bedroom is located over the living room. I guess that's what I'd want to see most, his bedroom. Somebody told me once that nobody's been in there since he died."

"Really?" I asked. "No one?"

Ann smirked. "Ah, well. Probably not true. But you know, there's bound to be weirdness up there, don't you think?"

Bound to be, we agreed.

FROM GRACED LAND

Laura Kalpakian

Emily pulled the county car under the jacarandas lining Santiago Street. She thought, Oh shit, without quite saying it. Her client's house was at the corner of Santiago and Sultana: 2924. Heartbreak Hotel. No mistaking it, but thirty years ago this tract was new and raw and these houses all looked alike: three bedrooms, one bath, separate garage, a scrap of lawn front and back, a parkway with jacaranda plunked, one in front of each house. The jacarandas had grown and prospered and now the lacy leaves formed a near-canopy across this forlorn street where the houses, by contrast, had shrunk into motley, sun-faded, hunched-over, ill-kept ranch-style stuccos with cement porches and fake shutters. She dreaded the coming encounter, although by now she'd been a social worker three months and knew how to conduct a Home Visitation. But was she ready for this? These people must be as weird as owl pellets.

She checked her briefcase for notes, a ridiculous gesture that only proves that hope springs eternal because (contrary to all Mr. Hansen's instructions in training class) Emily had not read the case histories prior to her fieldwork. The time she ought to have been dutifully acquainting herself with the paperwork on welfare clients, Emily had been busy writing something funny and clever and cute and caring to Rick. She put something in the mail to him every day, so she would always be present, there, in a manner of speaking, waiting for him when he came home from a hard day at law school.

She locked the county car and wondered if her supervisor had singled out this family for special contempt because Marge hated Elvis. Impossible thought. Aside from Sousa marches and possibly "From the Halls of Montezuma", music alone would not have moved Marge Mason in the least.

A rusted BEWARE OF DOG sign hung on the chain link fence, and Emily felt about in her purse for her mace canister. ("Not necessary, but not unwise," that's how Howard Hansen had phrased it.) But no dog approached and no barking disrupted the drowsy afternoon. She opened the gate and started up the walk, which was flanked on either side by slender gray crepe myrtle trees with long black satin streamers fluttering from their lower branches. The grass was dry and brown, but neatly clipped and clearly swept. No dead leaves gathered in the crevices of the steps, which were covered in carpet remnants of sky blue. The whole porch was an immaculately maintained open-air chapel sacred to the memory of the late Elvis Presley.

Nailed up across the two front porch windows there was an American flag and a Confederate flag and below them, a picnic table covered in a sheet, bleached, starched, and ironed. The table reverently displayed a Gideon Bible at either end. A wreath of plastic daisies lay before a poster-sized picture of the mature Elvis wearing a white spangled bodysuit with a flaring cape, his knee bent in a posture at once dramatic and humble, emphatic and supplicating, tense and intense; he held the mike in a white-knuckled grip. Emily gulped and turned her engagement ring several times. The picture was framed in quilted black satin with four satin rosettes at each corner, and long mourning ribbons twitched and gyrated at the behest of the April wind. Also on the white-clad table, smaller pictures of the young Elvis sat, some cut from newspapers, all in cheap metal frames, and at either end a vase of tall gladiolas in clear, unyellowed water. More red glads were tucked in the flag holder on the porch posts above yet another picture, Elvis in a Hawaiian lei. Nailed to a trellis, a huge hand-lettered sign read:

Sacred to the Memory of This Prince Among Men
Elvis Aron Presley
1935–1977
Long Live the King
His Truth Goes Marching On

Twining up the posts around the signs, encircling the big, black-framed portrait, strung between the two flags, and draped across the white sheet on the picnic table were hundreds of Christmas lights of the tiny, twinkling variety. The wind, more insistent now, bristled uncomfortably at Emily's temples, ruffled her denim prairie skirt, and lifted the sheet covering the picnic table. Underneath, between two speakers, she saw the biggest, hairiest, strangest-looking mutt she had ever seen, who seemed to be shredding a blanket with his fierce, sharp teeth.

Emily's hasty knock was answered by a woman with a mouth full of pins. she removed the pins with one swift gesture and hollered, "Get out of here!" Emily was appalled, speechless really. This particular contingency had never been addressed in training class, the recalcitrant client, perhaps, but never this. The woman yelled again and the dog tore out from underneath the picnic table and ripped around the side of the house.

"That Colonel," said the woman. "He knows this porch is Sacred to the Memory of Elvis. He has shade around the back. He just always wants what he knows he can't have." She gave Emily a look of complicity. "Like any male, right?"

Emily nodded affirmatively.

"You must be the new social worker. Mr. Johnson's replacement."

The woman was green-eyed and fair; she wore no makeup and her hair, darker at the roots, was neatly caught in a barrette. She was about the same height as Emily (except Emily was not barefoot) and she wore a loose Mexican dress, bold colors in a fine weave, which surprised Emily as most of her welfare clients wore clothing frayed and drab as their lives. Emily introduced herself, adding gallantly that she had indeed taken over Sid Johnson's caseload, but everyone said he could have no replacement.

The woman smiled. "I'm Joyce Jackson, but I guess you know that. Come in, Miss Shaw, and get out of this heat."

In the dim living room, starched, ironed clothing hung from the doorways, dismembered dresses pinned to patterns lay on the floor, and clean clothes still stiff from the line were folded and stacked in boxes marked MEN, WOMEN, CHILDREN and BABIES. The ironing board and the sewing machine competed for preeminence, and Elvis was everywhere. Emily asked her professional questions and noted Mrs. Jackson's responses on her clipboard. Then she mentioned she had a headache.

Joyce Jackson moved her to the La-Z-Boy, told her to take her shoes off, brought in two aspirin, a glass of iced tea, and a selection of generic cookies. For the first time since she had moved to St. Elmo, Emily felt the pleasures of shared humanity. Never mind that Joyce was almost twenty years her senior, clearly LMC, and dined on unbuttered bread. Emily relaxed into the La-Z-Boy, up against a comfy quilt, while the swamp cooler sluggishly keeled air currents about the dim room, cool with the smell of spray starch and something else— sweet, reminiscent, but elusive. Pigeons cooed up close to the house and their fluttering contentment seemed contagious. Across from Emily, Joyce sat, knees tucked up, stitching a hem while they chatted about music and men and money. The county, of course, paid Emily to talk with Joyce about men and money, but music ought not to have been on the agenda. How could you help it with Elvis pictures, Elvis posters, Elvis all around you, clustered on the table, filling up the top of the upright piano, tacked even on the lampshades? "You certainly have his whole life here," Emily remarked politely, "young and old."

"Well, he never got to be old, did he, Miss Shaw?"

"Emily, please."

"He died at forty-two. That's exactly how old I am now. Forty-two." Joyce sighed. "Leaves you with a lot to live up to. Look at all the good he did in just those few mortal years, the gifts he gave the world. Are you a fan?"

"Oh yes," Emily lied blithely in the service of good manners.

"I'm so glad to hear that. People who don't like Elvis, well, you can't trust them."

"Oh, you can trust me." Emily's gaze rested on the young Elvis in his leather jacket, slender, dark, intense, and beautiful, on a framed poster from *King Creole*.

"That's an original," said Joyce, as though Monet were under discussion. She launched into a funny tale of how she and her best friend, Sandee, had seen that movie a dozen times and lusted. "And that's the right word, Miss Shaw—"

"Emily."

"—we lusted after that poster. That was Elvis's favorite of all his movies. It was a real early one, '57, in those glorious early days before he went in the army."

Joyce took the ironing board down and cleared stacks of folded laundry from her path, put them beside the open sewing machine while she continued telling how she and Sandee had snatched not one, but two posters right off the wall at the old, long-vanished Dream Theater right downtown, one of those great old theaters with a ticket booth shaped like a wave. How she and Sandee had run into the ladies' room, strapped the posters to their thighs with masking tape they'd brought for that very purpose, and how, under their full skirts, no one ever guessed. "We went back in and watched the movie for the seventh time. Of course, peeling off the tape was no fun," she added. "Sandee got hers too close to the short hairs. Now Emily," she said, stepping over the patterned dress and going to an old stereo, "I'm so glad you love Elvis! It means I don't have to convert you. You just choose your favorite song. Name it. I have all his music."

"I'm not very good at titles," Emily confessed. Neither had she been very good at Interdisciplinary 451: American Pop Culture—The Postwar Years. She should at least have learned a few Elvis titles from Dr. Parks, a huge man who reminded her of the Jolly Green Giant, though he was not at all jolly. Quite the reverse. He was sallow unto greenish, with a grizzled, balding head, and he seemed gigantic because he walked so that his hands swayed in front of him and brushed against his knees. Dr. Parks gave Emily a C. Her GPA was high enough to keep her in the Tri Delts, but C's seemed to dot her grade reports, a spray of crescent moons. To a more perceptive mind than Emily's, her image of crescent moons alone might have suggested why her grades were so mediocre. Emily was afflicted with imagination—not, alas, the focused sort that betokens great things in the big world, but the other sort. Random and inappropriate thoughts ricocheted constantly across her mind like the lights and bells of a pinball machine, and the stimulation from all this flash and noise distracted her continually. In class she found herself wondering what the professor looked like naked (even someone like Dr. Parks, where the thought was really too too terrible) or wondering what he'd be in his next life, maybe a frog, wondering if he might suddenly sizzle down and hop away. Bits of verse suggested themselves to Emily at inappropriate moments, snippets of plays and poems and lyric; Shakespeare and Yeats and Louisa May Alcott elbowed their way to the front of her mind and stayed there, pushing out dutiful thoughts that had been waiting in line for a long time. She couldn't always quote these poems or bits of fiction correctly, but they stayed there, taking up space that ought to have gone to Interdisciplinary 451. Sometimes Emily spent class time wondering, if you were a fly, would you rather drown in cognac or honey?

Emily had confessed this failing to Rick and he said it was part of her charm. Anyway, he said, he would be the brains of the family. This was doubly comforting: clearly he meant to have a family with her, and Rick was very smart. Got very good grades. Top grades in his frat. Would do splendidly in law school (everyone said so), would come back to California, pass the bar exam first time through and join the lucrative butter-slathered practice of her father's Newport firm, Shaw, Swine, Swill, Slime, and Turdlock, which is the way Emily usually thought of her father's partners. Rick did not think this funny at all. Quite the contrary. He reminded her that Shaw, Shine, Brill, Syme, and Turlock would enable the two of them to have a lovely, opulent Laguna Beach life where they would entertain lavishly and tell their guests funny stories about the time they'd had to spend apart, he at Georgetown in D.C. and she in St. Elmo. Their dinner guests would laugh, *St. Elmo! How did you ever stand it, Emily? I hear that's the Armpit of the Nation!* Emily would roll her eyes and raise a glass of sauvignon blanc and say with a smile, *Oh, it's not that bad, it's worse!* Everyone would laugh, because of course those deserty counties were sinks of smog and poverty and desolation, except for Palm Springs, but someone would say even that wasn't the same, and then the conversation would shift. The comfort Emily gained from these mythical dinner parties always waned when she realized Rick would be years in law school and she would be years and years alone in St. Elmo. Years and years and years and

"Who? Excuse me, I—"

"Elvis. There never was a man like him, born a poor boy that God gave a great talent and a great destiny."

Emily sipped her iced tea, nodded, remembered Dr. Parks nattering in Interdisciplinary 451 about poor white trash Elvis Presley whitewashing black music. Elvis was a musical phenomenon only because he made black music respectable—which is to say white. Presley's success had more to do with his being a good-looking white boy than any so-called talent. The history of Elvis, Dr. Parks said, dismissing him in about ten minutes, properly belongs to the history of marketing and has nothing really to do with music. Dr. Parks said Elvis could only play three chords on the guitar, and, as for his famous shake-them-up-and-make-them-scream electric pelvis, well, black performers had been doing that for years in black clubs. But when Elvis brought this sort of thing before white Americans, they thought he had invented it. In truth, he'd only plundered and pillaged black art. Dr. Parks said, at the end of his life Elvis Presley was a great fat bloated toad of a drug addict who could hardly speak, much less sing. Dr. Parks said you need only look at those sequined capes and gaudy bodysuits to know that money could not buy good taste. He concluded with the observation that Elvis was one of those American pop icons morally, mentally, physically, spiritually, and emotionally unequal to his own success.

As Emily sat in Joyce's dim living room with "Love Me Tender" billowing across the room, pushed in slow, alluvial currents by the swamp cooler trailing an elusive fragrance, she recollected standing in a coffee line beside Dr. Parks and noticing he had big blackheads in his ears. She marveled now that she could have even listened to, much less taken seriously, a man who had blackheads in his ears. The line from *Midsummer Night's Dream* rang in her head: With the help of a surgeon, he might yet recover and prove an ass, she thought, forcibly returning her attention to Joyce. She wondered how they had got from Elvis's destiny to marriage. She was interested in marriage.

"The man you marry—I tell my daughters—can be rich, or poor, or plain, or beautiful. Girls—I tell them—you can marry the broom monkey at the Union 76 and you won't hear a word of complaint from me, but never, *never* marry a man who does not like his mother. A man who doesn't like his mother will never like you. Wedlock will feel like headlock, deadlock. Terrible."

Emily could not remember if Rick liked his mother. Could not remember his mother.

"The man who does not like his mother is the man to

have an affair with, but not to marry. My husband, Jack, he was a devoted son to his mother. Devoted."

What was that woman's name? Emily had been a guest in their Pasadena home and Rick's mother was—Frances. Right. Frances. Did Rick like her? "Did Rick—I mean, did Elvis like his mother?"

"I tell you, Emily, Gladys Presley was the most important person in his life. Ever. You don't know how close I came to naming Cilla, my first girl, Gladys, after his mother. And I would have too, if I'd known she was going to divorce him."

"Gladys?"

"No. Priscilla, his wife. She divorced the King in '73. Gladys was his mother. She loved Elvis absolutely unselfishly. Why, you know the first record he ever cut, he did it for her, right there at Sun Records in Memphis. He paid to record it. 'My Happiness' and 'That's When Your Heartaches Begin.' He gave her the record for a birthday present. She died in '58 when he was only twenty-three. Imagine."

"I'm twenty-three," said Emily, without anything more substantive to add.

"You can see pictures of him, when he got out of the service in 1960 and came back to a house with his mama gone, dead—it breaks your heart to see his sweet face. The look on that sweet face. He was never again that close or loving with another human being. His whole life would have been different if Gladys had lived. Who knows what suffering God allots us and why—and what that suffering means." Joyce dropped her sewing, her lips twisted with pain. "At the end of Elvis's life, the suffering on his face—" She gulped, swallowing emotion. "They say he took massive amounts of drugs at the end, that he was so drugged and fat, he was a zombie. They make cruel fun of him for that—the boy who didn't drink or smoke, the King of Rock and Roll who snorted drugs like a pig. Oh, it's terrible what they say. Don't they understand? Drugs were part of his punishment. They were part of his suffering. No one could save him from the suffering. No one. He sang himself to death because he loved us, all of us—the fans, the audience. He needed us as much as we needed him. You can tell that just by watching his movies. He didn't need the camera, he needed the people." Joyce's eyes filled with tears. "He loved us as much as we loved him. He died for us."

Emily sat spellbound in the La-Z-Boy, wishing like mad she'd paid closer attention in training class, where no doubt they had covered this sort of thing—Dealing with the Crashing and Inexplicable Sorrow of a Perfect Stranger—while she, Emily, had been tallying up who was married. Emily extracted herself from the La-Z-Boy and sat beside Joyce on the love-seat, patted her back, expecting that Joyce would say, *Oh, you'll have to forgive me.* . . . People always did say that, wanting to be forgiven for having emotions and showing them, but Joyce did not. Her shoulders shook and she wept for the suffering of the man whose death had broken the heart of the world. Emily went to the box of Kleenex on the TV and pulled a few, placed them gently in Joyce's hands.

"The drugs only prove he was human, born to suffer like the rest of us. We're all born to die and sin and suffer. The drugs were a disgrace, of course they were! Didn't Jesus suffer disgrace? Wasn't the cross a humiliation? The crown of thorns? What was that? There's no disgrace in his suffering. There's only his humanity."

Emily patted her again and thought, oddly, of Howard Hansen and his earnest face and voice.

Joyce blew her nose. "You remember your First Corinthians."

" 'Suffer the little children'?"

" 'By the grace of God I am what I am.' God gave Elvis the sweetest, most powerful voice He ever gave to a mere human being. God never bestows grace in vain, does He?"

"You wouldn't think so," replied Emily with what she hoped was an affirmative tone.

"You know, when I'm out, at a restaurant, or shopping, or even just in the car, and his music comes over the radio, I just have to smile because I know he's present. His voice was a gift of God and he's still giving to us. His spirit's in his music and his music is everywhere." Joyce toyed with her Kleenex, smiling. "When I wake up in the morning, every day, one of his songs is right there, at the edge of my mind, playing when I wake up, and I know, whatever song it is, that's the way the day's going, that there's a reason for it. I know if it's going to be a 'Peace in the Valley' day, or a 'There's Good Rockin' Tonight' sort of day, or a 'Wear My Ring Around Your Neck' day. When I hear his music, Emily, on the bus, or the Muzak at the mall, I just turn to whoever's nearby and I say, well, the King's still with us, isn't he?''

Emily glanced at the pictures of Elvis all around: the sideburned, heavy-jowled man, the near-boy with his openly vulnerable, invitational, appealing expression; the too-groomed, too-smooth, slick Hollywood face; the artist photographed in the intensity, the act of spontaneous creation: music. "He was certainly very good-looking."

Joyce blew her nose. "Elvis wasn't just good-looking, honey. Why, I could walk out of this house and point to half a dozen men who are good-looking." She chuckled. "Well, maybe not out of *this* house, but looks—looks are nothing, only fleshly clothing. When you die, you drop them like a pair of pants before you get into bed. Your spirit goes naked. What Elvis had was spirit, Emily. It wasn't painted on him. It came from here." Joyce hit herself squarely in the solar plexus.

"I guess I just don't remember very much about Elvis. I wasn't even born till 1959."

"You poor girl. You missed everything, didn't you?"

Joyce went into the kitchen for some more iced tea and Emily walked slowly back to the La-Z-Boy, wondering what she'd missed. She'd been to USC, after all. She was a Tri Delt. She was engaged. She looked at the laundry stacked in plastic LMC baskets and the starched ironing hanging in the doorways, the patterns lying dismembered on the floor. The eyes of Elvis everywhere seemed to bore into her and she reluctantly returned his burning gaze.

Joyce came back with her face freshly washed, hair brushed, and a bright sash tied around her loose dress. Emily was struck with the paradoxical evidence: Could a woman be beautiful without being glamorous? Impossible. All Tri Delts know you must be beautiful *and* glamorous. And rich. You have to be all three. And yet, here was Joyce Jackson, on welfare, middle-aged, manless, maintaining an LMC shrine to a drugged-up rocker, but she had the air of wanting for nothing. She carried a tray with a plastic pitcher of iced tea and more generic cookies. The tray was as LMC as they come, yellow metal with the names Joyce and Jack twined around wedding rings, and the date, June 24, 1959. She offered the iced tea with a palpable generosity of spirit that had clearly kept her buoyant. Her mouth was poised between candor and concentration and her green eyes were at once shrewd and innocent. She went to the stereo, pulled out a two-record set, and the needle clunked down on a rasping, oft-played "Jailhouse Rock." An irresistible flush of energy filled the room, enlivened even the sluggish swamp cooler, and Joyce picked up her hemming, humming, and between the music and the work in her hands she seemed whole, complete.

Emily Shaw fought a sense of envy. Wrongheaded, ridiculous envy, she told herself, rounding up all the usual suspect phrases—*I am young, pretty, educated. I have wealthy parents and a career and prospects and I'm engaged to a wonderful man who will be rich and prominent.* She arched her left hand for comfort and played with her ring.

"That's the most beautiful engagement ring I've ever seen."

"Thank you. My fiancé chose it. Rick. Rick has very good taste."

"Well, anyone can see that. He's engaged to you, isn't he? When are you getting married?"

"Well, I—we, that is, he's in law school back east, but he'll come to California this summer, during their break. This summer he'll be doing paralegal work for my father's firm. I call them Shaw, Swine, Swill, Slime and Turdlock, even though that's not their real names—except for Shaw, of course. Rick hates me to do it, even though I promised him that when he gets to be a partner, I wouldn't do that to his name. Our name," she corrected herself. "Rick thinks I should be more respectful."

"Why?"

Emily pondered. "Well, I guess because, well, because it's the law and whatever the law thinks is supposed to be right. Personally"—she lowered her voice—"I agree with whoever it was in *Oliver Twist* who said, 'If that is what the law thinks, then the law, sir, is an ass!' But I wouldn't say that to Rick. He doesn't like novels. He thinks books are full of unbuttered bread, except for lawbooks, like those." She pointed to a stack of 1934 lawbooks, footstool high before the loveseat. "Are you interested in the law, Joyce?"

"No. Those are family heirlooms."

"Rick is very interested in the law. Very smart. Works very hard—" And then, never mind Howard Hansen's instructions re Listening Skills, and never mind that spilling your guts is not exactly in the quiver of aids, Emily found herself going on about Rick. Sort of nonstop about Rick and how Georgetown was second choice and he'd been turned down by Harvard Law School and how the rejection was such a blow, the worst thing that had ever happened, and "You can't believe how devastated he was, Joyce."

"Oh yes I can."

"He thought his life was over and he'd just go—go be a broom monkey or something. He wanted to die. What was the use living without Harvard Law School? It was just awful, you know. 'That White Sustenance—Despair.' He was in a perfect coma of despair and it took all my strength and passion, really, passion, to get him to come out."

Joyce dropped her sewing. "Of the coma? Oh, Emily—"

"No. Out of the Motel Six. He took a room at the Motel Six in Inglewood and refused to come out. I had to bang on the door and beg him to listen to me, to let me in." Emily paused and then gave Joyce a rather more prim version of the incident there in front of room 132 at the Motel Six in Inglewood, where she had knocked, then fist-and-flat-palm pounded, shouted that she wasn't going to let him think his life was over because Harvard had turned him down. *That's shit, Rick! Shit!* she had screamed, and because they were in Inglewood, passersby paid her not the least bit of attention. "I finally convinced him it wasn't the end of the world and Georgetown was very nice. It was like 'The King's Breakfast,' you remember? The King wants butter for his bread and there isn't any, and the Queen says, well, 'Marmalade is nice if it's very thickly spread,' " she concluded, wondering where that had come from.

"You saved Rick's life, Emily."

No one else had ever thought Emily had saved Rick's life, but perhaps she had. "I guess it was a sort of far far better thing that I did than I have ever done before."

"That's the way it is," Joyce sighed. "Men will always need us more than we need them. You just have to feel sorry for men. They're just not independent like women are. Oh, you probably don't notice it so much, young as you are, but you just wait till you get a little older. Honestly. A middle-aged man without a woman is just pathetic."

Emily considered this thoughtfully with her generic cookie. "But you almost never see a man without a woman, young or old. You see a lot of women without men." The Old Maid's Prayer. The cookie went down dryly.

"That's because men are afraid. Why do you think they're always scrabbling after women?" Joyce bit her thread. "It's the fear that moves them. The old gut-thumping fear."

"Of what?" Emily cast back through her subscriptions, *Cosmo*, *Redbook*, *Glamour* (to say nothing of *Bride*). "Why aren't there a lot of men's magazines telling them how to shed ten pounds, or cook well and look good and make up so they'll always be pretty and have orgasms and keep a nice house and manage their time?"

"Oh, that's just gnats dancing, Emily. None of that matters. The truth of it is, a woman can look after herself and a man can't. It's that simple. Women always have a lot of friends and family and people at work and church, neighbors. They're not afraid to get personal and listen, tell stories, call someone up just to laugh and scratch, have a few beers or a cup of coffee."

"Or an iced tea."

Joyce grinned. "But a man? A man is only allowed to have a woman. And the truth is, a man can't relax with a woman until he gets her into bed. Poor bastards."

Emily decided right then to cancel her subscriptions. She did, though, mention a story in the April *Cosmo* about a man "who was all torn up, worried that his wife was having an affair. Mostly you always read about women who are bent out of shape wondering if their men are, well, screwing around. But in this story, you got to feel sorry for the man."

"You should always feel sorry for men. Men can't look after themselves. Cradle to grave, they're always asking women, *Where is my . . . ?* Start to finish. If they couldn't say that, they'd be mute. They begin with their mothers, *Where is my . . . ?* And end up asking the visiting nurse, *Where is my bedpan?* Pathetic. Women don't do that. Women know how to take care of things and people, starting with themselves." She held up the skirt she was hemming, nodded, put it aside, and started ripping the seams in a pair of pants. "I have to take out all Sandee's pants. She just refuses to buy a size eighteen."

"Still," Emily returned to the question of constant fascination, "you need men. Well, you need *a* man. A husband. You have to be married. If you don't get married, you end up an old maid. Oh, I know people don't use that expression anymore, not like the Old Maid's Prayer, but you can still *be* an old maid. People still think of you like that. Like the card game." She shuddered: the hideous, lost, alone old maid, to be stuck with her was to be the loser.

"Oh, Emily, that's got nothing to do with marriage! Why, my sister Bethany's an old maid and she's been married for twenty years! She's a grandmother! It's love that saves you from that kind of aloneness, not marriage! Look at me. My husband's not here right now. Sandee's always telling me, Joyce, why don't you just dump Jack, divorce him and get a new man? And I just say, why should I? I'd have to fling the new man out the back door when Jack comes in the front. And he's coming back. He is coming home." Joyce lifted her chin, awaiting the placating, professional social worker's response with its implicit *harrumph* and form-thwacking, but Emily (who had not read the case file) only said the weekends were the worst if you didn't have a husband, if you were on your own. Joyce picked up the refrain from Elvis's "Lonely Weekends" and said the King knew all about it.

"I don't mind being alone, really, it's just—" Emily slumped "I feel like while Rick's in law school, I'm in jail. I'm serving out a sentence. I'm a prisoner and I have to wait for him to bail me out."

"When you love someone, time is nothing, time is just as false as the flavor in a frozen burrito."

"Oh, I *know* that! I love Rick like Juliet loved Romeo and Desdemona loved Othello and Cleopatra loved Antony and Elizabeth Barrett loved Robert—you know what I mean? But it's awful, because the nights I wait for—the nights I love and look forward to—those are the nights I dread! I sit there every Wednesday and Sunday night and I do my nails, and the closer it gets to eight, I'm chewing my nails. I'm afraid the phone won't ring."

"Does it?"

"Yes, but I can't stand the tension! It's terrible. It's like—" And then she was telling Joyce this story. "The Operator," she'd read once in a magazine, about how a woman's fiancé had to move to a new city far away, and she tried to call, tried and tried and asked the operator to help her, and when she finally got through, a woman answered the phone. "I keep thinking of that story, of the last line. I can't remember what it was, but I can't get it out of my head." Emily went to the TV to get some Kleenex. She admonished herself to be professional and not get worked up. Listening Skills. The quiver of aids. Sociology 414. She vowed to sit and listen to Joyce's story. She would have a story. They all did. Probably something about the Jack on the yellow tray who Lost The Best Thing He Ever Had. In her three months on the job, already these stories had begun to furrow and rut with repetition. Emily had read hundreds of case files, and there, on paper anyway, these tales all had the flavor of coming attractions recollected in tranquility. Wasn't there always a husband, a dim and distant memory, the pledge of promise unfulfilled, the wedding picture with color going to yellow in all the faces, as though the wedding party all suffered hepatitis of the heart? Or, if not a husband, then some Other Man Who Didn't Work Out and left her with the infant token of a night's pleasure, his smile and the light in his blue eyes, and the sweet baby then brought squalling to his mother's arms and breast, where love bloomed anew. The baby who, according to the files, inevitably grew up to be smart-mouthed, bad-assed, snot-nosed kid, who had his old man's blue eyes and found himself some girl he could . . . "Where did you learn to do that?"

"What?"

"Sew like that. I've never seen—" Joyce's hands flew over the dismembered dress that had been pinned to a newspaper pattern, re-membering the dress swiftly, certainly, and without a single pause. Joyce seemed to carry the tensions of her body in her shoulders and hands and wrists. "How can you do that so quickly?"

"Oh, I was born being able to sew well. It's nothing, but you should have seen me in home ec at SEHS," Joyce chuckled. "They had to pass you if you were warm-blooded, but me and Sandee, we got the only D's in the whole class. We just loved to watch Miss Gruski get her dander up. We'd take a pillowcase up to her five times in a row, sewn inside out. Miss Gruski! Imagine her, teaching a bunch of teenaged girls home economics—and her never having a man or making a home, or any idea what any of it was like except what she'd read in a book."

Emily winced as though manacles cuffed her to Miss Gruski's manless and pathetic fate: the Old Maid's Prayer.

"She taught us to sew cute little aprons," Joyce went on without looking up. "Heart shaped over the bosom and gathered at the skirt, but we were never supposed to wipe our hands on them when we cooked—if you could call it cooking." Joyce laughed out loud. "Eggs goldenrod. That was Miss Gruski's idea of cooking. That and Jell-O salad. Can you believe it? Oh, kids like Jell-O well enough, but did you ever meet a *man* who wanted to do anything with Jell-O except maybe lick it out of your belly button?"

Emily endured a pleasurable shiver concocting a scene with Rick in her own double bed. Peach Jell-O. The very next time . . .

"Me and Sandee worked for those D's. Even the retarded girl got a C."

"But look how talented you are!"

"Yes, but it was 1957."

Emily had no idea what this meant and her face showed it.

Joyce clarified. "I didn't give a shit."

"You mean home ec was a required course?"

She quit sewing and smiled. "No, honey, I mean it was 1957. It was *too much.* The world had only just discovered Elvis, and rock and roll was only just born and bringing us all to life, liberating us, really, and that's all we could think about—rock and roll, and Elvis and having a ball, and boys and cars, and parties and sneaking out of the house. Well, Sandee didn't have to sneak out. But there were parties in the orange groves—where there aren't even any orange groves anymore. It's just no-man's-land now, all torn up and—" Her hands rested briefly in her lap while she looked soulfully to the young Elvis on top of the upright piano. "Anyway, how could anyone be expected to care about eggs goldenrod when you could be—'All Shook Up'?" She laughed to hear that very song come on the record player.

"When I was in high school," Emily offered (after all, she had not missed *everything*), "home ec was an elective and you didn't have to take it if you didn't want to. I didn't." It would have been too LMC for words, but Emily didn't say this. "I was college prep."

"My girls are going to college. UCLA. Cilla especially— so smart! And Lisa Marie, she's smart too. What an imagination! But she's lazy and Cilla's a go-getter."

Emily glanced from her clipboard to the yellow metal tray, noting the nine years between 1959 and Cilla's birth in 1968. "You must have postponed having children for a career." This is what all Emily's married friends intended to do. "Were you sewing professionally then, Joyce?"

"No, Emily, I was crying my eyes out. I guess it was a career. It certainly was a full-time job." Joyce paused thoughtfully. "Though, you know, when I watched Elvis's '68 comeback special on TV with Sandee and I had my baby, Cilla, in my arms, rocking Cilla and watching Elvis, hearing him sing like the King that he is—I thought for sure we were both safe and free."

"You and Cilla?"

"No. Me and Elvis. I guess he was for a couple of years there. Till Priscilla left him and then—well, you know what happened then."

Emily had no idea what happened then, but since she had billed herself as a fan, she nodded knowingly.

"Me. I was all right. I had my baby and I knew my husband would be back. I knew we'd be all right." A fleeting look of pain crossed her face. "Of course we weren't, or you wouldn't be here now, would you, Emily? I guess all that muck and misery is plastered on paper somewhere in the files of the welfare department." Joyce straightened her narrow shoulders. "It's not the whole truth, Emily. It's not even the whole story."

Emily, who had not read the files, squirmed visibly, opened her briefcase, wishing she could find there some human response that would not make her sound like a bureaucrat or an idiot.

"I know what everyone at the welfare department calls my house. What everyone calls it. Heartbreak Hotel. That's just not true. But I don't care. Call it whatever they want. Elvis was an eagle who soared over all our lives and freed us."

" 'Does the eagle know what is in the pit?' " asked Emily for lack of anything more pertinent. " 'Or wilt thou ask the mole?' "

"You really are a fan, aren't you? You really understand about Elvis."

Emily shrugged. " 'Can wisdom be put in a silver rod? Or love in a golden bowl?' "

"The King has lots of fans, but not many people understand him. They make fun of my porch. They think I put that shrine up for publicity, or some other low reason. But that porch is there to honor Elvis, to honor the eagle that he is. I'm honoring his goodness, which he didn't want anyone to guess at, his genius and his energy, his humbleness and his music. And his spirit," she added simply. "And of course, they're one and the same. You hear Elvis's music and it's just like you're standing, palms up, in the spring rain. That shrine is on that porch to educate people, Emily. To teach them about Elvis Presley."

"Yes. Well." Emily cleared her throat. "Education is very important. Education is the key to independence." She clipped efficiently through the files in her briefcase, that quiver of county aids offering acres of acronyms. "The county has this program, the GGP, the Good Grades Program for AFDC mothers on Family Assistance, and if you keep your grades up, the county pays your fees at SECC, St. Elmo City College. Or your books. Maybe they pay the fees but not the books. I think they help out with the gas and parking too. Something like that. Anyway, it's sort of like a sorority. You can stay in the GGP as long as you keep your grades up. You should go to St. Elmo City College, Joyce. You could do anything you set your mind to." Emily glanced at the 1934 lawbooks stacked footstool high. "You could go to Georgetown Law School if you wanted!"

Joyce scoffed, "My law school was the county courthouse."

"Well, what do you want to do with your life?"

"I'd like to carry on Elvis's work."

Emily coughed, shuffled her papers. "You want to be a rock-and-roll star?"

"That wasn't his work." Joyce walked to the stereo, flipped the records over, and one clacked down like an old man's dentures. "Burning Love" came scorching out. "That was his job."

Not until they heard the back door slam and Cilla called out she was home from school did Emily look at her watch. Inwardly she groaned and the generic cookies roiled in her stomach. And of course by now she had to pee because she and Joyce had shared the whole pitcher of iced tea, to say nothing of having shared stories and swapped histories, Emily offering up the long sweet saga of her and Rick, from their memorable first meeting during Rush Week to their glorious engagement party. In return, Joyce shared her stories of Elvis, his being born in poverty, just like the lyrics to "Dixie." one frosty morning in the Deep South, the gospel roots of his music, the genius that was just a gift of God, the destiny that connected him to Sun records, his traveling the South in the mid-fifties, playing any gig he could get, electrifying everyone who saw him. He wasn't even twenty-one when he signed with RCA and started going on national TV, where, even on those tiny gray screens, people thought he was dangerous. Small-minded, tight-livered, pump-sucking righteous types, like Joyce's own father, hated Elvis, accused him of obscenity. It got so bad, Joyce confided to Emily, that on the Ed Sullivan show once, they only photographed him from the waist up. That's how afraid they were. No matter. Elvis drove the fans wild with his voice, his posture, and just one hand free. But after he sang "Peace in the Valley," Ed Sullivan himself came out and assured the American people that Elvis Presley was a fine person. Emily and Joyce had got through all this (plus how to survive in St. Elmo without air-conditioning) while they worked their way through the pitcher of iced tea and the drowsy spring afternoon.

When Emily came back from the bathroom she shook hands with Priscilla, an immaculately starched and polished girl. She was dark, strong-jawed, probably the image of her absent father, tall for thirteen and perfectly poised. In five minutes Priscilla Jackson had reckoned up Emily Shaw alto- gether, from the rock on her left hand to her Pappagallo shoes, figured on the Christian Dior lingerie and Estée Lauder cos- metics. She figured up the cost, the maintenance, and the im- plications. She was shrewd, swift, and nothing got past her. "Where's Mr. Johnson?"

"He got transferred," Emily explained.

"He is a saint," Joyce declared. "It was Mr. Johnson noticed Cilla needs braces last year. He said, *Joyce, I bet that girl needs braces. Take her to the orthodontist.* Show Emily your braces, Cilla. Two thousand dollars, right there in that girl's mouth. Emily. Can you believe it? I bless MediCal every night."

"I hate them. They still hurt."

"I used to have to wear braces." Emily grimaced.

"Is that why you smile with your mouth closed?"

"Do I?"

"Oh, Cilla, would you run down the street to the Phans' and bring Lisa Marie home? I told her she could go there after school."

"Can't I call?"

"They don't have a phone, Cilla." Joyce turned to Emily. "They're Vietnamese and you never met such workers in your life, but there's so many of them and they're just getting by. They don't have a phone because only the little girl can speak English. The adults, they're still just wrestling with English."

"They should take ESL!" said Emily, making some notes on her clipboard, without considering that if the Phans could not speak English, they could hardly read the brochures, but she vowed to send some extra night school material for Joyce and information on the GGP and SECC especially for mothers on AFDC. She packed up and prepared to go, first reflexively fluffing and refolding the quilt on the La-Z-Boy. "I see a lot of country quilts at the boutique my mother shops at, but they are nothing like this." She fondled the hand-sewn hem. "Those are just run up on a machine to be sold. You certainly can tell the difference."

"It's an antique," said Cilla.

"It's been in the family for years." Joyce picked it up and put it in Emily's arms. "It's yours now."

"Oh no. I couldn't. I don't think it's allowed." Emily knew it was not allowed. In training class, Mr. Hansen had specifically addressed this issue, which was a Strongly Suggested unto Thou Shalt Not: Never get chummy with clients. Even given our shared humanity, Mr. Hansen had said, you can best serve your clients by keeping the relationship professional. If you once let it get personal, you open up the possibilities of heartbreak. For everyone. Mr. Hansen cautioned them to use good judgment. A cup of coffee on a Home Visitation, fine. Gifts, personal phone calls, a few brews outside work, no. "I can't, Joyce. Thank you. Really."

"We have lots, Emily. My grandmother made lots of these the last years of her life."

"Could she sew like you?"

"Better. Even with arthritis and old as she was. We've

kept all her quilts, but I know she would want you to have this one."

"It's so sweet of you, but I just can't—"

"Please. Take it. If you have this quilt, you won't be so lonely in St. Elmo."

Emily's resolve wobbled at the mention of loneliness. She bit her lower lip. "I shouldn't have gone on so about myself."

"We're all pilgrims and strangers on this earth, aren't we? We just have to comfort one another when we can."

Emily hugged the quilt, hugged Joyce, Cilla too, and moved toward the door, which Cilla held open for her. But there on a drop-leaf table in a forest of family photographs, a huge magnolia bloomed out of a Coke bottle. So that was the sweet, elusive scent. Emily bent down, breathed deeply into its creamy golden heart, its ancient fragrance. She noticed a glossy color picture of two little boys.

Joyce dusted the photo off tenderly. "Aren't they just the cutest little peaches? Justin's almost five and that little sweet pea there, that's Little Jack. He's just two."

"Are they your nephews?"

"They're little bastards."

"Cilla Jackson! You say you're—"

Cilla sulked and apologized while Joyce explained that these were her husband's children by Dorrie Vardy, the woman he lived with over in San Juan County.

"Hmm," said Emily, who would have known that if she'd read the case file.

Cilla hustled Emily out the door and off the porch and had her nearly to the gate when the Colonel ran from the back and jumped Emily, covering her with dog kisses, dropping his dirty blanket at her feet. Cilla collared him and dragged him off. "Don't take it personal," she cautioned. "He'd do the same for the Hillside Strangler." She shooed the Colonel away and opened the gate. "I guess Mr. Johnson didn't tell you then, huh?"

"You mean about your dad"—Emily coughed—"living with . . . away from home?"

"What? Farty Vardy? What a whiner. We don't know how Dad stands her. My mother treats those boys better than Farty does any day. If Farty was my mother, I'd beg to be adopted. No, I didn't mean that at all."

"About what then?" Emily rummaged for her keys.

"About coming—you know, coming in the mornings. See, I called Mr. Johnson a long time ago. I told him, don't come in the afternoon. Sometimes me and Lisa bring friends home from school. But if you bring someone home and the county car's out front and the social worker's in there, well then everyone knows, don't they?"

"Knows what?"

Cilla gave her a look of exasperated beatitude. "Look, I tell everyone my parents are divorced—there's no shame in that. Lots of people are divorced I tell them my dad's a drug buster always out on dangerous assignments, or maybe a fire fighter in the mountains. Something like that. But no one knows we're on welfare and that's the way I want it. At school I'm one of the Bobbaloos. You think I could be a Bobbaloo if I was poor? Poor people stink—but I guess you know that, being a social worker."

Emily could not bring herself to comment on this, but she felt oddly humbled by this candid girl, her protective pride and submerged pain. "You can count on me, Cilla. I'll always do Home Visitations in the morning." Emily shook Cilla's hand, gravely, not knowing a brush of yellow magnolia pollen yet remained on her nose.

SPROING!

Eri Makino

Well, you *do* see what I mean, right? Say what? Oh, the beers? Hey, you didn't have to return them now. No rush. But listen, you come on in. It's cold out there. Did I *tell* you what happened yesterday? I *didn't*, did I? At the PTA meeting—no, that wasn't it—Parents' Day—no, wait, at the whatzitcalled—at the Parents' *Social*. What for? You know, like I *told* you, for the nursery school. Oh? Yours didn't? Buffet lunch in this department store banquet room. *And* they had beer! I'm practically bubbling, "Beer too, eh?" as I pour myself a few. Funny looks? Nah, not *me*. I'm the type people don't notice. You know, just a *kuroko*—a shadow behind the scenes. Well, well, beer left over? So there I am, helping myself to more. Just once, when I spill some, people start giving me the eye. Later, there's talk of singing *karaoke*. But you know, I can't stand that silliness. "Hate to run *but*, today, it's the husband's day off," I tell 'em and come straight home. He's not here. *Perfect!* I'll get working on my novel, but then my stomach starts to ache. And then my son comes home from school. On his own. The bus stops in front of this building, though, so it's not like it's a real big deal.

I'm working at the *wa-pro*—my word processor. And my son comes up and starts talking about what happened at nursery school. No, *not now*, I don't wanta hafta hear *that* when I'm at the word processor. Still, mother's duty and all. I listen, "Uh-huh uh-huh," with half an ear.

"Mommy, know what?" That's how he starts up, the kid. "Today I . . . at school I . . . I drawed a picture, of Jack 'n the Beanstalk."

"Really? Drew Jack and the Beanstalk, did ya?" *Tip-petty tap tap*. That's the word processor.

"Jack's face! I drawed it."

"Uh-huh uh-huh." *Tappetty tap*.

" 'N then, I drawed the body, square. 'N then, I drawed hands 'n I drawed feet."

"Drew it good, did ya?" *Tip tap*. What a *nuisance!* Me with my stomach all aching, too. Hurry up. Quit talking and go out and play somewhere.

"No I, uh, Jack's fingers, uh, I could only draw two 'n only three toes."

"Hmm, that so?" *Tap tip*.

"Mommy, know what? I . . . "

"What is it? *Enough* already! So you drew Jack and the Beanstalk. So *what?*"

"Mommy, know what? I . . . the blue badge person, she told me to stop drawing already, so I stopped. That's why, Mommy, I . . . I couldn't draw all of Jack's fingers 'n toes."

"What's your *problem?* You can draw them next time."

"But Mommy, know what? The blue badge person told me to stop, so my Jack 'n the Beanstalk . . . "

"I know, I know. You couldn't draw all the fingers and toes. Fine, okay, enough. Hurry and get changed. You're starting to *rile* me."

"Mommy, know what?"

Sure enough, my stomach is shot, and now my head's going too. I can't stand it. Then he goes and starts *sniveling*. No, really. *Always* ends up like this. Here I am, happily working at the *wa-pro* and I end up feeling *guilty* 'cause I'm too busy to listen to the kid.

"Listen, Mommy's not mad. Mommy's just saying you can draw it again tomorrow."

"But Mommy, know what? Um, I, the blue badge person told me to stop drawing already, so I . . . I put my picture of Jack 'n the Beanstalk . . . I went and left it on my desk . . . " By then he's *boo-hoo-hooi*ng away. " 'N . . . now, my picture, I don't know where it went to!"

"It's all right. Teacher'll take care of it for you."

"But my picture, it'll end up somewhere. Teacher'll forget 'n it'll get lost!"

"Teacher'll keep it *safe* for you."

"But Mommy, I . . . does Teacher know I left it on my desk? Does Teacher put it away? Mommy Mommy, I dunno what happened to it!"

"Look, how's *Mommy* supposed to know? Listen, Mommy's got a tummy ache, *okay?*"

By then it *really* hurts, so I take something for it. But 'stead of getting better, it only gets worse. I figure I better lay out the *futon* and lie down. *Really!* What did I expect? Taking medication during the day like an idiot! And then my son sits down, right by my pillow, sniveling away.

"But Mommy, I . . . what's gonna happen to my picture of Jack 'n the Beanstalk!" I feel like crying *myself.*

"Why don't ya ask Head Teacher? Head Teacher knows everything. So if Teacher don't know, just ask Head Teacher."

"But Mommy, if I ask Head Teacher sump'n like that, won't she get mad at me?" *Snivel snivel.*

"She won't get mad. That's Head Teacher's *job.* Mommy doesn't know everything about nursery school, so if there's something you don't know, you can ask Teacher or Head Teacher. It's *okay.*"

"But if I asks 'em sump'n like that 'n they get mad, what'll I do?" *Snivel snivel.*

Gee, I'm *sorry.* Here I haven't even given you any tea. What would you like? English tea? Oolong tea? Say what? Hot? Okay, hot oolong tea. Anyway, no kidding, yesterday, I slept the whole day away. First time I've slept right through my husband's day off. And then, get *this*, this man—who up till now woulda yelled "Where's my dinner!"—just picks up the phone and orders Chinese food.

"Mommy says her tummy aches," the boy tells him. "That's what she said when I got home, too," our daughter chimes in. Then, who knows *why*, but the boy tells his father, "Daddy, don't worry, I, when I get bigger, I'm gonna get Mommy t'learn me how to cook." Beats *me.* Maybe that's why he phoned out, without so much as a word. That *really* surprised me. Then afterwards, he washed the dishes even. Tears came to my eyes, lemme tell you. It's got to be the first time he's *ever* done that in our entire married life. This is the same person who shouted "What am I supposed to do for dinner?" when I was sick in the hospital. Maybe the talk about divorce the other day did some good after all.

You, you're lucky. Your husband's a prince. Pulls in good money, doesn't play around or nothing. So how come I got married? Didn't I ever *tell* you? Wasn't like *I* wanted to get married, you know. Marriage—uh-uh, *no way*. I must've told you it was a *forced* marriage? C'mon, why would I do the forcing? It was me who got roped into it. You better *know* it. We were working at the same place. Uh-huh. How come? Well, *me*, I liked the place 'cause men and women got equal pay. Fact is, I entered the company telling everybody, "I'll be here till they make me president." How long'd I last? Eight months. They laughed in my face when I quit.

Oh? So you think I must've liked him since I went out with him, eh? *No way*. I just wanted to have a little fling. Hadn't had *any* fun till then, so figured I might as well have a good time. No, *really*, I'm the serious type. This guy, though, it's like he never even *spoke* to a girl before, he looked like such a dear sweet boy. Wasn't till afterwards I find out he's been playing the field. It's not fair. *This* is what happens when someone who's never fooled around screws up, but bad. Sleeping with him was *one* thing, but next thing you know, the whole office's buzzing about engagement rings and marriage and you can guess what. Like they stuck a "been-sleeping-with-him" badge on me.

So how come someone running around all over the place took it into his head to wanna get *married?* Must have been the right one for him, huh. *Me*, I didn't want to get married. Been *choosier* if I had. All I wanted was a little *fling*, so I took what I could get. Turned into one *big* mess, though. Every time I tried to get rid of him, I made things worse. Everyone figured us for lovebirds. *Pure* hell. I didn't want to get married. *He* did. I tried to run away. He wouldn't let me go. I kept my distance, made up all kinds of reasons like "I'm too busy." Me, *I'm* not the type to come right out and say *no*, but *forget* about talking roundabout to soften the blow. Saying *anything* was the mistake! What's worse, though, he's the kind who yells just like *that*. Emb*arr*assing! Getting yelled at in front of everyone! Anyway, he even guarded the door after work, waited for me outside. So that's how I slid into this *swamp*. Not me, *no way*, wasn't *my* intention to get married. Knew exactly what would happen if I did. And, well, that's exactly what *did* happen. Maybe even worse.

Listen, I've got a story you wouldn't *believe*. It's confrontation time, right? He's saying, let's get married. I'm telling him sweet of you but no thanks. We're at his place. It's a showdown. I've been thinking, if I agree, then it's curtains for me. I've got to *end* this thing once and for all. Hey, I don't go for casual sex, after all. Which is also why cheating's out of the question for me.

Atmosphere's tense. And he's wearing such a *look*, you wouldn't believe. Then, he whips out this *knife* from somewhere.

"If you won't marry me, I'll kill you first and then I'll kill myself."

Boy, am *I* in a fix. This is what I get for my little fling. Talk about *disgrace!* The mere *thought* of dying over something like this! Like one of those crimes of passion. I think about my parents and friends. This would put the whole *family* to shame. Gotta get out of this mess. Get scared and I'm a goner. Gotta think straight here.

"Well, I'm not saying I'll never, ever get married, you know."

"Okay, then, when's it going to be?"

"Now, let's not get hasty here, but, say, sometime, maybe."

"That may be fine for you, but not me."

I'm buying time like this. Pretty soon, he's got to go to the bathroom. I'm looking cool as can be. But *inside*, I'm rattling like a bag of bones. He locks me in the apartment and heads to the bathroom. I can hear him going down the hall. You're telling *me!* The stinking apartment didn't have but a rooming-house toilet *down the hall!*

"Now!" I think. It's the second floor. I practically *leap* up onto the windowsill and start kicking, *hard* as I can. A couple good kicks and the whole thing goes *flying*, frame and all. I jump to the ground. Pitch black, can't see a thing. No matter, I run and run. *Barefoot!* Scramble up a big old fence, jump down on the other side, dogs barking, I'm cutting through somebody's yard, even maybe knocked my way through a wall. Weirdest thing is, I didn't have *not one* scratch on me.

Finally I come to a bright street, look around and find a *sushi* place. I run inside.

"Please! There's some *weirdo* chasing me!"

The old guy there gets right into the act. Pulls down the shutter, puts some young guys on the lookout.

"There's a strange person wandering around out there."

"What do you want me to do? Call the police?" he asks. But I don't want *no* such thing.

"Oh no. I'd like to go home. Could you call me a taxi, please?" Just *listen* to me, like some *debutante*. I borrow a pair of slippers and get into the cab. Once home, that's it for me. I come down with a fever and hit the sack.

Next day, I don't even bother to call in sick. First time I ever done that. Head's completely out of it. Each time one of those police cars goes by *eee-ooo-eee-ooo* my heart just about stops. Wonder what happened to him after I split. Maybe they found his dead body somewhere. It'll get into the papers. I'll have to leave Japan. Gone and screwed up my whole *life*. What I get for doing such an idiotic thing. Have to bear the mental and physical scars for the rest of my days.

Ding dong!

"Anybody home?"

Can you *believe* it? There he is, all suited up, necktie and everything, up at my place with a what-was-that-all-about-last-night? look on his face.

"Hey, there's a man here to see you," my mother says. That *useless* mother of mine.

"I *don't* want to see him. Tell him to go *away*. Tell him I'm sick in bed and can't see him."

"Such a thing to say! After he came all this way to see you. What's the matter with you, sending him home?"

And *then*, Mother Dear goes and invites him in. 'Course, far as looks go, he's *not* bad. Impresses you as the serious type at first. And need we mention he's a graduate of *the* Gakushuin University? So much for my mother. She and he start acting like long-lost friends. I kid you not. She just couldn't *wait* to marry me off. Got to keep up appearances, after all. Didn't matter *who* the guy was.

"Honestly! Here this fine gentleman is paying you a get-well visit, stop being so rude and show your face," she tells me. Mother Dear gets me outa bed and I wind up having to see this guy. I *tell* you, this guy's like . . . like Jekyll and Hyde. *Flip flop*. In such good spirits now, you'd think yesterday didn't happen. He's so cheerful, *and* he's still going on about getting married. I'm flabbergasted. I mean, what can I say? My head's so mixed up, I just sort of blank out as I walk him to the train station.

Here I'm saying, "But I don't want to get married," and here he keeps making plans.

"Okay, forget about marriage. At least meet my parents." So I do. And can you picture it? I'm getting the full *fiancée* treatment. Now I'm not the sort to make *waves*, so I sort of go along with it.

Figuring it'll *never* happen, I tell him, "Only if we get married in Hawaii and buy a condo." Then, just like *that*, he calls to say, "I've made reservations for Hawaii. Everything's set!" And I don't even *want* to get married. Then our parents are meeting each other, and my mother, Mother Dear, she's already preparing for the big day. And no one even *bothers* to ask *me* what I think of all this.

Pretty soon what with all this anxiety, I'm flat on my back in bed. And then,

Ding dong!

Oh-oh, not *again*. I get this funny feeling. The guy, he's gone and hired a moving van, hauled all his things from that *flophouse* of his and while he's at it, he's come for mine! Somebody *help* me! I feel like screaming, but who is there to help? Dad's fighting it out in business, *nowhere* to be seen, as usual. Which just leaves my *useless* Mother (Dear).

"Oh, *Mother*," the guy says, "hurry it up, please." So she flutters about, throwing my things together, the whole kit and kaboodle which he and the driver load into the van. We aren't even *married* yet and, before I know it, they are cramming *me* into the van too, carting me off like another piece of luggage. I mean, what *is* this? I got *rights*, you know! So then comes the Hawaiian wedding and the honeymoon. And like some kinda *bad* dream, married life begins. Right, like they always say. Everyone says I was the *perfect bride*. Wunnerful wunnerful. Nothing but *lies*. A girl shouldn't get married 'less she really wants to.

Might as well be a slave. Marriage is just one big slave trade, anyway. Lots of people who don't love each other go and get married, just so's they can make some sorta *life* together and call it *marriage*. Took me a while to get that down.

Oh, hey, I'm *sorry*. I've kept you so long with this story. What? Changed your mind about going shopping? Well, if that's the case, no hurry, eh? Don't have to work today myself. A little *early*, maybe, but there's beer in the fridge. Kids won't be home for a while. Wonder what *did* happen to the kid's Jack and the Beanstalk picture? Maybe I shoulda called in about it. Well, gave him a note for the teacher, anyway. Teacher's got it tough, too. You *said* it. Right now she's probably getting this "Head Teacher, guess what? Know what? I . . . Yesterday I drawed a picture of Jack and the Beanstalk, but know what? I drawed the body and the head okay, but know what? I couldn't drawed hands and feet . . . " The principal's probably getting a stomach ache. *Somebody*, *do* something with this kid, she'll be thinking. Wait a sec, let me fetch the coldest ones. I can be pretty choosy. With beer, at least. Always gotta be cold. Oh, *c'mon*, once in a while won't hurt. Figure I'm on the road to alcoholism anyway. Say what? You've been drinking for 20 years? You're way ahead of me. Let's see, I been drinking since I was 18, so that makes 10 years plus. Okay, okay, so maybe I'm a little loose with my numbers. But hey, who's to worry.

Me? Gee, I don't know. Well, I like my kids. What? You can't *mean* it. You *hate* kids? You *always* hated them? Well, take me, I didn't much like them myself when I was young. But I'm *glad* I had 'em. Say what? *Painless* delivery? It's like, *the* worst, says this friend of mine. Labor pains are just like climax with the *good* part missing. By the last of it, anything goes. No more no more, I can't *take* it! I can't *take* it! For*get* the kid! Cut me *open*, pull it *out*, do *any*thing! But by then *boom*! out comes the baby. Yeah, feels like you just took one *enormous* crap.

"*Did* it!" you think. "Done born, *finally!*" That one moment, all the pain, the whole nine heavy months, everything hits. I got so *emotional*. Soon as I saw the baby's face, I burst into tears. Talk about *happy*. This is *my* baby. What I been carrying all this time. I was *lucky*, 'cause I had the baby in a university hospital. With a whole bunch of nursing students there. Pure and kindhearted still. They're working hard, massaging my back, holding my hand. And *me*, I'm trying to make it easy for them too. No, *really*, I'm telling jokes, making them laugh. We're having a *great* time, having a ball, like, when the pains come. So we start having chats between the contractions. *Until* I can feel the baby's on its way.

"I think it's coming," I tell the doctor. But they're all

in an uproar right then. Two delivery tables are in use, so this other woman and me, we have to wait on labor tables.

"No, you've got a while to go, from the looks of you," says the doctor.

The delivery attendant checks, just in case. "Doctor, I can see the head already!"

So they have me change places with one of the women on the delivery tables and within *five* minutes, the baby's born. *Honest*, it's gotta be one of the most important chapters in a person's life. I'm *so* emotional and excited, soon as I see the baby's face I start to cry. *One* attendant makes sure to tell the others in my room and soon everyone's crying, all the student nurses and delivery attendants, like in some fairy tale. Honest, my oldest was *so* cute. Well, who *knows* what anybody else thought, but I could *look* at her all day long. She was just *so* cute, I couldn't hardly stand it. *And* I was still young and healthy. Could do housework, child raising, work, and *still* have energy to burn. Didn't even bother me that my husband brought his pals home all the time. I'm such a softie, anyway. Anytime anyone tells me "It's a wife's duty . . . ," "It's a mother's duty . . . ," "It's a daughter-in-law's duty . . . "— which is what my mother-in-law says—I'd do it. Now I realize how *selfish* my husband was, thinking only of himself. But I went along with it. If even the *teensiest* thing wasn't how he liked it, boy, did *he* yell! He was *always* yelling. He's a little better now, but *really*, I was miserable for the *longest* time. There I was doing my *darndest*, but if anything wasn't right, he and the mother-in-law *sure* complained. Most of the time, they'd blame the way I *did* things. *Really*. Me, such a *lovely* wife and a *lovely* daughter-in-law. And a *good* mother, too. On top of that, I was even studying. Wanted to think that tomorrow'd be a *little* better than today. Guess I honest-to-goodness *believed* it, too. *Some*day, better times, they *had* to come, . . . a big bright happy future. *Really*, I was so young.

I had second thoughts about having another baby. You know, whether I could go on working with two kids. Wasn't as young as when I had the first. And work was going well too. But the sad truth was, even though my husband *did* make fun of my job—called it *women's* work—we wouldn'ta had enough to eat without it.

"It's tough being an only child," my husband says and, well, I guessed I agreed that it was.

"You can stop working as soon as it gets to be too much," he says, like it was nothing. Is the guy *dense*? Like money grows on trees or something. I tell him, his golf trips and *whoop-dee-dos* with his pals, they happen only 'cause of my working, but he simply can*not* understand. Yeah, just a big *baby*. His mother's a tough old bird and his father's impossible too. Like father, like son, *right*? Yells at the drop of a hat. Only *later* does he start to feel bad and acts, I dunno, like a big *old* baby. Then he's fighting with the mother all the time. Every New Year's they have one *doozie* of a fight, and she ends up saying, "That does it, I'm leaving." I'd really rather not be around them as it's lousy for the children, but as long as we're together, my husband is always dragging me along to his folks. Figures if *I'm* filial to his parents, then I'm doing *his* share, too. The very *idea*. Hates to dirty his own hands. Doesn't matter how dirty *mine* get. That's just how he is. Queer fish, eh?

Anyway, it was one *hell* of a year. For one thing, my English tutoring—I'm doing pretty well if I get, say, two new first-year junior high students. This time I get *eight* kids. It was *insane*. The primary school kids I had were all coming on graduation. For a while there, looked like I'd be left high and dry. Thought I'd be *desperate*, so I made up these flyers and passed 'em out every day. Even had the neighbors in on the act, handing 'em out like it's their business. Still, housewives are housewives. No *offense*, but, *well*, it's true. You used to work yourself, so it's different with you, but *them*, they hand out one measly flyer and it's a big thing. I'd been thinking to hand out maybe two *thousand*. Was even planning to knock on doors. A real *drag* and that's the truth. The neighbors? Picture it, they'd as soon play a *leisurely* game of tennis and here they are lugging a huge bag around in the drizzling rain. They get tired after a half hour. Not the fun they thought it'd be. One woman even got all dolled up to hand 'em out. *That* and their know-it-all comments like, "This'll be fun" or "One house call and they'll sign up for sure." As if it were *that* easy. With flyers alone, you're doing great if you get one taker for every thousand you hand out. And knocking on doors, fifty house calls might snag you one student. And you know, it's not cool for a teacher to be drumming up business herself. Looks like you're *begging*, and the parents and students give you no respect. Best to hire yourself a pro, but *expensive*.

Fifteen thousand yen per student signed, *plus* five percent of their monthly tuition. When I heard *that*, I knew I was in the wrong business.

I sure didn't expect so many new students! And then, of course, this is the year I go and get pregnant with my second. Soon as the second semester starts, I feel *awful*. Go to the hospital and you bet, I'm pregnant. "Give yourself a break before the next one," I'd been telling myself, but I get pregnant *just like that*. *One* time did it! What's worse, I'm verging on a miscarriage. The next-door neighbor gets the word, sees me fixing dinner, and breaks out crying. A regular rooming house, that condo. Walls like paper.

"Why should you have to fuss—your husband this, your husband that? Shouldn't *you* be relying on *him?*" the neighbor says. Hits like a *gong* right over my head. Here my husband's getting the full treatment and I wouldn't have dreamed of asking for a little tenderness myself. Pretty *dumb*, now that I think about it. All my friends' husbands, they're *so* kindhearted, every one of them. Yet, somehow, I'd figured them for the exceptions. And *now*, seems even my neighbors' husbands look after the children and fix dinner when their wives are sick. Oh, really? Well, aren't *you* the lucky one. *Wha*—? You mean he fixes meals on his days off? And does the shopping, too? C'mon, enough already.

Wasn't much later, my ovaries got all screwed up. Ended up in emergency. Thought I was built solid, but went and overdid it. Never rains till it pours, in buckets. *Really*. That's the time my husband yelled up a storm at the hospital.

Yelled when I had my first too. He's sure sweet with *other* people, though. When his pals bring their wives over, he's passing out cushions for the pregnant ones and all. Real nice to his pals. Even when we were just married, had his pals over practically every day, one or another staying overnight more often than not. No, *really*, if you add up all the guys who stayed over, comes to *quite* a number. And here's the bride, sleeping all alone, while he spends the night with his pals. I wondered if he was gay at first. Too bad, woulda made a *dandy* divorce case.

But back to going into the hospital. I was in my third month with the youngest. Had an operation, full anesthetic. They make a mistake the first time, had to operate a second time. How come? Well, I dragged myself into the hospital the day before a three-day weekend. Mother Dear was visiting. Heard I was in danger of miscarrying and was only *too happy* to drop by. Can't even visit her own daughter without a reason. You'da thought she was over for a good time. The woman, she doesn't give a *hoot* about my welfare. But, that's the kind of mother she is. I can't barely walk down that dark hospital hall, and what does she do, she settles her fanny in a chair and says, "Boy, am I pooped!" Sounds like my husband, *don't* it?

Me, her own *daughter*, so edgy now, I'm ready to *cry*. Same as when I'm in the hospital and I say I'm in pain and, my husband says, "So what, can't be as bad as I feel."

"Bet it wouldn't matter much if I up and died would it?" I half dig at my mother, and she tells me, "But then I wouldn't have a place to go!" without so much as batting an eye. No joke. It's the *truth*. All the grief she's put me through, and then I have to go and get stuck with this husband. Is this fate or what?

So okay. It's the night before the long weekend and all the doctors and attendants are dying to get *out* of there. They're going, "Say we operate first thing next week" and making ready to leave. Fiddle around in somebody's insides, then up and go home, just like that. I figure, you can't just *leave* me like this, after poking around where it hurts. Come on, *do* something—*any*thing! Cut me open, anywhere you like. The doctors, they fiddle around a bit, but they don't see how screwed up my ovaries are. All they say is there *might* be a problem with my uterus or something. They have this big discussion, and they give in. Emergency surgery it is. *Banzai!* I'm thinking. If they operate right away, things'll be okay. Intuition, I guess. Turns out, if they hadn't operated, I coulda gone into shock—maybe *died*—is what a nurse tells me later. They round up all the staff on the double.

"I'm right in the middle of eating some grilled liver"— the anesthesiologist. "Wouldn't ya know it. I just got home" —a nurse. "My wife's going to kill me. Already told her I'm on my way home"—the chief doctor.

"Oh I'm *so* sorry. Just when yall are about to go on holiday and all for little ol' *me*," the patient smiles, all shy and ready to please. The picture of harmony in the operating room.

"I promise we'll sew you up beautifully," says the chief doctor.

"*My*, how *kind* of you. Thank you *very* much."

Intravenous feeding, catheter tubes, bedpans. I'm counting on my fingers the days till I'm released. Stitches come out, then one more week and I can go home.

"I made a big mistake at work, thanks to you," my husband says. That's right—turn around and blame it on me. Is this anything to say to a wife who flashes him a now-don't-you-worry-dear V-for-victory sign as she's being wheeled into the operating room? Well, guess that's doing good by him.

Bedpans, so of *course* I get constipated. My stomach's bloated. Which means no appetite. University hospital food stinks anyway.

"I'd love to have something nice to eat," I say to a husband who, 'cause of his work—or so he says—rarely visits. And *then* only to yell, "Stop being so selfish, you've had your operation, haven't you?" Just *once* my mother-in-law brings me *sushi* and gives me this *dirty* look.

Oh yeah, the *second* operation. Just one more week to go till I'm out. And I have to go and sneeze. *Ah-aah-aachoo!* A killer of a sneeze. Surprised myself, even. *That* did it. Hear this *swoosh* sound. What? Where? The incision? *Panic!* I grab my stomach and there's blood all over my hands. Every ounce of strength in my body just *goes*. They carry me out on a stretcher, to the operating room, again. Must be my lucky day, I think.

When they operate, I'm practically naked and it's winter too. What now? The heat's not on. That's right, the heater's busted. The anesthesiologist isn't the same old hand as last time, but some intern, learning as he goes along. I figure this is the end.

The anesthetic doesn't take. Not where it hurts in my stomach anyway. It's my feet that go numb. Pretty funny, huh. The doctors all go into a huddle.

"What'll it be? Sew 'er up as-is?" Meanwhile I'm *freezing* and the pain's even worse. Oh *please*, let's just get it *over* with. "We'll give you a little something to put you to sleep," they say and add something to my drip.

Then, next thing I know, I'm headed off to the great beyond. Didn't I *tell* you? Seems to me I told you this before. But anyway, here's what happened.

I'm in this dark tunnel. Just trudging along in there. I can see a small light far ahead. Must be the way out. Keep walking closer and this bright light starts flooding everywhere. Don't remember much about it, 'cept that it was real nice. People dancing 'round in a circle like children, flowers blooming, wonderful just to be there. Pure *bliss*. Probably the happiest I ever felt in my entire life. I wanted to stay forever.

"Time to go home," someone says. Oh no, I don't want to go back. I want to stay here. I want to stay here forever. I don't want to leave. But return it is, that much I *know*. This time, I'm strapped onto this trolley thing and zoomed away high speed.

"Come in contact with the darkness of the tunnel and that part of your body will be lost," a voice threatens, so I scrunch myself up good and tight.

Suddenly the trolley brakes and I'm thrown into space. I look down and see myself, under lights, there on the operating table, looking like this amazingly tiny person.

"I don't wanna go back there!" As soon as I think this, *there* I am, back in my body. Feeling absolutely miserable. I don't want to forget this, I figure, so I tell the doctors the whole weird story. Too bad I can't remember everything now.

"Well, if it was such a great place, maybe I'll just send you *back* there, huh," the doctor says.

"If I go again, I'm never coming back."

Now, you got to *watch* yourself around a sick person. They can see right through you. It's the *truth*. They can see clear into a person's heart. So that's when I start thinking of leaving my husband. And that's when I see my mother-in-law thinking, "Just as well she dies along with that half-formed kid." Friends and neighbors come by. I can see, *plain* as day, who is worried about me, who was glad, who was disappointed I am getting well. My friendships sure changed course from then on. I was smiles-all-around up till I got sick. Used to be nice to everybody, doing all kinds of things for people. But when I realized that this life and this body is all I got, well, what's the point of sacrificing myself, and even my kids, for someone else's sake? I hadn't told you this yet—the *ugliest* part. My husband and mother-in-law told me to get rid of the baby. Mother-in-law said the same thing about my first one. Said, seeing as I was likely to lose it *anyway*. My being a tutor's pretty rough on the body, besides, she said.

"The old lady says you're too free with your time," my husband tells me even. Had to contain myself after *that* one.

Later, well, it's one hell after another. I never *do* get my health back. Looking after two kids. Work's tough, too. The husband, he wouldn't *dream* of lending a hand. Wants it sweet and fresh-squeezed and nothing but. Let *others* have it not so good. All the *tasty* parts, he wants for himself. Oh well, same old story. And my youngest, he's not too strong—been to doctors, in and out of hospitals. Got to be I couldn't even find the time to think. Each day, a struggle just t'get through. Once a week, my mother-in-law'd come to visit, s'pposedly to look after the kids, but it's "Do this, do that"—nothing but *orders*. And good daughter-in-law that I am, I *do* it all. Listened to everything my husband said, too. Habit, I guess. You know what they say: tie a slave down long enough and they forget what freedom is. Well, that's how it was with me. Still, I held up somehow, making do by hook or by crook.

Then, last summer—you know *this* part—I discovered *Elvis*, right out of the blue. Never been busier at work, with most students studying for entrance exams, half of them for the university. It was *one hell of a year*. Wasn't feeling well *at all*, but here I was still scurrying 'round at top speed. "Keep this up and you'll burn yourself out," I told myself. "Burn myself out and what'll I have lived for?" All of a sudden, *every*thing lost its meaning. Life's still moving right along, but inside—*nothing*. Wasn't s'pposed to be this way. Wasn't this the best year ever for work? Come next year, the youngest goes to nursery school. Things'll get easier. You'll be able to do what you want. Oh, I *told* myself this over and over, but the emptiness just hung around. That's when it was, *Elvis*'s singing suddenly came through to me. *Really*. 'Course I liked him before, in junior high and high school. Liked him ever since, too, but lost his records somewhere along the way. And I'm not like my husband, with *time* on my hands to enjoy music—well, the truth is, I'd forgotten *all* about Elvis. Then, suddenly, Elvis's songs were *there*, slipping into the hollow places in my heart. Boy, was *that* a surprise. I liked Elvis before, but I never realized how *great* he was. With his singing, he shakes a person to the *bottom* of their soul. There I am, listening to his songs and collecting his videos, and I realize that the harder I look, the more my own life is losing its color. Or, no, my life has in fact always been like that—only I hadn't ever noticed. To me, wasn't no one *living* so much as *him* singing there in the videos. So full of *life*, it was a *miracle*. Too full of life to be *true*. You'd think, this is the only person in the whole *world* really living. He's so *full* of life. And that depressed me. 'Cause I saw how I had been *dying* away in life. I knew I was one *mess* of a sorry person. I'd been *lonesome* all this time and hadn't even noticed.

No, I'm not drunk. Okay, you're pretty happy, ya? *But*, could be you just think so. Bottom line is, people are *lonesome*, lonely things. They just cover it up somehow. Me, I hadn't even figured that one out.

What have I *done* with my life? I was thinking.

And then *he* sang:

> *No day goes by wasted—*
> *Each and every day's special—*
> *Each life's got its own special meaning.*

Way *I* figure it, that's Osaka dialect he's singing in. Now isn't that *some*thing! Memphis—the Osaka of America!

Really. From then on, I was *born* again. A *new* woman. Oh, you've seen it. I started writing like a soul *possessed*. To me, that was my reason for living. Maybe if I had a voice, I woulda been a singer. But I started writing as I can't carry a tune. No, I'm almost tone deaf. Isn't it *some*thing, though? Here I am tone deaf, and Elvis's songs get to me all the same? It's in*cred*ible. You know something? Elvis, the man, he helps alcoholics go straight. He saves physically and mentally handicapped children. *And* he helps me.

No kidding. I was able to talk back to my mother-in-law for the *first* time. And *that* did it—cut me off for life. What a relief! *Really*. My husband, he was pretty mad. That's right, he tells me, "I want a divorce." Actually came out and said it. Who'da thought that? And *me*, I just said, "Nope."

My daughter says, "Mom, I've never seen you get mad at Grandma before. First time you gave Dad what he deserves too." Even she's on my side. Up to then, I *hated* myself. My life was just sort of drifting here and there. Even now, I can't say I like myself *that* much. But I sure do like myself a *whole* lot better than before. I like myself a little more each day.

Thanks to *Elvis*. If I'd kept on the way I was, I probably wouldn't even be in this world right now.

Sproing! The strings of fate just snapped.

Really. I didn't know it, but I had really high blood pressure. Two hundred over one-forty, they said. Can you *believe* it? Happened when they announced the results of the entrance exams. Went to see my students' scores, but all of a sudden, I felt just *terrible*. Called for an ambulance, then and there. You didn't know? And here we live in the *same* building.

"Teacher, it'd be a disgrace to have you die on us like that," my students told me. *Honest*. And I wouldn'ta known what I'd lived for either. Sure, when I think about it, I *do* like kids. Well, a *little*, anyway. I like my own, and I like my students too.

Ding dong!

Darn it! Went and forgot about the nursery school bus. Hey, I'm *sorry*. Here I've kept you so long, huh? Poor you had to go and listen to the whole boring story. Say *what*? You want me to listen to *yours* next time? But *you*, you've got it made. You're happy enough with your husband and kids, *right*? Got a *saint* for a mother-in-law too.

"Okay okay, forgive me. I went and forgot. Coming *right* this minute. So, tell me, what happened? What about the picture of Jack and the Beanstalk? That *so*? Well, there you are! Just like Mommy told you, huh? Teacher kept it for you."

Oh, okay, see you later. Drop by *any*time, you hear.

When I'm not busy with work, I mean. That time's no good. Sure I'll lend you an ear. Okay, *gotcha*. When the kids are away, eh? Kids can be *such* a bother. Okay, be seeing you.

TRANSLATION BY MONA TELLIER

AN ELVIS FOR
THE AGES.

Lynne McMahon

What the billboard
proclaims in this careful composition where black
    diamonds find a rhyme in the motley
the model wears, and the pink grass he's outlined
against repeats in clouds caught on
    reflector shades,
    is a slogan we can put our hearts in—

    a future atavism
that lifts us up by the snarl, by the brilliantined
    forelock, and sets us down
in the back seat. When he cants his hip
    in homage,
in memory, in making-it-new, when he starts
    that slow gorgeousness
and his shoulders begin their train over

    the trestle tremor,
the I-can't-stand-it vibrato, dropped to one knee,
    sweatdrop stoppered in a phial, phylactery,
when he hits the high long drawn overnote,
stretched over hushed drums, eternity pulls itself
    across the black gap
of the universe, thinned to a wire and holding

seconds past the breaking
point until it does finally thank god break,
the blood
drains away and he's gone, that's it, nothing: no
heart, no breath, the earth shocked still for
the eon
it takes the guitar to kick in and he's at the mike
resurrected, the butterfly
in the leather pulse damaged, but unmistakable.

ELVIS'S BATHROOM

Pagan Kennedy

O n Elvis TV specials they tell you he "passed away," makes it sound like he died in bed. Truth is, Elvis died on the can, then he fell on the floor and curled up like a bug. Great huh? The king of rock and roll dead on the floor with his pants around his ankles.

I never would've found out about that, or any of the cool stuff I found out about, if I hadn't got my tattoo. We'd just hitched to New York, my bullet-headed boyfriend and me, out two days of school to see a band play. Before the concert we were hanging out in the park and I fell asleep—must've been the shit pot we'd bought. I had this dream about an upside-down Jesus hanging on an upside-down cross. Jesus's lips were all covered with spit and blood and I thought he was saying, "You got to stop ignoring me, Spike."

After the concert, me and my boyfriend went down by the docks—where the slaughterhouses are and it smells like fish—and into one of those all-night tattoo places. Underneath the eagles and naked ladies and anchors hung up over the counter is this tall guy with his eyebrows grown together.

I said I wanted that one on the wall, the cross, only upside-down and with no Jesus on it.

He goes, "Look, kid, I only do what you see up there. I ain't no artist." Then he started telling me what a bitch a tattoo is to get off—but actually that's why I wanted one. When I had the dream, I knew this upside-down Jesus was my Jesus, and he wanted me to do the coolest stuff, like stay in New York and be in a band instead of hitching back to New Hampshire the next day, where I would be bored as shit in high school.

But I couldn't figure out how to stay in New York, cause I didn't know anyone. So getting the tattoo was like a pact with the upside-down Jesus.

The guy's hand was on the counter, and I put my hand on his and went, "Aw, mister, aw, pretty please?"

So he finally said okay, and let me up on the chair, which looked like a dentist's chair, except it was all stained with dark brown spots, maybe dried blood. The guy worked slow, one dot at a time and each one felt like a tiny cigarette burn on my arm. The tattoo didn't look like anything at first, but when it was finished it was just like I wanted. And I was thinking that's how my life would be if I followed the upside-down Jesus—one cool thing after the other, and later I'd see how all along it'd fit together.

A year later, when I'd just gotten out of high school, I was thinking I'd try to move to New York. Then this friend of mine who went to my high school in New Hampshire, but a year ahead of me—Oona—called. She was living in the seedy part of Boston, place called Allston, where the hardcore and garage scene was. She said they needed someone in her house.

I went down for a day to look and the place was just my style: graffiti with the names of bands like UFO Baby and Reptile Head (Oona said they used to practice in the basement), stolen gravestone leaning against the banister on the staircase, big plastic Santa with gas mask out on the porch, and in the kitchen a bunch of chairs they obviously got off the sidewalk on trash day.

For all my life, if I put my feet up on the table or my cigarette out in a glass I was always getting yelled at. Not even yelled at, but worse, just Mom saying "Sarah," in that math teacher way of hers. In this house I could throw up on the floor, tear a hole in the wall, or slit my wrists for kicks to splatter blood on the ceiling, it was all okay.

When Oona and me got to the bathroom, I saw this upside-down crucifix hanging from the chain you pull to make the toilet flush. Seeing that made me realize I wasn't supposed to go to New York.

I went, "Oona, check it out—just like on my arm," and I showed her my tattoo. I wanted her to see that this was something amazing, cause for me it was a sign that I should live in this house.

She went, "That's all over Allston. It's a witchcraft thing." She wasn't freaked out like me. Oona's never freaked out by anything. She's great—a real curvy girl with long black hair, wears old lace dresses, smells sweet as a graveyard.

She started telling me about the house. What really freaked me out was that Juan Hombre, who used to be with The Benign Tumors, still lived in the living room. They didn't make him pay rent cause he was a celebrity. Even living up in New Hampshire, I'd heard of the Tumors. They'd do covers of songs like "Going to the Chapel," first straight, like they were a fifties lounge band, and then they'd let loose on their own version and everyone watching would tear each other apart. Just when they were starting to get airplay, they broke up.

They put out one record, which I had. I couldn't even believe I owned it, it was so cool. On the back of the jacket was a picture of each Tumor. In Juan Hombre's picture, he was jumping off the stage, twisted up in the air like a wrung-out rag—a skinny guy with heavy cheekbones, dark skin, and wild black hair. He was the coolest-looking one of all of them. And when I thought of that picture again, I realized he looked like the upside-down Jesus in my dream.

I met him the day I moved in; there he was, sitting at the kitchen table eating bread and reading the *New York Post*. He looked like a vampire, skinny as hell with dark circles under his eyes.

I told him I was the new girl moving in and sat down. I went, "I loved that record you guys put out."

"Thanks," he said, but he seemed embarrassed. I go, "So, is your name really Juan Hombre?"

He said, making fun of himself, "No, that's my stage name. My real name's Mark Martinez, and I'm not even Spanish, just a Portugee boy."

I go, "What?"

"Portuguese—you know, sausages, sweet bread, cork farmers."

I was spending a lot of time in the kitchen, wailing away on this African drum I had.

Juan would come in there a lot to get things—a beer or something—but then he'd sit down at the table and we'd start talking. Mostly we talked about Elvis. Me and Juan didn't give a shit about the early Elvis; we were into the late Elvis, like

what he ate—fried peanut butter, bacon and banana sandwiches—and all the pills he took.

Before I met Juan I didn't even know anything about
Elvis. I thought he was supposed to be like Pat Boone. But
we'd sit there at the kitchen table, and Juan would tell me
Elvis stories. When Elvis didn't like a TV show, he'd take his
cool-looking gun out of his belt and shoot out the TV; he stayed
in this hotel in Vegas where they brought him new TVs all the
time. He could swallow sixteen pills at once. He'd get all these
girls to strip down to their underwear and wrestle on top of
his bed, and he'd sit on the floor watching. He called his dick
"Little Elvis."

The weirdest shit was about how Elvis died: like, when
they did the autopsy on him, they practically found a drug
store in his stomach, but the thing is, though, creepy thing is,
none of the pills were digested. What I'm saying is, Elvis didn't
die from pills like everyone thinks; he died from something
else.

Right before the end, he did a lot of reading—right
there on the can. He got real religious, but in an Elvis way,
reading stuff about UFO cults, Voodoo, Atlantis, raising people from the dead, same time as he was reading the Bible and
considering himself some kind of big Christian.

Anyways, just after Juan told me about how Elvis died,
I had this dream about him sitting in the bathroom reading—
this book just like the Bible only it's the other Bible, and it
tells about Elvis's own Jesus. Elvis says some words out loud
from the book and this other Jesus comes in through the door.
He's a skeleton, with flames all around his bones and skull.
The skeleton-Jesus touches Elvis on the forehead with one
flaming finger, and that's when Elvis dies.

I said to Juan, "I want to go to Graceland. I feel like
if I could just see his bathroom, I'd have this revelation or
something." I was afraid to ask him to come, but then he said,
"Yeah, let's do it. When do you want to go?" Our trip to
Graceland—we talked about it a lot, but I think it was really
just a way of saying we wanted to sleep together.

A couple days later, Juan asked me out on a "Date With Hombre," as he called it. We went to Deli-King—the diner where
all the punks and street people hang out—and it was amazing
being in there with him. We could barely get to a table, what

with at least six people going. "Hey, Juan, where you been? We missed you, man," and they all want to talk to him. The only ones who didn't recognize him were the real hardcore street people—only thing they talk to is their coffee.

Meat Hook, crazy fucker who was thrown in the bin for trying to cut off his own dick, and also the former star of UFO Baby, stood up, and clapped Juan on the back. He was tall and skinny, with his hair in a greasy ponytail and a skull tattooed on his forehead. "Juan," he said, "we got a room open in our house. You want to live over on Ashford?"

"Right now I'm okay," Juan said as we sat down. Juan was so cool I could practically see an aura around him; I couldn't believe it was me there in the booth with him. He was wearing a leather jacket someone had given him, just like that, cause they liked the Tumors. His hands stuck out of the sleeves, brown and bony with scars all over them from his job in this lab hauling boxes of radioactive waste. I thought how his hands would feel like sandpaper sliding over my skin.

He started telling me Deli-King stories, like the time him and Kirk were in there and tried to steal one of the little pictures of the Parthenon off the wall. That was a few years ago.

"You sure've been here a long time—the way everyone knows you and shit," I said.

Then he came as close as I'd ever seen to getting annoyed. He said he was planning to move to New York real soon. He was fucking sick and tired of Allston—he couldn't get any good band going here cause he already knew everybody and he knew he didn't want to play with any of them.

Nothing happened on our date, except that we came up with an idea for a band. I was already just starting as the drummer in a hardcore band called Train Wreck, but I didn't see why I couldn't do a band with Juan, too. It was going to be called Elvis: What Happened? I was going to be the Elvis impersonator and Juan would play guitar. We'd do the music that Elvis would have done if only the Colonel hadn't put him in all those corny movies. Juan was sure that if it weren't for the Colonel, Elvis would've gotten together with Jimi Hendrix, so he was going to play his guitar like Jimi would've.

I said to Juan, "This is a good idea and all, but something about it seems weird. I mean, everybody talks about what Elvis would've been like, but I've been thinking that you couldn't have an Elvis without a Colonel Parker. That's just the way it works, you know?'' I was kind of kidding, but in another way, I wasn't. I said, "It's like, see, at the cosmic level there's an Elvis force and a Colonel Parker force, and the Elvis force is everything young and cool and the Colonel force is everything old and mean and money grubbing. But they're two sides of the same thing; they're the same person."

Juan was laughing at me, which made me kind of mad, but then he said, "That'll be part of Elvis: What Happened? We'll start with a dimmed light, and you'll walk out in your Elvis costume and explain that." Maybe that's why Elvis: What Happened? never got off the ground. Right from the beginning it was too conceptual.

Well, actually, the other problem was Juan. He kept playing out of my singing range, so I go, "Come on, you're only playing in B flat. I can't sing that low."

He goes, "I can't help playing in B flat. That's my key. I'm just a one-key Portugee."

And every time I fucked up, Juan seemed to take it like a sign that the whole thing would never work out. He'd hunch up over his guitar more and maybe run up and down the scales once, like he was already thinking about something else.

I kept going, "Juan, I know it sounds like shit now, but it'll get good if we practice."

This guy in Train Wreck used to play with Juan and he tells me, "Juan's a nice guy, and an amazing guitarist when he was with the Tumors. But he was so depressed when I tried to play with him that I had to drop him." I was wondering if maybe Juan was too good of a guitarist for all of us.

One day we went to a party at Timmy's. Timmy and her friends are the fashion kind of punk, like with dyed hair that hangs just right over their eyes, antique clothes, and pointy English shoes—and always look like they just took a shower.

Me, I'm tall, and I was muscular then because I worked at UPS throwing boxes onto trucks. Plus, I had a crew cut. This particular day, I was wearing what I always wear: combat boots, jeans, and a muscle shirt so my tattoo showed.

All the fashion punks were ignoring me. To top it off, Juan was kind of ignoring me too. He was talking to Timmy mostly and I was wondering whether they'd ever slept together. She had on this sixties miniskirt that showed just how toothpicky her legs were. I couldn't take it. I was sick anyways, so I told Juan I was leaving.

I walked home and got in bed—had chills and was lying under all my blankets shivering. I nodded out in that weird way you do when you get a fever, but woke up when I heard Juan come home. I was thinking, "Is he going to come up to my room?" and he did. He stood in the doorway for a minute, looking at me lying there.

"My face is numb," he said. "I can't understand it; I only had two drinks." He walked over to my bed like he was walking in a moving subway car, hands out in front of him. He looked around for a minute like he didn't know what to do, then he sat on my bed, his hip on my stomach through the covers. It reminded me of the way my Dad would sit on my bed sometimes.

I was sure they'd put 'ludes in his punch, the way he could barely stand up a minute ago but could still talk—which is 'ludes, not booze. I didn't want to waste this opportunity of having him wasted, so I go, "Juan, tell me something. How come people are always saying you were different when you were in the Tumors? And how come you guys broke up?"

He said, "I don't know. After a while it wasn't clicking. One day I walked out of practice and didn't come back. When the band broke up, I realized I was just some moron who carts around radioactive waste for a living."

I couldn't understand how he could think he was a failure. I go, "You're the best guitarist in Boston. You could play with any band you wanted. And, besides, what about New York? You're going to move to New York."

"I'll never get there," he said. "I can't even get a band together here."

"What about our band?" I said.

He massaged my shoulder, "Yeah, well, what we're doing is okay, but it's a joke, a joke band."

When he first came in my room, the sun was just setting, and I'd been watching the sky out my window going from reddish to purple. It was getting to be twilight, but I didn't turn on the lamp next to my bed. It looked like the air in my room was turning purple too. I couldn't see Juan's face anymore. He goes, "Spike," and rakes one drunk hand through my crew cut.

Then Juan, just a shadow, lies down next to me.

"Are you crazy?" I said. "I'm sick. You're going to catch my disease."

"I don't care," he says. Then he kisses me. The way he does it is sucks, like he's sucking all the air out of me and my lungs will collapse. But then his hand on my stomach is real gentle, and he's sweet and calls me Priscilla. And soon all the light fades and it's night in my room.

Later that night I woke up and saw Juan was sitting up in bed with his head leaned against the wall. I thought maybe he was watching me sleep. But when I asked him what he was doing, he said, "Just thinking."

I started thinking how when I was fourteen and didn't even know what punk was, he was hanging out with Meat Hook and all those guys.

I sat up beside him. The moon was over the electric plant out my window, and his chest was lit up white, with shadows where his ribs were. I stretched out my arm, twisting it around so he could see my tattoo. "Know why I got this?" I said. I told him about the upside-down Jesus. I said, "In my dream he looked like you."

"As handsome as Juan Hombre?" he said.

"I'm serious. Promise me you won't laugh at me?"

"No," he said.

But he didn't really mean it, so I said, "It seems like everybody who's really cool knows this secret. You know it; I can tell you do. I want to know what it is more than anything."

"Spike, that doesn't make any sense. Believe me, if there was a secret I would tell you what it was." But I thought he was just saying that cause I wasn't cool enough to know it: the secret was what Juan knew in that picture where he's screwed up in the air; what Meat Hook knew when he tried to cut off his dick; what Elvis knew, sitting on the can, when his own Jesus touched him on the forehead, right where his third eye would be.

"Look, it's now or never," I said, cause I was getting a week off from UPS soon. In a week, I figured, there wasn't time to hitch or even drive. We'd have to fly. I had the money, cause UPS paid good.

"Okay," said Juan. He said okay but I'd have to lend him some cash.

I was fine now—I always get well right away—but Juan was sick as a dog. He was coughing and sneezing and he slept even more than usual. He'd been sick for weeks, but he wouldn't go to the doctor. He wouldn't even take aspirin; all he'd do is pop downers once in a while. It was like he just wanted to lay there and suffer.

But he said he'd go to Graceland anyways. My UPS job was driving me crazy and I felt like if I didn't go somewhere, I'd go insane. Besides, I guess I had some idiot idea that things would be better if we were traveling. We hadn't fucked since that first time, maybe cause Juan was sick. We'd fool around, but then he'd say, "I'm sorry, Spike, I'm tired now."

This might sound stupid, but once we were in the airport and not in Allston, he looked different. I mean, nobody recognized him here as Juan Hombre, and when I saw him kind of slumped in his airport chair, coughing, looking older even than thirty, for the first time I saw him like he probably saw himself.

Plus, we were on this crappy, cheap airline probably just set up for punks and people like that who don't really give a fuck if they crash.

And Juan, he hadn't even bothered to take Contac or anything. We take off and suddenly he gets quiet, just sitting there with his head in his hands, going, "My ears, oh shit," cause his ears couldn't pop since they were all clogged.

We got to Graceland by afternoon. They make us line up outside, and the fat people with the IT'S HARD BEING THIS SEXY, BUT SOMEONE'S GOT TO DO IT T-shirts are giving me the eye. I tried to tone down my act for Graceland—sneakers instead of combat boots—but I still stuck out way more than in Boston.

This perky Graceland tour girl makes us file through the door all in a line. Juan and me were laughing at her accent cause when she told us to stay with the group it sounded like she was saying for us to stay with the grape.

Inside, in front of every room, was another Barbie-doll zombie tour guide who said stuff and when you walked to the next room you could hear them saying exactly the same thing all over to the next people.

The stairs are right there when you walk in, but we didn't see them at first cause we went with the herd over to the dining room. Then Juan grabbed my arm, going, "Spike, look." The stairs were roped off.

I was pissed, fucking pissed. I went up to one of those Barbie dolls and said, "Are we going to get to go upstairs and see the bathroom where he died?"

"No, I'm sorry, Ma'am," she said.

"This sucks. I can't believe this." I started raving about how pissed off I was, right there in Elvis's living room where he probably did a lot of ranting and raving himself. The difference was at least he got to see the bathroom.

We did it all, every last idiotic Graceland thing—toured the *Lisa Marie* and the *Hound Dog*, his airplanes; watched a corny movie called *The Dream Lives On*; took pictures in front of the grave.

When Graceland closed, we sat on the sidewalk of Elvis Presley Boulevard waiting for a bus to come and take us somewhere to sleep—a motel, a park, whatever. Even though it was six, the heat was still blowing off the highway, blasting us every time a bunch of cars passed.

Not having seen the bathroom, man, I still felt so burned I had to smoke a joint and mellow out. I told Juan he shouldn't cause of his cough but he did anyways.

We were leaning against the wall around Graceland, which had writing all over it. I started walking up and down, reading; each stone had one message to Elvis written on it like "Motor City Hell's Angels Know Elvis Is Still the King," or "Freddie from Alaska came here to see you 3/12/84." I found an empty stone and wrote, "Elvis I came here to see the toilet you died on but they wouldn't even let me upstairs."

When I sat down again, I noticed Juan had kind of fainted. His head was leaned up against the wall and his eyes were slits.

I hit him on the shoulder, "Come on, Juan, man, you can't sleep here."

He said, "Spike, I feel like shit," which was weird, cause in all the time he'd been sick, he hadn't complained once I don't think. He looked all pale under his dark skin, and when he coughed he sounded like an old man in a bus station.

I slid my eyes over his way, wondering what in the hell I was doing there with him.

It was starting to get dark and he'd fallen asleep leaned against the wall when this purple Pontiac, with fins and everything, pulls up to the gate in front of Graceland. A black lady gets out and, real businesslike, opens a vial, pouring white powder in a line across the road, right in front of the gate.

I got up and ran over to her. "Excuse me," I said, "do you know when the downtown bus comes by here?"

"Ain't no buses after six o'clock," she said. She had hair all stiff and wavy, like a wig, and was wearing a cotton dress with little flowers on it. She was old, about my mom's age, I guess. She looked at me for a minute, then said, "If you want a ride somewheres, get on in back."

"Wait a sec. Let me get my friend." I went and waked up Juan. He said, "You got us a ride? You're great, Spike," then limped along behind me and we got in the back seat of the car. I was kind of ashamed for her to see me with him, some old sick guy.

She already had the car running, and when we got in, she backed out onto the highway. I said, "If you could just drop us off downtown, like anywhere, that would be great."

"Don't you children want some dinner? Let me fix you some."

I looked at Juan, but he had his eyes closed. I go, "Sure, that would be really nice. Do you live in town?"

She half turned her face to me, only for a second, but I thought I saw a design of dots on her forehead, darker than her skin. "No, honey. I live way out in the country."

When she said that, it was like one part of me started freaking, imagining all kinds of ax murder scenes in this house of hers. But this other part of me knew it would be okay.

After a while, she turned off the highway. It was dark now, and I could tell we were in the boonies, cause all I saw in the light from her headlights was trees and mailboxes—tin boxes on top of sticks along the road.

Finally, she turned onto a dirt road and parked. We got out an followed her up this hill all covered with weeds and dead-looking bushes. On top was her house, which looked like a dark, big box blocking out the stars.

"You live alone?" I said. It kind of occurred to me that she could have a son who would beat us up.

"My husband, Henry, he's over at the Night Owl watching the game on TV. That gets him out of my hair once and a while," she said, kind of laughing. The door wasn't even locked. We walked in and it was dark in there and smelled perfumey, like incense. She turned on a lamp and said, "Now you sit here and I'll get us something to eat."

We were in a living room all crammed with weird shit—a big framed picture of JFK with ribbons hanging down from it, baby dolls, Christmas lights, a deer-head trophy with designs painted on its fur, a Buddha with a red lightbulb on top of his head, and a hubcap with a crucifix in the middle of it. Juan and me sat down on this couch the color of a tongue. Juan had waked up some and he said, "Looks like home," meaning our house in Allston.

The lady came back with bowls on a tray, and sat down in a chair opposite us. She handed me a bowl and I started eating this hot, spicy stew.

She said, "Now tell me how come you children are down here?"

I told her about Graceland, about how I wanted to see the bathroom where Elvis died cause of my dream about him. She laughed. "I shoulda known." Then she went off on a wild story. She looked at me when she told it, like Juan wasn't there.

"This is a secret," she said, leaning forward. "In the few years before she died, my mamma ministered to Elvis's hairdresser. Mamma was a spiritualist, born with a veil over her face. She lived here with us, and when the hairdresser came for love potions and such, I'd hear all kinds of things, cause he was so fond of talking about Elvis.

"Towards the end, Elvis, he was studying Voodoo. He goes down to Schwabs, the five-and-dime on Beale Street, and buys all of them fake books on Voodoo. He reads all them books and thinks he knows everything, like he's some kind of swami, even took to wearing a turban, I hear.

"Mamma, she tells the hairdresser to warn him; she just knows something bad is waiting to happen to him if he keeps this up.

"A few days later that hairdresser comes back and what do you think? He says Elvis told him he had a funny dream. He dreamed Jesus was standing over his bed looking at him. This Jesus got a crown of flames and he's holding keys.

"Mamma says, 'That ain't Jesus, that's Pappa Legba, king of the dead. Tell Elvis not to mess with Voodoo anymore. Tell him to stop taking them pills.' By now Elvis wasn't just reading the five-and-dime stuff; he'd got a hold of the real thing—bought it from some bad Voodoo men for near five hundred dollars. Listen, honey, if you go making money off Voodoo, that's black magic you're doing. Likewise if you make a spell that hurts anybody else. Those men, they stand down by the river at the end of Beale Street. They sold Elvis a book, spells on how to kill people, how to make folks do what you say.

"And a week later, Elvis died. He was reading a book, the bad Voodoo book. I found out from the hairdresser. And you know what page it was on?"

The lady leaned forward and I leaned forward, even though I thought she was bullshitting me. "What?" I said.

"It was open to a spell—a few words you say, that's all—for summoning up Pappa Legba. Now anybody with sense knows you can't make Pappa Legba do anything; only reason you call him up normally is so you can ask his advice kind of, cause sometimes things here get out of line with the spirit world."

I was playing along, since it was her house and her food. "Don't you wonder what Elvis asked him to do?"

"Yes, I do," she said, real serious. "Elvis must of told him to do something, then Pappa was mad and struck him dead. Or maybe that's what Elvis wanted in the first place—to be dead."

I looked at Juan. He was still eating, his spoon shaking when he held it to his mouth. He smiled at me, even though I don't think he'd been listening to her really. I was hoping the lady didn't notice how out of it he was.

I thought she was trying to fake me out, so I said kind of sarcastically, "How come you're telling us all this? Isn't it a big secret?"

She said, "I thought you should know, since you got the cross of Legba on you."

She was looking at my arm—at my tattoo I realized. "My tattoo is the cross of Legba? Well, then it's just some kind of coincidence, cause I didn't know that when I got it," I said.

She goes, "Ain't no coincidences. You're a child of Legba."

She goes into telling me about him. Says he watches over crossroads and thresholds—that's why the keys. When people die he comes to get them and if you want to talk to spirits, you got to go through Pappa Legba. He's like the bouncer of the spirit world, I guess.

And I had the same feeling I did when I saw the upside-down cross in the bathroom in Allston—like everything was falling into place, and would keep on falling into place as long as I didn't fuck it up.

Viv—that was her name—said to Juan, "Here, take this pill." She was standing over him, and he took it from her and put it in his mouth, before I could say anything. Juan, that guy never thought twice before taking a pill.

He looked up at her leaning over him and goes, "Do you mind if I lie down?"

"Not at all, sweetie, stretch your legs out," she said, and I stood up so he could put his legs where I was sitting. I took off his shoes for him. They were black lace-ups, the leather all cracked and scratched, with a hole on the bottom of each.

She showed me the extra room where Juan and me could stay after she made the bed. Like the rest of the house, this room was just full of stuff. There was an old wood cabinet with glass shelves and through the glass I could see all these amazing things, like a little mosaic bird made out of colored mirrors and something that looked like someone's cut-off hand.

She goes, "This was to be my baby's room, but she died before she was even out of me."

I was afraid to say something wrong, so I kept my mouth shut.

"It's okay," she said, "it was eighteen years ago—I've come to live with it." I was freaking, cause I was eighteen. I wanted real bad to look in that room, but already we were walking down the dark hall to the kitchen, and we ended up sitting in there. She brought us each a glass of lemonade. I start to drink it, but she laughed and said, "Hang on there," and poured something from a flask into each of our glasses.

The kitchen was all dark, and the floor was crooked, which made me kind of seasick. There were plants, herbs I guess, hanging upside-down from the wooden beams in the ceiling.

I ended up telling her practically my whole life story. She listens like she's heard it before. Her dark skin shines blue sometimes and I like that. Every one of her fingers has a ring on it, like Liberace's. While I talked, I heard her breathing in and out the way she breathes.

Sometimes when I said something she goes, "Ummm-hmmmh." When she heard my story, she said, "Most bad children are just bad, but some few are the children of Legba. They're bad cause they've got power but don't know how to use it, so it gets all gummed up inside them. Never happened to me, cause my mamma knew what to do, how to keep the power running through me. She used to sprinkle dirt from a graveyard on me when I was asleep."

"God," I said, "I wish someone'd done that for me, man. My childhood sucked."

Somehow we started talking about Juan. "He's not always such a mess," I said. I told her what he was like when he was in the Tumors.

She goes, "The more power you got, more can go wrong."

I said, "What about your mom? Didn't it go wrong with her?"

She leaned forward, even closer than before. She said, "She knew how to hang onto it. It ain't a secret, it's a science, something you got to follow at every turn and keep learning every day." She sat up straight again. "We women pass that science down one to the other cause you sure can't trust a man with the power. They spend it like money for booze, but we know how to keep it till we're all sucked up and old. Not that I have anything against men. They start out pretty, and when they're past that, they can work and earn you money, like my Henry. But they sure cannot understand about power, honey."

We were still talking an hour or two later when Juan walked in. He said, "I was wondering if you have any Kleenex?"

"There's paper napkins on the shelf there," she said.

"Thanks." He took one and blew his nose until he'd

used up the whole napkin. "Thanks for your help. I'm feeling much better." He can be real polite sometimes.

"You ready for a real bed now?" Viv said.

"Yeah," he said. It was only about ten, and Viv said she was staying up to wait for Henry.

After Viv finished the bed and left the room, I took a look in that glass cabinet. What I thought was a bird made out of colored mirrors turned out to be the edge of a picture frame. I pulled it out: it was a square made of clay with colored mirrors and gold stars and silver moons all stuck in it. Inside the square was a picture of a black girl. It was all old and faded, and the girl was wearing a black dress, which didn't seem like a dress on her cause she was so muscular.

Juan had been sitting on the bed while I looked around. I sat next to him. "The plane leaves tomorrow," I said.

"It's been a great trip, Spike. I'm glad you got us down here." He was always sweet like that, giving me the credit.

"I don't think I'm going to go back right now. Viv said I could stay here."

I expected him to freak out, but he said, "I thought maybe you were going to say something like that." He put his arms around my waist and leaned his head on my shoulder. "I always knew you were too cool for Allston. You're so cool, Spike." I guess that in his own lazy, half-assed way he loved me.

"I'm coming back to Allston," I said, kind of weirded out. "I'm just staying here for a week or something, not forever."

"Yeah, right," he said. "I don't know about that."

And then, by way of saying good-bye, we did it for a long time, real gentle. Later, middle of the night, I wake up and see he's staring at the floor where the moonlight, coming through the window, makes six squares.

"What are you thinking about?" I say.

"What I always think about. I'm trying to figure out where I fucked up." The hollow of his neck has a few beads of sweat in it, like a cup with only the last few drops of a magic potion inside. I lean over him to lick out each last one.

THE ANNUNCIATION

Rafael Alvarez

I n the brief moment before the Great Bolewicki Depression Clock swept past the end of the millenium, the restless spirit of Elvis Presley returned to Earth through the ripe womb of a 15-year-old Jewish virgin named Ruthie as the girl floated helplessly over the rooftops of Baltimore.

The clock said: "It's not too late, it's only . . . " and a new age of revolution began ticking away.

This good news was heralded throughout the cosmos but passed unnoticed on the blue planet where it was rendered; a fantastic event absent from Ruthie's long list of plans.

"Ready?" the angel asked.

"Am I ready?" shrieked Ruthie.

"Ready or not . . . " said the angel.

"Oh Jesus," said Ruthie, breaking down.

"Uh-huh," said the angel.

"Oh God," cried Ruthie.

"That's right."

Ruth Hadassah Singer had the face of a cherub, eyes like golden pools, an arrogant mind and an obstinate heart.

By the 10th grade she was certain that any success and all reward was hers for the choosing.

All so pretty and plausible, so sure and sweet: all before the choosers chose Ruthie.

Ruth spent most of her time reading about the gardens of Monet, playing the violin, hanging out at lacrosse games, talking on a private line in her private room, and shopping with inexhaustible plastic.

It was the life she was born for.

But when privilege dimmed to predictability and entitlement bought nothing not expected, Ruthie liked to go slumming in the Holy Land.

With her best friend Carla along for the ride, she would cut school early and drive down to the Baltimore waterfront to visit an old woman who lived in a little gin mill consecrated in pink and black as a shrine to the King of Rock and Roll: Miss Bonnie's Elvis Grotto, Graceland on the Patapsco.

Protected by the blessings of Miss Bonnie, the girls drank on the sly and drove middle-aged men crazy with their white blouses and plaid skirts, wading just close enough to the undertow to feel its pull.

When the silly men and their stupid tricks bored her, Ruthie hoped to catch Miss Bonnie on a good day, when the barmaid told stories about old-timers who pushed handcarts up and down the alleys selling pots and pans, men like Ruthie's great-grandfather who came to America with nothing.

"Aww, I was a little girl back then hon," she'd tell Ruthie, who felt invisible and safe in the long blue shadows of the Grotto. "Hell, I was younger than you are now."

After years of serving up 8-ounce draughts, boiled eggs, pickled pigs feet, and as much Elvis as Baltimore could handle, lean years of surviving when her feet swelled up from serving drinks for 16 hours, her ears rattling with the nonsense of drunks, and her eyes burning with smoke, the King had come through for Miss Bonnie.

Through it all her comfort came first and always from Elvis, soothed by the luxury of his voice and the multiplication of his presence. From time to time she took time out from her labor to glance around the sanctuary and say: "No matter where I turn, he's always looking at me."

Now, 22 years after his death, her homage had paid off.

A wide stream of people looking for something and willing to trade dollars for the promise that it existed in the voice of the King had made Miss Bonnie a wealthy woman, earning her the right to sit deep in an easy chair in the back of the Grotto, smoking cigarettes, sipping wine, receiving visitors, and watching her hero sing to her and only her on a television as wide as the wall.

Elvis was just another cartoon to Ruthie, and when she

thought Miss Bonnie was distracted she would ridicule the rich failure of his life.

Bonnie ignored Ruthie's bad manners in favor of something gold shining in the girl's eyes, a glint that gave her hope against the bad roads she saw there.

When the wine was going down easy, the old barmaid would preach from her chair, bragging on her little high school friends, girls with more education in their toes than all of her regulars put together, kids who came to visit more often than her own grandchildren.

At the first sight of Ruthie and Carla slipping in the side door, she'd crow: "Here come my darlins. Allda-way from up'air in Rollin' Park. Aww yeah, up'air whereda shit don't stink."

Up there where neither shit nor sin stank.

Up in the rarefied air of entitlement where Ruthie and her friends drove their Daddies' Jaguars to buy hamburgers and learned black history from the private lives of their housekeepers; girls for whom sneaking down to Port Street to drink and tell lies was more exciting than taking a shuttle to the moon, which for many of them was also an option.

And none had more options or beauty or privilege than sweet virgin Ruthie, the young and arrogant.

Ruthie who snuck down to the Grotto as often as she could, to be present in a place where things happened that no one could stop from happening.

Like Miss Bonnie's faith and fortune.

In tribute to both, the old barmaid commissioned a hot air balloon shaped to the last custom curve and crevice like the magnificent head of Elvis Presley, a $120,000 marvel tethered fast to the roof of the Grotto, bright eyes piercing the dark like blue lights, hours away from its maiden voyage.

The balloon was Miss Bonnie's thank-you and she passed over all the children in her own family to offer the first ride to Ruthie and Carla.

"You know, kids," she told them. "I believe in God and my certain saints . . . hell, you just don't turn your back on those who helped you up."

Up, up, up.

The King had delivered.

And would soon be delivered again.

The night before the big ride, Ruthie and Carla sat in

the back of the Grotto drinking beer, listening to the King sing of wise men and lonely streets, and flirting with a couple of guys twice their age, stringing the simpletons along for the kick of seeing their eyes pop out and their lips twitch when the girls crossed their firm, smooth legs or licked bubbles of beer from the corners of their mouths.

Carla was 16 with orange hair and freckles, a sexual veteran for a couple years out of back-alley fear, refusing to be bound by anything she didn't know.

Ruthie was a year younger with nut brown hair and ocher eyes, a virgin out of a sophisticated fear of what she didn't want to know and intending to keep it that way.

The man who wanted Ruthie had a vague idea that his desire could only come out wrong, a stronger notion that it was wrong to even try, but he'd never seen a peach quite so ripe and precious as the young girl next to him and he was ashamed but willing, in the part of his brain that showed movies on a very small screen, to strangle a yard full of dogs just to dip his cookie into a warm bowl of her milk.

His desire for Ruthie was so great it projected itself on the wall behind the child's head in a mural of twisted red neon.

"Whatever makes you happy," he told her, "whatever you want to do . . . " and Ruthie pushed her empty glass toward him for the third time.

The other man was fixated on Carla and from her stuffed chair in the back, one eye on Elvis and the other on her livelihood, Miss Bonnie regulated the game, ready to give the men their walking papers if they got out of line or forgot where they were.

Carla told the men: "at dawn . . . " and Ruthie kicked her under the table.

"What?" they said.

"The balloon leaves the park at dawn," she said, and Ruthie kicked her again.

"We'll come and see you off," said the man who wanted Carla.

"Yeah," said Ruthie's hopeless suitor, moving in close to her and leaving a smudge on her bare leg with his dirty pants. "We'll come and kiss you bon-voy-ah-gee."

Ruthie smiled into the man's delusion and purred: "Right asshole, and I'm Cleopatra."

* * *

A dozen balloons lay limp and flat on the lawn rolling down from the Patterson Park Pagoda, a strange and skeletal obelisk of the Orient a block away from Miss Bonnie's, a three-tiered jewel stuck like a pin in the heart of the Holy Land.

Balloons majestic and ridiculous, vast swaths of nylon shaped like lions and spark plugs and lollipops, greeted Ruthie and her hangover that nagged: "You should have . . . but you didn't . . . you did . . . and now you're here."

Stepping carefully through the early morning darkness, she made her way through a jumble of wicker gondolas and the gangs of people attending to them, her tired eyes straining through the crumbling darkness for the massive head of Elvis Presley as day broke flinty and gray around the tight row houses and tiny restaurants flanking the Great Bolewicki Depression Clock.

It's crystal hands filled with bubbling water, the clock glowed like an aquarium through the promise of dawn.

It said: " . . . it's not too late, it's only 5:51 A.M."

Ruthie didn't see Carla anywhere.

Typical . . . irresponsible . . . she thought, disturbed but not unnerved, drawn to the ride waiting for her and eager to add it to her collection.

Ruthie walked by a group of people working to inflate an antique balloon, an old bulb of a single color shaped only like what it was. Behind it she found Elvis, his thick and heavy sideburns laying on the grass like a pair of giant skillet-blackened pork chops.

Alongside stood a skinny man with a wrinkled face to whom Ruth would entrust her life hundreds of feet above the ground.

Gus was in his late 40s but looked a hard 60, a flask in his hip and a bulging strawberry on his nose, a sky pilot who was certain, as Ruthie approached, that there would be no need to hit the jug on such a calm and beautiful morning as this.

He was fiddling with a gas generator and a huge industrial fan when Ruthie asked, without introduction, if he had seen a red-haired girl named Carla.

Gus yanked a cord on the generator and with a whirr and a whoosh the big fan spun with the might of a hundred horses, filling out the folds and creases in the giant nylon envelope flapping on the ground and drowning out his answer to Ruthie's question.

The balloon grew in front of the girl like a giant mushroom, 80 feet tall with a pompadour on top, and by the time Ruthie scratched her head and blinked twice, its regal visage was upright and proud amidst a field of 11 competitors made from the same material, filled with the same force, but dwarfed in the mighty shadow of the King.

"Damn," said one man. "Wouldja lookit that."

It was a simple race. One balloon sailed away first and the rest took off to chase it.

Today, all the others would pursue Elvis.

Ruthie looked around the hillside as the park began to get crowded, her head throbbing and a cup of coffee between her hands, and she knew, when the pilot barked "get in," that Carla was not going to show.

Ruthie dawdled to defy the man, inching just close enough to the gondola for Gus to hear her complaints about an unworthy friend, the stupidity of a balloon shaped like Elvis and the vacant lives of those gathered in awe around his billowing head.

Putting his red and throbbing nose an inch from the young beauty's face, the pilot said: "Missie, if you're lucky the world will beat that shit out of you. If you're not, you will be ruled by it for the rest of your life."

"Uh-huh," said Ruthie, moving closer on baby steps, chilled and unsure of herself in an old, forgotten way, just frightened enough to ask an honest question.

"You think that maybe it isn't such a good day for this."

The pilot scanned the sky and found it as clear as the girl's complexion.

"Awww yeah missie," he said. "There's a storm comin' and we're gonna ride it."

Ruth decided the man was an idiot and her courage returned.

Laying the soft curve of her rear end on the railing of the small basket, she swung her feet over the side as the crowd around Elvis pushed in closer, noisy with excitement as the countdown began and the happy double-pump of accordions and clarinets from Fat Louie and the Silk Umbrella Boys erupted on the third tier of the Pagoda.

The band played the "In the Clouds Polka," people shouted and cheered, and the sun broke free from the last blue cloud of dawn as Gus followed Ruthie into the gondola, handing her a sack of rocks to toss to the ground on the count of three.

Ruthie cradled the weight in her arms as the balloon chafed at its tether, and when the pilot unleashed a jet of raw heat that pushed the struggle between bondage and flight to its limit, the girl thought she saw something gold sparkling inside the flame.

Gus called out: "One . . . two . . . three!"

Ruthie counted to four and dropped the sack.

The balloon shot up like a rocket!

With each roaring gust of flame the balloon sailed higher in the sky, slowing from a streak to a quiet waft as the distance grew between Elvis and the Earth.

Ruthie loved it.

Before the faces on the ground faded away to specks, she saw the man who had bought her drinks at the Grotto the night before, the man who would cut off his limbs to feel his lips on hers but was not yet availed of that opportunity as he ran on crazy legs and waved eager arms to reach the spot where Ruthie had been a few moments before.

Tilting back his neck until his head touched his shoulders, the man blew kisses and shouted words that died before they found their mark: "I'm gonna bring a lot of pretty colors into your world . . ."

Ruthie leaned over the side and laughed long and hard, her hangover melting in her laughter, the pain of it dripping down to the man's face like yolk.

With Elvis weaving his way through the clouds, the other balloons were cut loose for the chase and a happy Ruthie Singer sailed away from her troubles.

Casting a wider gaze across East Baltimore, she studied the eight-sided slate roof of the Pagoda, the black-tarred tops of row houses that looked like a line of Hasidic hats sewn together at their brims, and the tombstones of a cemetery on O'Donnell Street sticking up like Popsicle sticks in the old boneyard where a boatload of Chinese sailors was buried after it capsized in the Great Baltimore Hailstorm of 1917.

Tracing the harbor rim, Ruthie looked down at the twin gold cupolas of Saint Casimir's Roman Catholic Church, where old Polish pahnies with hard faces and fat ankles prayed to Buczha, retired packing house women with the ancient blood of Polska in their veins, blood like Ruthie's except that they believed the Messiah had already come to tell the world: "Mercy conquers justice . . . "

Beyond Saint Casimir's she could make out the long and wobbly pier of Orlo's Grand House of Junk as it jutted into the harbor down at the end of Clinton Street, the place where Ruthie sometimes went to buy antique skirts and hang her naked feet over the side of the seawall, where her great-grandfather used to come to rest and talk with Orlo about the way it was for peddlers in the New World, hucksters who longed to open a tailor shop, maybe a storefront, but wound up with pushcarts and junk wagons pulled by ponies.

The balloon drifted higher, and Ruthie's keen eyes followed a narrow brick walkway from the House of Junk to the crumbling pillars and peaked roof of a 19th-century temple called the Lloyd Street Synagogue.

Lloyd Street, where her family worshipped when they came over from Leoncin on the pivot of the last dead century, back when Jews worked and worshipped in Baltimore City; where Ruthie's great-grandfather came to pray long after all of his friends and family had died or moved.

Lloyd Street, where a five-year-old girl named Ruthie gathered her last memories that made any sense before retreating to the other side of a heavy door; where everything the child knew about the faith of her birth lay in the mystery of her Old Pop's face as his mourners trickled in from the suburbs to say Kaddish over his shrunken body.

It was the old man's sweat—"Pots and pans, Orlo, and once in a while, I'll sharpen a knife or a pair of scissors, fix an umbrella . . . "—his sweat that put a son through college who put a son through medical school who put Ruthie in with the bluebloods of Roland Park.

And it was his spindly legs that pushed a cart through the alleys of Baltimore to nurture a legacy of prosperity and disintegration, a broom that sweeps a girl of five behind the doors in her head only to wake her up ten years later in the vestibule of womanhood, a peach gone sour.

How many repaired umbrellas equal the bottom dropped out of a childhood?

Lloyd Street passed from view and Ruthie breathed

deep, fresh air, resolving to ask her Daddy for a hot air balloon just as soon as she got home.

Up in the sky was a great place to be.

The pilot was not so content.

All of the balloons that were supposed to follow Elvis were sailing northwest out of the park, far beyond the city limits to the Jewish suburbs of split levels and cul-de-sacs, sofas covered with baby blue crushed velvet, synagogues made of glass and steel, and dollhouses where no one was ever home.

All the balloons except one: the great inflated head of the King of Rock and Roll trapped in a double-crosswind pushing it east by southeast at three times the speed of the others.

"Goddam," said the pilot.

Ruthie stood across from Gus on the other side of the shiny cannister of fuel, rocked in the silence of an invisible lullaby and contemplating treasures that only waited for her to claim them; thinking, just maybe, that it suited her to become the world's most famous balloonist, Ruthie Earhart taming fickle winds in a balloon sculpted in the image of herself.

"Goddam," said the pilot.

In 30 years of piercing the sky as a gunner on the back of choppers in Nam to hang-gliding through the crevice of a valley named death, he'd seen it all, but he had never seen this.

Knocking back a belt from his silver flask, a trophy given by a rogue pilot who taught him to handle balloons long before Ruthie was born and Elvis had died, a man who told tales of balloons stitched from seas of silk, Gus recited an old lament behind his brown teeth.

"I know the wind like my own right mind, and I know it can't be knowed . . . ," he sang. "My heart wants to fly on a sweet summer breeze, but I don't know from whence she blows . . ."

The old shitbird was whistling in the dark.

There was no wind.

None.

The skies were dead, yet Elvis continued to sail toward the sea.

Leaning over the fuel tank, Gus dropped his face in front of Ruthie like a dark moon and pointed to the far spot in the sky where the other balloons had fled in a pack.

"Thar she blows, missie," he said. "The answer is blowin' in the goddam wind."

Ruth looked him square in the face and blew air through her lips, more confident than ever.

The ride was pure joy.

She loved the idea that this balloon, her balloon through the wisdom of knowing how to pick your friends, was traveling to a place where the others couldn't, an airship of precious and privileged cargo on a path denied the rest.

Below her lay the great star of bricks fixed in stubborn pride and christened McHenry, and beyond the fort's twinkling tentacles, out in the middle of the channel, little red tugs with white dots on their stacks pulled creaky freighters to safe berths as Elvis passed overhead, made fast to sky tugs no one could see, the veiled hand of fate pushing Ruthie down the Patapsco.

She turned her back to the pilot and lost herself in the adventure, a soap bubble floating in the breeze.

Even nasty Gus had to admit it, even with no wind and blind tunnels and the baby-sitter's burden of little Prissy Highpockets and her steamer trunk full of condescension, he had to acknowledge that the ride was one of the most pleasant he'd ever taken.

Except to enjoy it he had to ignore everything he knew about the way things worked. His tricks had no more effect on the balloon than the suffering of others had on Ruthie.

Every time he shot fire up into the envelope to find a responsive current or waited many long minutes without shooting the gas to bring the vessel down to a cooperative slipstream, it refused, continuing to move out of the deep water port of legend and down the basin of the Great Chesapeake.

Away from everyone she had to impress, intimidate, or avoid, Ruthie was at ease and free, wearing a face for no one as her true face lay open to the sky, a perception deep in the intricacies of her self-absorption that she wouldn't trade this ride for anything.

Rising in time with the sun, the balloon brought her closer and closer to the source of the world's illumination, her body bathed in a light that changed every color it kissed from far to near.

Ruthie's nut brown hair sparkled amber and gold by turns and her skin passed from pale to the lustre of whipped butter and dunes of sand.

She wore a big shirt, a man's shirt of Mississippi cotton colored wheat and brown and cinnamon, a garment musical with tinkling buttons smoothed from old soda bottle glass, disks of mahogany, and ornaments carved from tagua nuts of the Amazon rain forests, each trinket worth 100 times more than the few nickels she traded for the shirt at Orlo's House of Junk.

Around her knees lapped a skirt burning copper and cherry in the sun, made fast with a gray waist sash elevated to silver. Her small, clean feet were shod with leather sandals, cracked and brown since the day she hung her legs over the seawall down at the end of Clinton Street.

A string of beads made of silver and shell and small orbs of glass circled Ruthie's neck, sparks of sun forcing pinlight through the glass and speckling the girl's throat with color. The rays reflected off the baubles that denied them entrance, abalone and oyster competing for brilliance with her straight and gleaming teeth.

When the sun passed through the soft and downy flesh of her perfect ears, it turned them a luminous crimson, revealing tiny, connected veins of blue and violet life, the floodlights of history glaring through Ruthie's body and finding it uncorrupt, blameless in a way she would never allow herself to believe.

All was right in Ruthie's world because Ruthie was no longer in it.

But across from her the pilot was near the end of his wits, his face crumpled like an old brown bag.

"Maybe this," he said, unleashing a whooshing jet of flame into the nylon cavity, letting the flame burn for a full minute, the ship rising higher, Ruthie brought closer to the fixed script of her life, and the course of the balloon unchanged.

Looking up, her mouth tightened into a perfect, open circle and her eyebrows spanned high arcs as she blinked once, twice, three times.

Impossible!

A giant black man beamed down at her, his immense body warbling inside the shaft of burning gas and a gold trumpet glowing in his right hand, a bald-headed and billowing specter swathed in purple.

"Why hello dolly!" he rasped.

"Me?" said Ruthie.

"What's that?" said the pilot.

The angel's big eyes devoured the basket.

He said: "Any other virgins up here?"

Ruthie felt a sharp cramp just below her stomach and balled her fists until it passed. Even if Carla had shown up it wouldn't have changed the answer to the question.

Her peace had flown and her head pounded again.

She was talking to a giant black ghost glowing purple inside a column of fire.

And he was talking back to her.

The pilot turned off the flame and the apparition vanished.

Ruthie grabbed his elbow.

"Did you see that?"

"Missie," said Gus, "the only thing I see is we're heading down the bay . . . " and he pulled away to fire another jet of gas.

Again the angel appeared to Ruthie.

"SHUT IT OFF!!" she screamed and Gus fumbled for the switch.

The angel remained.

In the heat of his violet gaze Ruthie sank to the bottom of the basket, looking up, when she dared, with watery eyes fixed with fear and wonder at a massive shaft of gold and purple towering above her.

She was certain now that she was seeing what she was not yet sure was real.

So real.

Threads of gold whirled through the purple weave of his clothes, a scarlet shirt, ultramarine tie, and a white handkerchief folded in the breast pocket of his sport coat, a suit that melted into a silky robe from his waist on down, where it faded to pale sky and fire when the pilot fired the gas again.

Majestic and rich, the messenger mopped sweat from the curve of his wide ebony pate with the handkerchief and smiled at the child beneath him, his teeth glowing like moonbeams on a field of snow.

"Don't be scared," he said.

"Me?"

"Yes darlin, you," he said. "They ain't made a mistake yet."

"They?"

"Them."

Rising taller, the angel filled the inside of the balloon like a purple sunrise, the colors more spectacular than all the stained glass of Athens and Rome.

Ruthie shouted: "WHY ME?"

Shit, said the pilot, who in almost 30 years had lifted all manner of nuts, egomaniacs, and dreamers into the air, taking them up to be married, to copulate, to pass secrets, take drugs, and decide that their lives together would become forever separate the moment they returned to Earth.

But never had he played host to a spoiled rotten princess who held one-sided arguments with the empty sky.

"Shit," he mumbled again. "Why me?"

But no one was listening to him.

"I don't get the whys, honey," said the angel. "I just deliver the good news."

"GOOD NEWS?" screamed Ruthie. "GET OUT!"

The angel vanished.

In her moment of relief, when she clambered to her knees and steadied herself on the rail with slender knuckles hard and white, Ruthie peeked over the side of the gondola to find herself face-to-face with her tormentor.

The angel was now the size of a normal man and sat cross-legged in the air, the trumpet in his lap and arms spread wide in explanation.

Ruthie gulped.

"Sweetheart," he said. "I don't have a lot of time and there's something you need to know."

Fear in Ruthie's eyes begged: "What?"

Gus looked over to see tall and proud Ruthie on her knees, whimpering, talking to boogie-men, and he abandoned all thoughts of trying to manage the balloon or the day.

The answer came and Ruthie gasped.

"NO!" she shouted.

It was too weird, too sick, too gross to be true.

It was true.

"NO!" she screamed.

Leaning out over the railing, arching her thin back high

atop the curve of the Earth, on the edge of falling but safer than she'd ever been in her life, Ruthie shook her fist at the bloated head of Elvis.

She seethed: "Once wasn't enough? He's gotta come back? That's what this fucked-up world needs?"

"The world doesn't know what the world needs," said the angel, eager to finish the job, giving away more of the script than he should have just to be done with it. "It won't be him again. Everybody gets another chance. Even you."

"Always me," said Ruthie.

"Look," said the angel. "This isn't a game. They like you and that ain't nothin' to sneeze at."

Ruthie cried: "Everybody likes me . . ." and the angel wondered how the girl crossed the street every day without getting hit.

"Ruth," he said, "it's not my job to know. All I do is bring the news and blow the horn. Now please child, are you ready?"

The sound of her name tripped a circuit in Ruthie's head.

"GODDAMIT! GODDAMIT! GODDAMIT!" she screamed. "I'M READY! Give me twins: Elvis and Chuck Berry joined at the hip. Give me four and twenty blackbirds. Give me anything you've got and the minute this thing lands I'll run to the nearest clinic and kill it."

The angel said: "You can, but you won't."

Ruthie raged: "Oh won't I?" and wondered why she just didn't jump now and save herself the trouble.

Over and over again she shrieked "Oh won't I . . . won't I?" until, struck by genius and becalmed by eureka, she remembered something she read once in a book.

"I can do anything I please," she announced. "I have free will."

"You do," said the angel, "but you don't."

Pierced by truth, Ruthie's heart was bathed in a completeness she'd never known. Hymns to the silence fell down around her and she began to cry again, quietly, no fight left.

The angel pulled his handkerchief to wipe her eyes and Ruthie knew then, her cheeks wet one moment and dry the next, that it was really happening, she knew beyond thought that if a little bit of this thing were true, it must all be true.

"Okay, sweetheart," said the angel. "One more time. . . ."

"Oh Jesus," said Ruthie.

"Uh-huh."

"Oh God," she whispered.

"That's right . . ."

"Okay," said Ruthie, and the angel stood and turned to the sun.

Raising the golden trumpet to his full lips, he tilted his black head back against the pale sky and with the force of a gale blew a high C heard throughout the cosmos; a note of full and singular clarity that caulked all the cracks in the universe and made the art of man shimmer in its frames; the single purpose of its unwounded wail painting the skies across all the Holy Lands of the Earth in rich nocturnes of purple and gold; the purity of its current short-circuiting the rodent brains of the evil long enough for their victims to find the only way out and its vibrations fathoming the depths of the sea where it was received by millions of silver fish turning to jump in the other direction.

Ruthie wet herself.

The pilot's head rang like a hammered cathedral bell and the trumpet's peal passed into the tap roots of all the world's loamy forests as Ruthie hung over the side of the basket and relieved herself of the bile that had collected inside her for ten years.

The pilot said: "What in hell is going on?"

Ruthie called out: "God help me."

And the angel took the trumpet from his lips as the wind whispered: "That's right . . ."

Unattended, the balloon began a slow drift down to the tip of a South Baltimore peninsula called Curtis Bay, where Ruthie saw clusters of small, green shingled houses with cheap department store swimming pools in the backyards, kids riding bikes down crooked alleys and lines of wash stretched across backyards.

Vomiting for the last time, she was heartened to know that this was still life on Earth and she mourned for a planet that had always deferred to her as best it could.

The balloon passed over oil tanks standing squat-shouldered and side by side behind streets of shabby houses on old dairy land chopped up for industry a hundred years ago; churches, corner stores and row houses shoved into the leftover spaces for working families.

Beyond them, on a high hill off the corner of Prudence and Filbert streets, lay a field perfect for the landing of any ship with the audacity to defy gravity.

The wide green plane revealed more of itself with each echo of the trumpet's fading ring and the pilot's old confidence returned, eager to unburden himself of his passenger as soon as possible, confident like the Ruthie that was but would never be again.

Ruth raised her head and hugged the basket's wooden railing to keep from collapsing again. The angel turned to speak his goodbye.

"No luck, no coincidence," he said. "No faith without doubt."

Ruthie raised a weak hand to wave as the angel's form grew by doubles, his suit bleeding from purple to pink across the sky, a storm cloud drained of its fury.

On its own the balloon found the grassy field, home to a few sunflowers and a stone water tower capable of turning the deserts of Egypt into shamrocks and emeralds, and the pilot congratulated himself on skills that never failed as the people of Curtis Bay ran from their homes to see a once-in-a-lifetime prize drop from the sky.

With 200 feet to go, Ruthie stared down at them in ignorance of the morning's second miracle: the absence of an assumption that they were clamoring to see her.

Nothingness was her first reward; she was unaware that she even had a body, a body that had caused so much pride and pain in her young life, leading silly men and stupid boys to her like insects.

Why me had long passed and *what now* loomed with 100 feet to go.

It looked like half of Baltimore had gathered down below. Housewives fled their kitchens and rough men dropped wrenches to stand in a crowd of children and point to the sky.

Ruthie's heart leapt with the hope that maybe they could see the spirit who had burned tall in flame, sat cross-legged in the clouds, and blew a typhoon of truth over the arcs of all the world's constellations.

With eyes saffron and lemon bright she thought that maybe her fate would be shared, her burden distributed, that, just maybe, she was not alone in this thing.

"LOOK!" called a glue-sniffing freak.

"GO TO HELL," said a man who went to Mass everyday.

"YEZUS-KA-HONEY, dear Buczha . . . " prayed an old woman in a black dress.

Seventy feet, sixty feet, fifty feet.

"IT'S HIM!" screamed a young girl.

As Ruthie strained to see the last wispy outline of her visitor, the pink particles of all the faiths of the world disseminating throughout the firmament, the people shouting on the ground robbed her last thread of old hope.

"IT'S ELVIS!!" they screamed.

"THE KING!!"

No one had seen the angel but Ruth.

Glancing over at her while bringing the balloon down in the center of the hill, Gus felt sorry for the girl even as she confirmed his assumptions: Sweet Little Miss was just another overeducated straw bonnet who would never amount to half of what was expected of her, a zero on the left who talked to the air, screamed at the clouds, cried at nothing, and threw up on the promise of a safe landing.

Forty feet, thirty feet.

"Brace yourself missie," he said.

The gondola hit the field with a dead thud and ripped a wake of dirt and sod as the balloon dragged Ruthie and Gus across the lawn like a torn bag blowing down a gutter.

People raced after the sputtering head of Elvis to welcome their visitors, catching up to the gondola and grabbing it as the last gasps of life escaped from the balloon, the wide and honest face of the King of Rock and Roll flapping flat over the field.

Ruthie crawled out of the overturned basket and started pushing her way through the crowd.

Most of the well-wishers stepped aside as she forced her way through to walk across the field alone, stepping carefully around the arching shadows of the water tank that had graced the hill since the Great Depression.

"God she's pretty," said a kid about Ruthie's age as

she passed, the only person in the crowd to ignore the balloon in deference to the queen who had emerged from it. "They don't make 'em like that around here."

They.

Them.

Me.

You.

Deaf to the chatter of the crowd, Ruthie rode a wave of peace she couldn't name, blind to the faces mooning past her as she waded through a wall of bugeyes and twittering eyebrows.

She only wanted a cab to take her home and a new angel to explain to her parents what had been explained to her.

If one part of it were true, it must all be true.

The people on the hill melted as they jostled past Ruthie to get to Elvis, but the buildings appeared to her in sharp detail, especially the water tower, a useful work of art drawn from a palette of sand and mortar. The tank fell to the hill in 1930 from the dreamy mind of a book collector named Frank Heyder and seven decades later it twirled before Ruthie like an Aztec lampshade.

Walking a lonely road down to the real world, she watched the sky behind the tower change with every step and remembered what the angel had said: "It changes like the air around you."

But he hadn't said what.

The din on the hill faded to silence as Ruthie walked down Filbert Street, a voice that was not her own weaving through the margins of her mind, telling her not to worry, that the care of Ruth Hadassah Singer was no longer something she needed to think about.

The thought became more real to her with each step, real in a way that nothing ever was before, and her eyes opened to Curtis Bay as a place where people needed more than money to make it from one day to the next.

And the same voice that told her all was well in the midst of such a terrible reckoning sang to her that she would come to know such neighborhoods with an intimacy previously reserved for her selfish heart.

Making her way down Filbert Street, her head tilted out beyond the axis of her body, Ruthie approached Saint

Athanasius Church and its large windows of rainbow glass, white and green championing the inextricable connectedness of heaven and Earth; blue hope and blood red declaring the inescapable composite of beings called human.

One last time she looked over her shoulder to the hill where the ride had ended and her life had begun, one more look back to Gus and Elvis, the people celebrating them, and the Curtis Bay water tank through which all the water of the Holy Land came to be cleansed for a million waiting taps.

In that moment Ruthie witnessed the last sweep of the second hand that dispatched the great messenger back to the pale blue of just another Saturday in Baltimore and in it Ruthie understood why she had always held back, why she was always scared, why she was the only 15-year-old virgin she knew.

For this.

So this could happen.

With Saint Athanasius at her right hand, Ruthie felt her waist tighten and the pale pink of her nipples tingle in heartbeat cadence with the miracles shimmering in its stained glass.

A few steps farther, down at the curb, she was surprised to find a cab waiting for her, and as the driver opened the door Ruthie knew she was pregnant, at one with the child inside her as sure as she knew her name was Ruthie.

THE RESURRECTION OF ELVIS PRESLEY

A i

Once upon a time, I practiced moves in a mirror—
half spastic, half Nijinsky,
with a dash of belly dancer
to make the little girls burn.
I dyed my dark blond hair black
and coated it with Royal Crown pomade,
that stuff the Negroes used,
till it shone
with a porcelainlike glaze.
Some nights I'd wake in a sweat.
I'd have to take off my p.j.'s.
I'd imagine I was Tony Curtis
and I'd get a hard-on,
then, ashamed, get up
and stare at myself in the mirror by nightlight
and, shaking as if I had a fever,
step, cross step, pump my belly,
grind my hips, and jump back
and fling one arm above my head,
the other toward the floor,
fingers spread wide
to indicate true feeling.
But where was he
when I bit the hook
and got reeled in

and at the bitter end of the rod
found not God but Papa Hemingway,
banished too to this island
in the stream of unconsciousness,
to await the Apocalypse of Revelations
or just another big fish?

2

I don't know how it happened,
but I became all appetite.
I took another pill, another woman,
or built another room
to store the gifts I got from fans
till neither preachers, priests,
nor Yogananda's autobiography
could help me.
The Colonel tied a string around my neck
and led me anywhere he wanted.
I was his teddy bear
and yours and yours and yours.
But did I whine, did I complain about it?
Like a greased pig,
I slid through everybody's hands
till I got caught between the undertaker's sheets.
And now I wait
to be raised up like some *Titanic*
from the Rock 'n' Roll Atlantic.
Now as I cast my line,
tongues of flame
lick the air above my head,
announcing some Pentecost,
or transcendental storm,
but Papa tells me it's only death who's coming
and he's just a mutated brother
who skims the dark floor
of all our troubled waters
and rises now and then to eat the bait.
But once he wrestled me
like Jacob's angel
and I let him win

because he promised resurrection
in some sweeter by-and-by,
and when he comes to me again
I'll pin him down
until he claims me
from the walleye of this hurricane
and takes me
I don't care how,
as long as he just takes me.
But Papa says forget him
and catch what I can,
even if it's just sweet time,
because it's better than nothing,
better even than waiting
in the heavenly deep-freeze,
then he tells me don't move,
don't talk,
and for Chrissakes don't sing,
and I do what he wants,
me, the king of noise,
but in my memories
this country boy *is* singing,
he's dancing in the dark
and always will.

THE ELVIS CULTS

Michael Wilkerson

I returned from Arman on August 16. No one could remember offhand what year it was. Those of us who had been released by the militant assistant professors who occupied the embassy were taken to a small conference building in the State Department headquarters in Washington. I was questioned by the third assistant attaché to the associate secretary.

"What hobbies did you take up during your five years in the embassy?"

"The guitar."

"That will serve you well." She paused and fixed a Styrofoam cupful of instant coffee. "I think you will find your family a little different than they were when you were taken hostage," she said.

"How so?"

"Our sources in Pittsburgh tell us they have moved West and joined the Elvis Cults."

I crossed my legs. I pondered. We had been given little news during our time at the embassy. The assistant professors, most of whom had finished their dissertations while holding us hostage, had been kind in other ways, since the novelties of abuse and humiliation had worn off. They'd given us novels— the classics only—and musical instruments, and sewing implements. I'd made an Afghan, but I'd heard no news. The situation room had been turned into a racquetball court. We took turns keeping track of the reservations. Hostage basketball teams had defeated the assistant professors repeatedly in round-robin tournaments, but we hadn't heard of the Elvis Cults.

The third assistant attaché continued her briefing.

"Your wife and son have moved to Elvisville, Indiana."

"Indiana?"

"Elvisville."

"I never heard of it."

"It used to be called 'Ellettsville,' until three years ago." She looked at a tattered map. It looked as if it had seen a long time in a glove compartment. "It's in the south central part of the state. Do you remember the film *Breaking Away*? The one about bicycles."

"I saw that just before I went to Arman. That was the last film I saw."

"Your wife and son are living in that area now."

I asked how to get to Elvisville. The third assistant attaché said the government no longer had enough money for plane fare.

"Face it, you're no hero. It's been too long."

"I would have thought the hostages would have been a campaign issue. There is an election this year, isn't there?"

"I think so. There hasn't been much talk about it."

She drove me to the Greyhound station in a VW Rabbit and handed me a tattered twenty-dollar bill. "You can take a cab from Bloomington to Elvisville. This should cover it."

The twenty dollars plus my tax refund from 1979, which the IRS had held for me, should be enough for a few days, I thought. I expected my wife Lesley would have some money. I thought of her for a moment, forgetting the forgettable presence of the third assistant attaché. Lesley was a distinguished-looking woman—tall but unassuming, cleverly but casually dressed. In the Sixties we'd been protesters together. We'd owned all the Hendrix, Joplin and Doors albums. She was a friend of a friend of Bob Dylan. She'd worked for Allard Lowenstein, played Joni Mitchell songs in bars. I knew little of the Elvis Cults, but I certainly couldn't believe *she* would join them. The third assistant attaché shook my shoulder.

"Mr. Jensen, I don't believe you've been listening."

"Sorry."

"Let me just say this: you have been away a long time. A lot has happened."

"I'm only interested in finding Lesley."

"You may not find her as you'd wish. The Elvis Cults are a serious phenomenon in this country."

"I don't understand. She used to mock 'Heartbreak Hotel.' "

"I'm sorry, but the government is much too poor to pursue your wife's particular case. President Reagan has smashed our budget like a bowl of potatoes."

As I pondered her simile, she smiled. "Good luck, Mr. Jensen. You'll miss your bus if you don't hurry." A man who looked like Elvis took my luggage. Another sold me my ticket. The bus driver looked like Him. I struggled to the back of the bus, searching for a seatmate who bore no resemblance. I found one. He handed me a card that said, "DON'T TALK TO ME. I AM A DEAF MUTE AND I CAN'T HEAR YOU."

Delighted, I seated myself. I counted seven Elvis Look-alikes on the bus. I can say that now without flinching. At the time, I wanted desperately to find another mode of transportation. I counted my money. I noticed that His picture did not appear on the smaller bills. Yet. I heard the engine—deep, throaty, rhythmic, and strained. I looked at my seatmate. He turned toward the aisle, away from me. I slept through most of Maryland, Pennsylvania and Ohio, dreaming of my room in the embassy and Hafez, the assistant professor who'd been my tennis partner.

Before I knew it, before I was really ready to venture to Elvisville, the bus had glided into Bloomington. I stood in the small station holding my suitcase. It's odd that sometimes you tell your whole story to a stranger; that's what I did, there in the station, to a man who bumped into me while I stood motionless.

"C'mon, pal, buy you a taco," he said. There was a "Taco Tico" next door to the Greyhound terminal. I had soft shell, he had hard. I told him about being a hostage.

"You seem to have liked it," he said, licking grease from his ring finger.

"It was secure," I said. "I got pretty good on the guitar, too."

"I guess you guys know the whole story of how you got out of there," he said, obviously expecting me to say I didn't. I'm glad I said I didn't, because I didn't. There had been a nationwide "Forget the Hostages" campaign since 1983, he said. Most Americans had flown their flags at full mast and displayed bumper stickers that said "What Hostages?" on their Toyotas.

"It took a few years to catch on, but after a while absolutely everyone just plain stopped caring," he said, crunching his shell.

"So that's why the letters from my wife stopped coming," I said. The assistant professors had told us of a crackdown in censorship; now it was apparent that they'd lied. "I'm in Indiana to find my wife. She lives in Elvisville," I told my acquaintance.

"Elvisville. Boy, you sure picked a hell of a time to come out here."

"Oh?"

"Today's the anniversary of His death. The place'll be jammed."

"Do you think I could get a cab out there?"

"Cab, hell. You can get a bus. They run every half hour from the front of the courthouse." He offered me a cigarette; I declined. His face—fair, freckled and decidedly un-Elvis-like—was refreshing to look at. His hair was red. His eyes were blue.

"I was going to move out there to Elvisville myself once," he said. "Didn't want to be a Jordanaire, though. Your wife a Jordanaire?"

"A what?" Although I vaguely recognized the word by its sound, I didn't know what it meant.

"The members of the inner circle are Jordanaires. That was the name of His backup group, you know. The Jordanaires are the ones who run the place. It's a terrorist conspiracy in there. Hell, I like his music okay, but I can't see worshipping the guy. My dog can sing better."

"But why did you think of moving out there if you didn't want to be in the inner circle?" Perhaps it was his tone of voice, hollow-sounding against the false adobe decor of the Taco Tico. Perhaps I was just being nosy. Perhaps I'd forgotten American habits. In any case, I needed to know more.

"Two reasons, really." He didn't seem offended. That's one good thing about Indiana people. You ask them a question, they'll talk. Forever if you don't stop them. As I write this, I can see that he answered my question backwards. Those Hoosiers! "One, I'm not much for administration. Two, I couldn't afford the surgery."

"Surgery?"

"Sure. You have to get redone to look like Him." My friend paused and sipped his Coke, studying me. "You've seen the Lookalikes, haven't you, pal?"

"Sure, but—"

"I know, you're thinking about your wife. I'll tell you: the women get the surgery too. Makes most of 'em look a lot better. If you happen to like Elvis, of course."

"I have to get out there," I said. "I have to see Lesley. Surely she isn't a Jordanaire. She wouldn't do it. But she does like to get involved." I must have been talking very rapidly. I smashed the remains of my taco.

"Calm down, pal. The Elvis bus is four blocks that way. They're running them special, right from the courthouse lawn, today only."

As I left my friend at the Taco Tico, I saw a newspaper machine at the door. The headline said only: BIG, BIG ANNIVERSARY. I spent the quarter, and read as I walked toward the courthouse. The disc-like sun grooved sweat on my back. The newspaper featured several Elvis Cult stories, including a lengthy history of the movement. Elvism had become the second largest religion in America. There was a picture of Bloomington's mayor, who looked like Him. The cults were centered in the south and midwest; they ranged from the quiet, meditative "singalikes" of Wisconsin and Minnesota to the more severe, cloistered "lookalikes" of Elvisville, portions of Illinois, and the Deep South. All Elvists were required to visit Memphis once during their lifetimes. Each day they turned toward that city and sang His lyrics; the songs varied from cult to cult. Approaching the courthouse square, I heard a soundalike band doing "Jailhouse Rock." A huge crowd waited in several lines for bus tickets.

I wondered what the words meant. It had been a long time. A young girl pinned a button to my lapel. A pennant was put in my hand. Teenagers with glue bottles stuck sequins to my soggy shirt. I was ordered to gyrate. There was a crush. Screams. I heard "Love Me Tender." I missed my wife. I was hot. A hunk of burning love. Where had I heard that before?

I guess I fainted (perhaps I was drugged, or slugged); in any case, someone took me to a bus, where I revived during "Teddy Bear."

Rituals ensued. The noise of the choruses was nearly

unbearable, yet somehow endearing. So many people united in one cause. I remembered the demonstrations outside the embassy, back in the early days when it seemed that every Armanian wanted us out, tortured and slaughtered. Those were horrid times—before the racquetball and the guitar lessons—yet we all were awed by the Armanians' solidarity.

Hundreds of plush toy Teddy Bears, all of them apparently dressed in sequined clothes, some sporting miniature guitars around their necks, were tossed in the air in a mob-style game of catch. Two years ago, the crowds outside the embassy had hung the President of Arman National University for refusing to approve one of the militants' dissertations. The terror of that day matched what I began to feel as the Elvists continued to shout outside the bus.

"He's awake," I heard.

"Let him be." The voices all sounded nearly the same. Everyone seemed to be speaking from that region of the throat just below the Adam's apple. The sound was strained and guttural. I was taken out of the bus, longing for the security of the embassy, the solid walls of the racquetball court, even the dreary politics classes Hafez had made me endure when I had thought I could tolerate no more.

The music had stopped. The talk nastified.

"Outsider."

"Infiltrator."

How had they discovered me? Had I talked in my sleep, or had I gyrated improperly to "Jailhouse Rock"? I still don't know.

My hands were bound with a guitar strap, and I was jammed into a long, two-toned 1957 Cadillac sedan, in which I rode through the ten miles of two-lane highway, past the grocery stores (all 7-Elevens; I was getting used to that) and gas stations (all Exxons; I was used to that, too, after the long ride from Washington.) We arrived at the gates of Elvisville. Guards in sequined suits waved us through. Thousands and thousands of Elvists swarmed, but finally cleared a path for the Cadillac. I asked my captor, who rode in the front passenger seat, why the people had moved. He sat silent, idol-like. The chauffeur said my captor was a third cousin of the King Himself.

The sight of the crowd was stunning, literally unforgettable. I wondered if that many people had attended Woodstock. Lesley and I had gone there. Now, I surmised, she was here. Somewhere within that mass of dark-haired, tanned bodies who wiggled strangely choreographed, decades-old dances in an enormous field ringed with speakers, I thought I recognized the Bunny Hop. The car continued, past the field and through a small set of gates, which were turquoise and guitar-shaped. Small buildings, shaped like mansions despite their size, lined the driveway on which we drove. Finally we arrived at what appeared to be the command center of Elvisville. A man in a white smock, who was attended by two Look-alikes, greeted me as I got out of the car. He too looked like the King, but I surmised from his commanding presence that he was a Jordanaire.

"Said-a-hello to you today," he said.

"Hi."

"We gonna have some fun tonight."

I did not really know what to say to this man. I asked him to untie the guitar strap that offended my hands. We began to walk down a side street that had no buildings on it. He pointed to the structure at the end, with a curved front and a sign I couldn't read.

"Your new place to dwell," he said. The aides beside him broke into "Heartbreak Hotel."

I laughed. The man in the white smock slapped me. The aides continued undaunted.

The odd spectacle paled. I could read the sign in front of the building "HEARTBREAK HOTEL," it said. "GUEST MODIFICATION AND JORDANAIRE TRAINING FACILITY."

"Is my wife in there?"

The man in the white smock said nothing. The aides chortled. One asked if I had any requests.

"My wife," I said. "I want to see Lesley."

"Dunno it," they said, and prepared to play guitars. My ears began to ring—first shrilly, then with a hissing noise like that of huge, idle amplifiers with pilot lights ablaze. I fainted when the chords came.

The story's almost too painful to tell. They wouldn't let me see Lesley—or maybe they did: I stayed there sixty-four days, locked in the cylindrical center of that, uh, Heartbreak Hotel. They took me to dinners and concerts. They made me wear sequined clothes. They gave me an electric guitar that was designed to shock its user if anything other than Elvis songs were played on it. My son came to visit me; he'd had the surgery, which had apparently been inexpensive, swift and relatively painless. The man in the white smock was the head surgeon, as I'd feared. I saw no one who looked like anything other than Elvis, other than my reflection in the mirror. I did not find the Lookalike women pretty. Gradually, I realized that one—which one?—of the women in the inner compound of Elvisville had to be Lesley; still, I hoped, ever so slightly, that she might have escaped, might have found a way around the surgery. I knew that all of the Elvists had essentially the same personality. My son and I had talked; we'd had all the time together I could stand, but all we had in common was the guitar, and, oddly, my hands wouldn't let me play those insidious Elvis songs. The more I remained hostage in Elvisville, the stubborner I became. They wanted me to stay. They wanted me to become a Jordanaire. But I couldn't make the right noises. I had no sense of rhythm. I can't, to this day, gyrate.

They were keeping me around because I had been an officer in the diplomatic corps. Dispassionately but metrically, they told me they were planning to secede the states they dominated from the country, and that they'd need diplomats when that ensued. How cruel my career choice had been—the foreign service had given me nothing, nothing but the chance to compare two ways of being held hostage. This time, I was no cause célèbre, not even briefly. There was no racquetball, no one to whom I became close, as I had been with Hafez. The Elvists were universally alike, universally uninteresting. Day after day the Soundalike bands played; my son, stranger to me that he was, had become something of a star among young Elvists. His twitches and tics were inspired in their faithfulness to the King. I was obliquely proud, but I felt little sense of paternity.

They hoped I'd change my mind, that I'd submit to the near-painless scalpel and join their ranks. It's easy to say now that I would never do anything like that, that I never felt any sympathy for their cause, that the Elvists couldn't move me at all. But it isn't true. I consented to the surgery, not without huge misgivings, but because I had been a hostage too long. I had little will remaining. They promised me living quarters with Lesley if I'd submit; no matter how transformed she might be, I thought, she would still be Lesley. How much could a surgeon change a person, anyway? I was told the man in the white smock would come for me on the eightieth day of my captivity.

The seventies passed, mostly. I grew more and more nervous. Tentatively, I sang in a band of Elvists. I tried to remember the lyrics to "Return to Sender." But I kept getting them wrong; I feared that I was not ready. Perhaps I would never be ready. Still, I tried to adapt to their ways, to His ways.

A noise on the roof interrupted my singing.

"Tennis? Would the American like to beat his buddy in some tennis?"

"Hafez!"

I heard the blades of a helicopter and the tinkling of Plexiglas as Hafez kicked through it. A rope ladder lowered. Alarms went off. "Jailhouse Rock" played throughout the Heartbreak Hotel. I had no time to think; I'd selected the surgery, but Hafez was tugging at my arm.

"Come on!" Hafez had placed my hands on the rungs.

The voice in the alarm song was female. Despite its Elvistic qualities, I thought I recognized it.

"Lesley!"

Hafez pushed my hips up the ladder.

I shouted. "Lesley, come with me!"

Tinny guitar notes whined and bent toward me; Hafez shoved me into the helicopter and slammed the hatch. I tried to spot Lesley in the crowd of Elvists below. I still believe I saw her; I'll cling to that. Hafez says it's an impossibility, that she would not have been discernible in that large a group of Jordanaires. The helicopter landed in Bloomington. Hafez took me to the Taco Tico. I don't cry very often, but that night tears diluted the Salsa.

POSTLUDE

Hafez's story was simple. Without the hostages to keep him busy, he'd had to apply for tenure, and he hadn't made it. The Revolution soured swiftly for him then, and he'd heard so much from me about America and Lesley that he came over. Money was no problem; even on a junior professor's salary, he'd piled up a hefty savings during the rent-free embassy occupation. Disgusted with the Revolution, he'd found the third assistant attaché, who sent him to Elvisville. Hafez, too, had treated himself to Taco Tico and had met the old man there. A month's savings in Armanian money paid for the helicopter. We've found this guy several times since; he hangs out at the Greyhound station and seeks dinner partners. If you would come to Bloomington, and look just a little lost in the bus station there, he'd take you next door and talk you to death over tostadas, enchiladas, quesadillas, whatever. Turns out the guy's brother manages the restaurant, so he's sort of on the take. Takes tacos off his taxes, I guess. Hafez is standing behind me, planting lines like that in my ear. Come on Hafez, this is a serious memoir here. There's more to tell; I'll try to summarize. We're playing Australian doubles in twenty minutes. That's a bizarre story too. Hafez found this woman—I'd better back up a minute.

That surgery the Jordanaires got, and that I almost got, really is easy. It's irreversible, you know, but there are a lot of people who simply hate their own looks. One of the things I used to do at the Embassy was tell Hafez, in the minutest detail I could muster, just what Lesley looked like. It was a way to keep the fires burning, you know, and it was curiously satisfying, almost as if I had been with her during the whole occupation. So when we got on the helicopter, Hafez told me he had this surprise for me in Bloomington. We downed our tacos, and he took me to meet this woman, a Bloomington native, who had just taken the bandages off from her surgery. Yes, she looked like Lesley. It was stunning. Hafez thought, you know . . . that I'd fall in love with her. I tried, and she tried, but it was just trying. There was too much resemblance to Lesley, and, at the same time, not enough.

But good old Hafez—he'd even bought a duplex before he'd rescued me, and Melinda, the new Lesley, was living in it. So, even though she and I couldn't make a go of it, she stayed, and just sort of drifted over to Hafez's side of the house. I don't mind—they're great together, and I can beat them at tennis. I guess we've settled in here now. Hafez sells rides in his helicopter and works occasionally with one of the acting companies that summer in Bloomington and make those bad bicycle gang movies you see in the drive-ins. He's a lot better rider than he was a teacher, I'll tell you. The only revolutions he cares about are the ones bike wheels make. That's America for you.

Melinda manages an apolitical bookstore downtown. She's always holding meetings at which students get together to not talk about the issues.

I've hooked up with Indiana University. One of the professors got a grant to set up a Department of Elvis Studies, so I'm doing some research and teaching a couple of classes. I just dig in and listen to the music, and trace the histories of the cults, and project what'll happen to them. I think they've kind of leveled off. The secession isn't going to happen, and new surgeries are in a decline that parallels that of the birth rate. Next year, RCA will publish my first critical book, *Hound Dogs and Suspicious Minds*.

Oh, every now and then I think of Lesley, and of how I could have been a Jordanaire. But I've got a cure for that. I just pick up my guitar and, as seriously as possible, sing "Hound Dog."

And that cures it. Rock and roll has survived; it eradicates the blues. Even He knew that.

ELVIS

Brian Gilmore

1.

elvis presley is alive and well
and the world scrapes near the ground

at the north pole, a flag remains unplanted
in egypt, there are no pyramids.

elvis presley is alive and well
but there is no such thing as superman,
there was never a thing called slavery
there was never a rape of africa.

elvis presley can beat jesse owens
because jesse never ran a race
bob gibson is throwing knuckleballs
kareem is shooting jumpers.

elvis presley is alive and well and i swear i
saw him in harlem
everyone bolt your doors!
everyone board up your windows!!
everyone stop taking singing lessons!!!
no one is writing this down!!!!

elvis presley was a black man
and al jolson didn't need any make up,

for it is proven
and i believe it to be true

elvis taught bruce lee karate!

2.

elvis shouldn't have been allowed
to
register
and vote

3.

shoot him with fire hoses

4.

such a mass,
such a disturbing mass. such a wallowing in the mud
mass   such a dangerous mass.

couldn't live up to it,
couldn't be it, ain't that great,
ain't that bad, ain't that cool.

the mass didn't make up those moves, didn't make up
that voice, those clothes, those ways of crooning
and swaying and fooling the world with that whole
weird way of doing things.

they bought it. swallowed it. bathed in it.
ate it   with a gin and tonic but shit,
hold the tonic because i don't understand it,
i can't face it unless my head is spinning!

the mass couldn't do it all because mud is like
blood;   mud is about emotional outrage!

the mass could never be it all because
america is an illusion and for those of us
watching
tv
all the time—iranians don't care about some white
boy acting like a nigger snorting velcro.

that goes the same for the middle east
and asia
and afghanistan
and afrika
and most of the
world.

but now you're saying—'japan loves elvis,
seen those impersonators . . . '

but japan ain't been japan since 1945;
japan is manhattan or chicago or london

damn sure ain't japan!

you're saying the same about other
countries too who are into it
long after we were into it

but really they aren't into it
because once you are into it
you can't call yourself an
afrikan or
an asian
or an arabian.
call yourself whatever you want,
but don't upset the ancestors,
they know about the mud and that
emotional outrage.

still there is that mass.

that huge monster looming over us larger than life
a wailing soul simulating bantu and yoruba wearing
zoot suits and breaking more black sisters' hearts

than chuck berry could mend with 'maybelline' or
'thirty days.''

so the mass swelled and got muddy. the mass got so
big and muddy it couldn't see or walk, realized it
couldn't be superman
couldn't be the lone ranger
couldn't be captain america throwing his mighty
shield.

the mass knew different.
knew about chitlins, whiskey
and juke joints.
knew he stuck out like a sore thumb.
knew he didn't make it because he was better than
anyone
else
because memphis had 500 young white boys around
1950 whose old man or grandmother bought them a
guitar and some ray charles' records for christmas.

he just knew better than the rest that velcro was a
magic potion.
and magic makes people snort velcro.
and snorting velcro makes people wallow in the mud at
night.

and mud makes us look like something we aren't.
because
the mass wasn't white,
he had too much mud in his hair
and snorted too much velcro.

and the mass wasn't black because
he had too much velcro in his hair
and not enough mud hanging off his lips.

the mass was just dangling on a vine holding a
guitar
and some watermelon wondering

why did he want to be what he truly despised?

5.

sick the dogs on him!!.

6.

where the hell is bull connor?

7.

elvis lovvvvvvvvvvveeeeesssss
pig knuckles.

ELVIS IN PERSPECTIVE

Cathryn Hankla

> *But poets should*
> *Exert a double vision; should have eyes*
> *To see near things as comprehensively*
> *As if afar they took their point of sight,*
> *And distant things as intimately deep*
> *As if they touched them. Let us strive for this.*
>
> —Elizabeth Barrett Browning,
> *Aurora Leigh*, Book V

There's something about looking down on Graceland that can make you feel all shook up inside. You can drive there making all kinds of jokes about maybe seeing a Ken doll–sized KING hitchhiking on the side of the road, somewhere on 181 looking for Memphis, but it's like when you get there, you have to shut your mouth, paralyzed, and just gape at the whole of this weird, wild creation that contains such a thing. It's too much. I don't know. The hardest part for me is that I get so sidetracked thinking about the husband of the woman who is Elvis's biggest fan in Roanoke, Virginia. The husband actually built Miniature Graceland with his hands, a testament to human ingenuity, and a devotion to his wife, who is devoted to Elvis. It begins to remind you of the food chain, only this is a chain of love. As such, I figure it's as good a place as anywhere to test a new relationship, so I try to go there on the first date. I've found that it saves a big hunk o' time.

TELL ME WHY

Ernie and I had known each other for a century I guess, but one day as we were walking out of the office in the new bank building downtown, that looks like King Tut's tomb, he sort of *looked* at me while we were talking about the weather, and I knew he was going to call.

Ernie called that night and asked me to go bowling on the weekend. It sounded well-lighted. I hadn't bowled since high school, but bowling was a sport no one could take seriously anyway, so I said, "All right."

Ernie said, "I'll pick ya up at four and we can get some food after the game, all right?"

Before I could speak again Ernie hung up.

Ernie roared into the curb outside my apartment building right on time. A great beginning, I thought. I hate men who are late or women either for that matter. A person should be where they say they're going to be approximately when they claim they're going to be there, and not fifteen minutes later. Ernie was driving a Nova that was at least two feet off the ground, but he was on time. And when I hoisted myself into the car he shut my door for me—always a plus—and the car was clean, like he had thought about me.

"How do you like my car?" Ernie asked, when he had the steering wheel in his hand.

"It's very clean," I said.

Ernie was turned toward me, holding the wheel, and his foot wasn't moving off the brake. A little wave of panic swept through me for no good reason, I thought. But it seemed we weren't going anywhere until I came up with something better about the Nova.

"It's a pretty shade of gold," I said, even if the interior was red, I thought.

Without smiling, Ernie just looked at me. He said, "You don't know much about cars." But his foot finally came off the brake and we left the curb. We drove in silence to the bowling alley, but at least he didn't try to tell me about his car. Later, though, I realized that car question had been Ernie's test, and I had been written off before I even had a chance to test Ernie. I guess that's one difference between men and women. Women like to give the benefit of the doubt. We let them dig their own grave if they're going to before we write them off. But for men it's a lot more cut and dried. You don't know shit about engines and you're out of the race.

Since I didn't know that until later, I was still planning to give Ernie my Elvis test, right after dinner.

When he had shoved the last limp French fry into his mouth and chewed sufficiently, I popped the question.

"Ernie," I said, casually, but just forcefully enough, I thought, to let him know what I wanted, "have you ever seen Miniature Graceland?"

"Yeah," he said.

And when he said that I thought I saw a few stray locks of hair fall over his forehead. Ernie wasn't bad looking if he would shave that mousy mustache and stop wearing such ugly clothes. But I could always work on the wardrobe. Clothes make the man, they say, but clothes are the easiest thing for a woman to change, since men typically don't give a shit about them anyway.

"Great," I said. "Do you want to go?"

"Now?" Ernie asked.

"Why not?" I said, still trying to sound casual.

"Why?" asked Ernie. "You've seen it, I've seen it, so why bother?"

"When was the last time you saw it?"

"A couple of years back."

"It's expanded since then, there are new buildings, even a model of the Roanoke Civic Center, and a car museum." I thought I had him where I wanted him; his logic was just about to run out of gas.

Ernie was ahead of me. "Now that you've told me all about it," he said, "there's no reason to drive all the way over there."

"But I haven't really described all of it. There's a lot more to see." I knew I was beginning to whine.

"Anyway," Ernie said. "My mother lives over there, and if she sees my car going by it'll hurt her feelings if I don't stop, and I'll never hear the end of it, so there you go."

Ernie had played his ace. I knew it and Ernie knew that I knew it: the mother was the kiss of death in any relationship. That's when I knew that Ernie had written me off much earlier. No man who was really interested in a woman would bring up his mother on the first date. Since it was all over I thought I'd at least enjoy myself, so I said, "We could stop in at your mother's for a few minutes." I smiled the sweetest and most devious smile I had ever smiled.

"You know," Ernie said. "I don't really feel very well."

I thought he did look pale, even if that was the lamest line I'd ever heard. I was disappointed in ole Ernie. I thought he might be more creative.

He drove me home and we were both polite at the door while I found my keys in my purse. I thought about scaring him to death by inviting him in, but I was tired of games by then.

When Ernie's Nova growled off I came back out of the door jangling my keys. I'd drive over to Riverland Avenue myself. You never knew who you might see there. Even Jimmy and Rosalyn Carter had shown up to pay their respects one hot summer night, just like this one.

HOW DO YOU THINK I FEEL

Tom was a shy man and skinny as a pencil, but I thought there was potential because he wore sideburns. When I see a man with sideburns I see a man with flair. You just know he's got a secret weapon to his personality if you can just get to it. I spent a whole fall season trying to find Tom's backbone, and all I got was thirty different kinds of flowers.

Oh don't go on about how wonderful it is to find a man who brings you flowers. You wait until you have to hide inside your house because a man is encircling your premises with gladiolas or making a big cross out of pink miniature carnations on your front lawn that the KKK would be curious to see. Women and flowers, well I've had enough baby's breath and roses and irises to last me a lifetime. But there was a moment when I thought it might work out with Tom, even though I didn't ask him to visit Graceland on our first date. If I had stuck to my plan, though, I wouldn't have had to sneeze through all those flowers. I've learned my lesson now.

As I said, Tom was a shy man and so skinny his wrists were like two bones, not one. His pants drooped in the seat, and his shirtsleeves flapped off his bony shoulders. But when he was seated at his computer terminal, pored over his display screen with that green light reflecting off his face, and those perfectly trimmed bell-bottom sideburns, well, he looked almost like a poet. And that's another thing we women have to fall for. Poets and musicians have made a career living off of women, and it's our own faults if we don't have the gumption, if we'd rather slave for a guitar player than do the easy thing—just sit down and write our own damn poems. That Elizabeth Barrett Browning is the best, isn't she? But this happened some time ago, when I thought the closest I'd ever come to art was to kiss Tom's sideburns. Well, he can kiss mine—but that's another story.

Every day on my coffee break I'd pass Tom's desk and look at his sideburns. He didn't seem to ever take a break, and he didn't look up either. But I kept brushing past him day in and day out until—I didn't plan it to happen, this way, but it did anyway—I brushed too close to his chair and dropped my full cup of coffee down his back. You know I don't think he would have looked up then, if I hadn't started apologizing and trying to sop up the coffee with a tissue.

Tom stood without speaking, and I kept saying, "Oh, I'm so sorry, I'm so sorry, let me try to clean up your shirt." All the time I dabbed at the wet coffee with a tissue, leaving clots of tissue here and there on his unnaturally crisp blend shirt. I went to the ladies' room and brought back a handful of paper towels. Tom was still standing beside his desk, a little hunched in the shoulders. He was staring down at the screen, and his sideburns twitched. I was beginning to think maybe the coffee had scalded him, and he was in shock, so I kind of shook his shoulder and asked him if he was all right.

"I'm quite well, thank you," Tom said. "But I have work to finish."

"I am sorry as I can be about your shirt," I said.

"Don't think about it a second longer," Tom said.

I thought that was a nice thing to say, even if we didn't go on and have a real conversation. Tom just sat back down at his screen, and I walked back to my desk thinking it was almost scary, but kind of cute, the way he was so devoted to his work.

Not that week, but the next, he sent a bouquet of carnations to my desk with a note asking me to go out for a cup of coffee after work. I felt tingly when I read the note, thinking I'd been right about Tom all along. Still waters run deep and all that crap I'd bought hook, line, and sinker from the magazines. Women, if you see still water you can bet it's really a well you'll like to never climb out of, so I'm telling you, don't dive in.

On my first date with Tom we went for a cup of coffee, just that. He took me to this yuppie coffee shop that hadn't been open long. I got a big piece of chocolate double fudge cake and some coffee with milk foam on top, which I think is addictive because now I think I have to have one of those at least twice a week. That first visit with Tom hooked me on the coffee, but I don't hold it against him too much, because that foamy coffee is something I can have alone or with someone, and it tastes just the same either way.

When Tom took me down there to the coffee shop I wasn't so high on going. You know it was in that part of town. When we got there, though, none of those people were in there, but the crowd looked just as strange before I got used to them. A lot of the people in the shop were wearing the most expensive athletic clothes you can buy out of catalogs. And the teen to early twenties crowd was dressed in black from shoes to berets. A couple of tables pressed against the back walls seemed reserved for groups of men or women. Pink bandannas trailed from the men's back pockets, and the women never looked up from their conversations. Every time I've been in the coffee shop I've seen a couple of single men or women either reading or writing at a table, and nobody bothers them. When I pointed out a woman who was writing in a notebook to Tom, he said,

"She's a local writer."

I couldn't think of anything to say back to him at the time. But now that I think about it more, I don't think he knew her personally. Anyway, if a person is sitting there, doesn't that mean they are local? I wish I'd of said that. Instead, I ate some cake, which was delicious, some time went by, and then I said something that gave me away completely, I said,

"I don't think I see a single person I know." That was the nicest thing I could think of to say.

"Yes," Tom said, as if he belonged to the in-group. "This is a bohemian crowd."

The way he said *bohemian* pulled the wool right over my eyes. It was like all I saw was Tom's voice, not the geek who sat before me with outdated facial hair. When a good looking man with a beard and a black turtleneck brushed by our table and then looked back and said, "Hello, Tom," I was lost. Later I found out they had gone to high school together. I'm sure the man in the beard was as popular and good looking back in high school as now, and that's why he could afford to be nice to someone like Tom.

Tom and I didn't say much to each other, but I liked the cake and the coffee, and it wasn't until after Tom had dropped me off—he drove a Honda Civic, by the way—that I remembered about Elvis, and about my car which I had driven to work and forgotten in the parking lot. I convinced myself it was a sign; a sign that Tom might be the one. Maybe my rules had messed up my opportunities. That can happen, can't it? Let go and let love, right? So I tried to forget about the Elvis test and be content with remembering what Tom had said and done at my door.

Tom pulled us snug to the curb and practically leaped out of the car. I sat tight. When a man moves that fast he's old fashioned. I waited and sure enough he opened my door for me from the outside and extended his hand to help me out. We walked to the door of my apartment house hand in hand. I stopped under the yellow glow of the bug light and faced him, still holding his hand.

"May I kiss you?" Tom asked.

"Of course," I said and began to pucker my lips. He was so sweet to ask first, I thought. My eyes were nearly closed when Tom raised my hand to his lips and brushed it lightly with a kiss.

"May I call you again?" Tom asked.

"Yes," I said, stunned.

"Thank you," Tom said.

I floated through the door as he said, "Good night."

The next morning when I left the apartment on my way to my car that I'd forgotten wasn't there, I stumbled over a white envelope on the mat. A couple of my neighbors had already clomped over it. I could see my name written in a curly hand, shining through a boot tread, so I picked up the smudged envelope, and my heart began to pound. I opened the letter, black fountain ink on pure white, forty pound rag. I read: **"Good morning, Beautiful."** It was signed, **Sincerely Yours, Tom.**

I looked up from the words and there was Tom getting out of his silver Honda Civic and coming toward me. He remembered I'd left my car downtown. I was trembling, still holding his letter in one hand. Tom led me to his car by the other hand.

From that point on, until I finally asked Tom to go to Miniature Graceland, I thought I was in love and I was sure Tom was, which was even better. Every day it was flowers or a sweet little note, or flowers and a note, or a little present on my desk, like a couple of chocolate petit fours that I was afraid to eat until Tom told me what they were. When I got in bed every night, just before I closed my eyes and shut off the light, my princess phone rang. I picked it up and said good night to Tom. That was all, just good night, so mine was the last voice he heard before he went to sleep. And he kept picking me up for work, so his was the first voice I heard in the morning. We went on like this for several months. When it started to get cold I was even gladder someone other than myself had to scrape that damn frost off his windshield every morning.

The night I asked him about going to see Elvis, my test was already an afterthought. I mean Tom and I hadn't *done* anything but hold hands and a little kissy face, but a woman knows when a man is interested, and it's all up to her to let it happen when she feels like it. I thought it was like this between Tom and me. He was just waiting politely for me to unleash his animal passion. I was waiting for the proper time. It couldn't happen too soon, either, I knew from hard experience. A woman has to maintain her mystery. But a woman can't let the mystery get too deep, either. Suspense about the inevitable can't last forever. I was just about to stop biding my time, and for some reason my old Elvis test floated to the surface in my mind, and before I gave it a serious reevaluation, I popped the question. Of course we were sitting in the coffee shop at the time—we had become as regular as the man who read *Crime and Punishment* alone—sipping that coffee that I can't remember how to pronounce. I know it's Italian, so don't think I'm a fool.

"Tom," I said. "Have you ever seen Miniature Graceland?"

"No. Is it open in the winter?" Tom asked, his face as nice as pie.

"Hummm," I mused. "You know, I've only been in the summer, but I think it's open all year 'round."

Tom shifted in his chair so he could look out the plate glass into the night lit by streetlights. I saw the flakes blowing through the air before he announced, "It's snowing."

"Yes, it is." I love snow, always have. Seeing the fluff trailing down through the light mesmerized me so that I was taken by surprise when just a shake later Tom said,

"Well, let's go."

He meant we were going to Graceland.

Tom drove without hesitating once at a turn, which I thought was a good sign. He must be the only person I've ever gone to Graceland with who knew the way. Now I think that being sure about the way doesn't guarantee you're going in the right direction.

We pulled up alongside the monument and before we got out of the car Tom reached over and squeezed my hand. Just a little squeeze, the kind an adult might give a child before going through the tent flaps into the first circus of your life.

I sat tight as Tom had trained me with his gentleman act, my eyes staring no place in particular, and waited for him to come around and open my door. Something made me look out the window. Maybe it took a second too long for my door to open—and what I saw I couldn't even believe, and I couldn't take my eyes off it, and it's hard to say what it was even now, because I think maybe nobody will believe it could happen, nobody but my mother who knows what scum can walk the earth in tailored pants and well-trimmed sideburns. Well, it was Tom of course, but at first I wasn't even sure, given the snow and all, so I rubbed at the fog on the window and kept looking. How he got off his clothes so fast I'll never know. But he was shaking his backside at my side of the car. Not mooning me, but just like he was dancing—blinding white backside shaking, and then I saw that Tom wasn't wearing a stitch, and he was going to turn in my direction any second. Just about when I started locking the car doors a floodlight came on all over Tom and nearly blinded me.

He was wearing something—his socks. And he was

bending down in that light and slipping on his shoes. Without looking back at me or his car—he ran. I hoisted myself over the stick shift and into the driver's seat, turned the key and instantly taught myself to drive a standard shift. I stalled out a few times but managed to leave the curb. I felt as though I were the criminal. Here I was in a stolen car, bucking along the neighborhood streets, in a snowstorm, on the lookout for a naked man. You had to be kidding, right? But there I was, skidding a foot or two whenever I lurched into a different gear. After a while, when I didn't see hide nor hair of Tom, I drove his car home.

When I woke up it was Sunday, but I had to think a minute and remind myself it wasn't a workday before I fell back to sleep. When I woke up the second time it was ten o'clock and the phone was ringing. I pulled the receiver to my ear.

"Baby," I heard a voice I'd know anywhere say. "My Lear's fired up for you."

It was Elvis. I couldn't speak and then I heard a click.

It's true. Tom had flipped. After that it was flower after flower in front of the house, blanketing my car, my desk, my Cross pen set, until I liked to died, and every night and every morning I'd get a phone call from that maniac who slumped over his computer screen at work like nothing had happened. "Baby," he might say when he called, "You rock my roll." I wanted to slap him. I wanted to pour a whole pot of coffee down his polyester shirt. Who would believe me but my mother, and even she had trouble with it.

A year later I was still afraid to answer the phone at night because I might hear, "Baby, are you lonesome?" And you know I was. But I've learned my lesson. If I never see another sideburn in my life it'll be too soon.

I BELIEVE

My mother has called me everything from picky to "gone off in the head" and looked at me like maybe there's something else the matter with me, and we both know what she means. So I spend a lot of time with women, but who else is there I ask you? A woman could die waiting for a date in this town, and the depressing thing is that this is the biggest town in two hundred miles. I tell my mother, sure it gets old waiting, but believe you me two Mr. Wrongs don't make Mr. Right. And I should know. "Honey," my mother tells me, like she's deaf, "Go to church with me and you'll meet a nice man." Seems like my mother has the shortest memory allowed by law when it comes to things in my life that are genuine traumas, and I mean that stuff with Tom and some other things, too, that would warrant at least two years of therapy and curl your hair besides. In a mood of desperation is not the time to start lowering standards, so I don't. I just go about my business, but the time is passing and I wonder what—if anything—is in store. Maybe I should just get a dog.

Every Sunday I kick back with my coffee and read the Personal Ads from start to finish. At first I was looking for someone, but now I just read them for entertainment. How much can you learn about a man from twenty-five words or less? Well, I know a lot of men don't say that many words during a whole marriage, but that's beside the point. Most men jaw their heads off about themselves when they're dating—if they like you they bore you to death, it's the only true golden rule. I liked this ad that began, **Are You She?** But as I read on I realized that grammar was about all that he had to offer. He made himself sound like a hairy Suzy Homemaker. "I like quiet time with my cat, reading, writing fiction, and baking— that's right—baking. I rock climb and kayak. Looking for companionship, maybe more." But I always like it when they say **"maybe more."** It's so much more alluring than when they say they're looking for **romance** (which means they want to do it on the first date) or looking for **"a monogamous relationship"** (which means they're recently divorced and probably tired out from a custody battle for two pitiful, but let's be honest, obnoxious little boys). All of life is a code, but the Personal Ad code is like Real Estate and what they say of love and war—all's fair. And you can bet lies abound, believe me. The trick is to find the truth in the lie, because I believe people are always revealing themselves no matter what they are concealing. Personal secrets are like that stolen letter in the story that's hidden in the open. You know that if a person is consciously concealing something in particular, it's all over their face and in everything they say, but most people don't notice, because it's too obvious to be the truth.

Last Sunday I found this ad that began with the headline **Holding My Own** and went on "when I could be holding 5'5"–7" D/SWF, 125–130lbs, 25–40. I am WWWM, N/S, tall, dark and handsome, successful professional with an interest in the outdoors. Children okay. Let's stargaze together."

If this sounds all right to you, let me clue you in. First off, that punny headline is just gross if you think about it. And if he's so interested in height and weight he's either a shrimp or a fatso. Forget tall and handsome. But wait, you say, maybe he's a shrimp but he looks like Tom Cruise or Robert Redford or Paul Newman. Believe me, he doesn't. And how do I know? Because he's placing a personal ad. "Interest in the outdoors" means he wants to yodel in the open. "Children okay" means he's a grandfather—you notice he doesn't specify his own age. And face it, "Let's stargaze together" is the worst kind of cliche, and that widowed thing kind of makes you wonder if he killed his wife.

The seasons keep changing in circles around me, and I keep going to work and coming home and answering the phone and it's nearly always my mother. Except for a couple of times and nothing came of it. You know I haven't waited this long to be bored to death or to take in some lost man like he was a stray. Well, if he was cute enough I might keep him overnight, but it's always more trouble than it's worth, and with this new disease I don't even think about that kind of thing anymore. But it's almost summer and I've got to do something besides read the personals because I'll be forty in two months, and that's all I need to say.

I decide to start off the summer by going down to the coffee shop because I haven't been there in a while. I order that Italian foamy coffee and sit down with my back to the wall so I can watch the people. Seems like the same crowd or at least they're dressed the same, and I feel right at home. The woman at the counter even says, "I haven't seen you for a while." It makes me feel like family. An art show clutters up the wall, some weird pieces of wrinkled paper with hair and fur and ribbon stuck on them, and I don't much see the point in that, but at least the paper is inside plastic boxes so the hair can't drift around and get in the coffee. I don't know why I haven't been here all winter long. I must have been depressed and didn't know it.

There's another place I haven't been in a while—a

good long while—so when I finish my coffee I march straight to my car and drive over there.

A line of cars stretches a half block since it's the first summer night and some people are parking but others are just looking at what they can see from their cars and then driving off. For a few minutes I can't decide what I want to do, so I stay in line, and when I'm about three cars from the front gate I think, Why not walk through the shrine? so I get out of line and park. Before I leave the car I reach into my purse and find a dollar bill to donate. Most of the time I don't give money, but tonight for some reason I think about how it must take a lot of electric power to keep all those strings of lights shining on.

I go first thing to the donation box and slip my dollar through the slot like a letter. From the speakers I can hear one of the late period songs, "My Way." It's not too loud, but I can hear all the words as I walk along the sidewalks and peer at the monuments. Something overhead catches my eye, swooping down on a wire suspended from the house: a model of the Lear Jet. What a nice touch, I think; it's like Elvis himself might be landing at any minute. But I see that he's already here when I look to the front steps of Graceland. His plane must have landed at the new airport. His arm is raised in a stiff wave of welcome or goodbye. It makes me want to pick him up and pat him on the head or rock him in my arms like a baby doll, but this Elvis is descended from Ken or G.I. Joe, not Baby Thumbelina with a big mushy body and sprawling arms and legs you can love.

On this cool early summer night Elvis wears an off-white linen suit, a black shirt buttoned to the neck, low black boots, and the same expression he will always wear, I guess. I wonder how he'll be dressed tomorrow, because every single day of the year this Elvis wears a different outfit. I saw a picture once in a local magazine of all his clothes lined up, and it said there was an outfit for every day plus some special costumes for special days—like his wedding day. Or his funeral. At Christmas, colored lights stream from all of the little buildings, and a pared-down poinsettia decorates each step leading to the doors of Miniature Graceland. I read how the woman had to cut store-bought plastic poinsettias down to size with cuticle scissors. On the saddest day of the Elvis Calendar Year you can find little black wreathes where those red poinsettias were. But tonight everything is cheerful, I think. The wreaths are in storage until August. I don't know how long I've been staring at Graceland, but now I can hear a different song, "I'm Left, You're Right, She's Gone." I think these people own every Elvis song ever recorded.

My knees ache from squatting so long, so I just plop onto the narrow sidewalk and let folks walk around me. They don't seem to mind or maybe I don't notice after a while. I just sit there and think about my love life and what a big failure I am. It's a train of thought that goes like this and reminds me of that children's song, "There was an old woman who swallowed a fly": I'm not married; and therefore I am unattractive; and therefore I will never have children; and therefore I will never have grandchildren; and therefore all I have to look forward to is taking care of my aged mother; and therefore I should just kill myself while Mother is still basically healthy and I won't feel too guilty about leaving her. But I am a coward; and therefore I will never kill myself; and therefore the end result is that I'll wind up alone, missing my mother— unless she drives me crazy first.

I also think about how it won't be long until I turn forty, and how this friend of mine told me to just quit worrying about it because in reality I'm already living through my for- tieth year and my next birthday will mark the end of it. I can't even begin to say how depressing that was to hear. I know nobody wants to hear what else I think about while I'm sitting in the middle of that little sidewalk like a rock in a river that other people have to steer around, but I really wonder some- times if a person can live very long without ever having sex. I guess I'll find out. Maybe I can leave my shriveled-up body with my hairy palms to science, and they can research the long-term effects of sex-deprivation on what used to be a nor- mal middle-aged woman, whose liberated expectations were forged by birth control pills and free-love in the sixties, re- pressed by Reaganomics and jazzercise in the eighties, and finally replaced by voyeurism and auto-eroticism in the early nineties. "You've come a long way, baby!" I think I'll tell my mother I want to leave my body to science, without telling her exactly why, so she can tell me how sick I sound and I can enjoy knowing that it's even worse than she thinks.

Elvis, I think, staring into his frozen eyes, at least we understand each other. I lower my head and listen to the strains of "There'll Be Peace in the Valley." I think he's singing just for me, and the song even starts to cheer me up a little bit, and I think maybe I'll break down and actually go back to church—why not?—because the only reason I haven't is because my mother keeps telling me it's a good place to meet men. Whenever she says that I feel like a hypocrite to even consider it. I'm thinking about which church I'll attend this Sunday—maybe the big stone church downtown. I don't even know which denomination it is, but what does that matter? I'm so involved in imagining myself walking into the stone church in my new suit that I hardly feel it when someone puts a hand on my shoulder, and I hardly hear it when someone asks, "Ma'am, are you all right?"

But I finally open my eyes when I hear the question again. "Hi," I say, and look into the face of a pleasant looking man I've never laid eyes on before. "I'm fine," I say, and start to get up, and this tall man reaches down his hand and helps me.

"My name is Edward," he says, and releases my hand when I'm steady on my feet. "I was worried about you there for a minute. I hope you don't think I'm rude."

"Not at all," I say. "I was just thinking about things."

"What?" Edward asks.

I hesitate just long enough for him to apologize for asking. "There I go again," he says. "I'm really not a rude person."

"I don't mind telling you I was thinking about my life," I say. I check the clean-shaven spaces in front of his ears for sideburns. So far, so good. "Where are you from?" I ask.

"Down South," he says. "I just moved here."

I look up into Edward's open face. "How did you find this place?"

"The city or Elvis?" he asks.

"Either," I say.

"By accident. I was just learning my way around last month, trying to find my way to that neon star on the mountain, and I stumbled onto this. This is my second visit. I wanted to see it at night." Edward smiles, and I count two boyish dimples. The gray mixed up in the blond at the temples means he's probably my age.

I think about half a second and decide why not, I've

got nothing to lose, and anyway, he's already passed part one of my test. "So what do you think?" I ask Edward.

"What a kick," Edward says, and smiles. "I wish my sister Judy could see it."

That's plenty good enough, I think. I don't say anything else for a minute. People are walking around both of us, but we don't move. We're staring down at Graceland together.

"What's your name?" Edward asks.

"Jane," I say simply, still staring at Elvis. I wonder whether tonight he's waving hello or goodbye with that stiff little arm.

"Jane," Edward repeats, thoughtfully. "Would you like to go to church with me in the morning? I've been going to that big stone church downtown. Or maybe we could just go get a cappuccino, what do you say?"

That's it, I think. My back stiffens and the blood rushes to my head and starts pounding. Things like this start out so perfect, but they always end up awful, I know it from experience, and when I look down at Elvis and he's a doll, so young, and we all know how he ended up, just drugged out and fat—but he could still sing. That concert from Hawaii can break your living heart it's so good. And it's like you can forget how soon afterwards he was dead. And anyway, I remember watching that concert when I didn't know he was going to die, and I didn't really even notice how bloated up Elvis was in that white cape, singing, "Can't Help Falling in Love." All the fans who later claimed they could tell by watching him that night that he was as bad off as it turned out to be were full of shit, I think, in retrospect.

"Jane?" Edward says.

My neck hurts like hell, but I can feel my heart flutter up in my chest because I know I'm finally going to see the inside of that pretty stone church. "I love cappuccino," I say. Edward and I start walking away from Elvis, toward our cars. "I can show you how to get to the star," I tell him. "It's not very far from here."

CONTRIBUTORS

AI is a native of the American Southwest. Her first book, *Cruelty*, received unusual aclaim when it was published in 1973. Her second book, *Killing Floor*, was the 1978 Lamont Poetry Selection of the American Academy of Poets. Her third book, *Sin* (1986), won an American Book Award from the Before Columbus Foundation. Her most recent book of poems is *Fate* (1991).

RAFAEL ALVAREZ was born in Baltimore in 1958. He has been a staff reporter for the *Baltimore Sun* since 1981. He recently completed *The Day Elvis Died & Other Tales from the Holy Land*. He is a big Johnny Winter fan and the father of three.

ELIZABETH ASH is a writer living in Washington, D.C. Her work has appeared in the *National Enquirer, People*, and the *Washington Post*. She teaches at Georgetown University. Born in Birmingham, Alabama, she has loved Elvis since she was twelve.

NICK CAVE is one of the most gifted and widely discussed figures in music. Founder of the legendary group the Birthday Party, his first solo album was hailed in *New Musical Express* as "one of the greatest rock albums ever made." He has since gone on to release a steady stream of discs with his band the Bad Seeds. He has appeared in the films *Wings of Desire* and *Ghosts of the Civil Dead*. He has written two books: *King Ink* (lyrics, plays, and short prose) and the novel, *And the Ass Saw the Angel*.

SAMUEL CHARTERS is the author of four novels: *Mr. Jabi and Mr. Smythe, Jelly Roll Morton's Last Night at the Jungle Inn, Louisiana Black,* and *Elvis Presley Calls His Mother After The Ed Sullivan Show.* He has written numerous nonfiction works on jazz and blues, including *The Poetry of the Blues* and *The Roots of the Blues* as well as poetry, translations, biography and criticism. He currently owns and operates a small jazz record company in Storrs, Connecticut.

MARK CHILDRESS was born in Monroeville, Alabama, grew up in the Midwest and the South, and now lives in San Francisco. He is the author of the novels *Crazy in Alabama, A World Made of Fire, V for Victor,* and *Tender.* He has been a reporter for the *Birmingham News* and an editor for *Southern Living Magazine* and the *Atlanta Journal-Constitution.*

ELEANOR EARLE CROCKETT works with the avant-garde music group Liquid Mice. She grew up in East Texas and is the founder of STRAW (The Society to Replace Asphalt with Straw).

CORNELIUS EADY's *Victims of the Latest Dance Craze* won the 1985 Lamont Prize. His other books are *Kartunes, Boom Boom Boom,* and *The Gathering of My Name,* which was nominated for the Pulitzer Prize. Born in Rochester, New York in 1954, he teaches and directs the Poetry Center at SUNY–Stony Brook.

JANICE EIDUS is the author of *Vito Loves Geraldine,* a collection of short stories, and two novels, *Faithful Rebecca* and *Urban Bliss.* "Vito Loves Geraldine" won a 1990 O. Henry Prize. She is a native New Yorker, now living in midtown Manhattan.

BRIAN GILMORE was born and raised in Washington, D.C. He is a student at the District of Columbia School of Law. His poems have appeared in *Obsidian II, The Sidebar, The Unity Line,* and in the anthology *Fast Talk, Full Volume.* His book of poems is *Elvis Presley is Alive and Well and Living in Harlem.*

CATHRYN HANKLA is the author of a collection of stories, *Learning the Mother Tongue*; a novel, *A Blue Moon in Poorwater*; two volumes of poetry, *Phenomena* and *Afterimages*. She teaches in the writing program at Hollins College in Virginia.

WILLIAM McCRANOR HENDERSON teaches creative writing at the University of North Carolina at Chapel Hill. His novels are *Stark Raving Elvis* and *I Killed Hemingway*.

LAURA KALPAKIAN is the author of the novels *Graced Land* (filmed recently by Roseanne Arnold), *Beggars and Choosers*, *These Later Days*, and *Crescendo*, as well as two award-winning short story collections. Born in Northern California, she now lives in Washington State with her two sons.

PAGAN KENNEDY writes about books for the *VLS* and *The Nation*. She has won a grant from the Massachusetts Arts Council for her fiction. Her stories have been published in *The Quarterly*, *Prairie Schooner*, *Story Quarterly*, and other magazines.

LYNNE McMAHON teaches at the University of Missouri in Columbia, Missouri. She has received the Ingram Merrill Award and a Missouri Arts Council Grant. Her book of poems, *Faith*, was published in 1988. She recently completed a new manuscript tentatively entitled *Develoution of the Nude*.

ERI MAKINO was born in 1953 and is a rebel against the long-standing convention of a separate "women's literature." She documents in *Turn-Down Tales* (1988) the entire rejection-slip process of trying to publish in a Japan dominated by what she calls "men's literature." "Sproing!" won the 4th Waseda New Writer's Award. Other writings include a novella, *Entertainment* (1987), and a novel, *A Voice in the Dark* (1989).

GREIL MARCUS is the author of *Ranters and Crowd Pleasers: Punk in Pop Music, 1977–1992* (Doubleday, 1993), as well as *Mystery Train, Lipstick Traces: A Secret History of the Twentieth Century Dead Elvis: A Chronicle of a Cultural Obsession* and editor of *Lester Bang's Psychotic Reactions and Carburetor Dung* and *Stranded*. He currently writes a music column for *Artforum*. He lives in Berkeley with his wife and two daughters.

SUSIE MEE is a native of Tyron, Georgia. Her first novel, *The Girl Who Loved Elvis*, was recently published by Peachtree Press. Her book of poems is entitled *The Undertaker's Daughter*. A graduate of the University of Georgia and the Yale Drama School, she currently teaches creative writing at New York University.

RACHAEL SALAZAR is the author of the novel *Spectator*. She was born in Paris, lived for many years in New York City, and now lives in Albany, California.

JUDY VERNON is an English instructor at Northwest Mississippi Junior College in Senatobia. Her novels include *Cousins*, *Hissong*, and *The Many Lives of Yokasta Sneed*. She has also published *Consequential Light*, a book of poems.

DIANE WAKOSKI was born in Whittier, California, and was educated at the University of California, Berkeley. Since 1967 she has taught at Michigan State University. She has published more than thirty poetry volumes, including: *Emerald Ice: Selected Poems 1962–1987*, *The George Washington Poems*, *Dancing on the Grave of a Son of a Bitch*, and *Coins and Coffins*. She also has an essay collection, *Creating a Personal Mythology*.

HOWARD WALDROP was born in Mississippi but has spent most of his life in Texas. His novels and short story collections include: *Them Bones*, *A Dozen Tough Jobs*, *Custer's Last Jump*, *Howard Who?*, *Night of the Cooters*, and *All About Strange Monsters of the Recent Past*.

MICHAEL WILKERSON is the Director of the Ragdale Foundation. His short stories have appeared in *Triquarterly*, *Iowa Review*, *Indiana Review*, and many other publications.

MARK WINEGARDNER, the author of *Elvis Presley Boulevard* and *Prophet of the Sandlots*, was born in Bryan, Ohio. He teaches at John Carroll University in Cleveland.

DAVID WOJAHN teaches at Indiana University, where he is the Ruth Lilly Professor of Poetry, and in the Vermont College MFA in Writing Program. His books are *Mystery Train*, *Glassworks*, and *Icehouse Lights*, which won the Yale Younger Poets Award and the William Carlos Williams Book Award.